Plazas and Barrios

T0163476

Society, Environment, and Place

Series Editors: Andrew Kirby and Janice Monk

Plazas and Barrios

Heritage Tourism and Globalization in
the Latin American *Centro Histórico*

Joseph L. Scarpaci

The University of Arizona Press   Tucson

The University of Arizona Press
© 2005 The Arizona Board of Regents
All rights reserved

Library of Congress Cataloging-in-Publication Data
Scarpaci, Joseph L.
   Plazas and barrios : heritage tourism and globalization in the
Latin American centro histórico / Joseph L. Scarpaci. — 1st ed.
      p. cm.
   Includes bibliographical references and index.
   ISBN-13: 978-0-8165-1631-5 (cloth : alk. paper)
   ISBN-10: 0-8165-1631-6
   ISBN-13: 978-0-8165-2602-4 (pbk. : alk. paper)
   ISBN-10: 0-8165-2602-8
   1. Historic districts — Latin America. 2. Historic
preservation — Latin America. 3. Cultural property —
Protection — Latin America. 4. Heritage tourism — Latin
America. 5. Globalization. I. Title. II. Series.
F1408.5.S37 2004
980 — dc22
2004008527

Publication of this book is made possible in part by the
proceeds of a permanent endowment created with the
assistance of a Challenge Grant from the National Endowment
for the Humanities, a federal agency. Additional support was
provided by the Department of Urban Affairs and Planning,
Virginia Tech.

Manufactured in the United States of America on acid-free,
archival-quality paper containing a minumum of 50% post-
consumer waste and processed chlorine free.

11   10   09   08   07   06   6   5   4   3   2

In loving memory of my mother,

Josephine Cicero Scarpaci

1932–1998

For embracing the best of the Old and New Worlds

Contents

List of Illustrations   ix

Preface   xv

1 Approaching Latin America's Built Heritage   3

2 The Historical Geography of the Spanish American Centro Histórico   38

3 Land Use, Building Quality, and Skylines in the Centro Histórico   97

4 The Social Construction of Latin American Historic Districts   120

5 Heritage and Land Valuation in Cartagena de Indias   148

6 Heritage Tourism in Habana Vieja: Restructuring in a Post-Soviet Age   184

7 Tourism Planning and Heritage Preservation in Trinidad, Cuba   206

8 Globalization's Pressures in the New Millennium   220

Notes   237

References   241

Index   257

Illustrations

Figures

1.1 McDeli's, a building up for sale in Cuenca (1997).   5

1.2 Advertisement for historic property near the entrance to Cartagena de Indias.   6

1.3 Neighborhood district sign in Cartagena de Indias.   9

1.4 Sketch of colonial-era streetscape, Habana Vieja, May 1998.   13

1.5a Trinidad's Main Town Square.   22

1.5b Trinidad's Plaza de las Tres Cruces (Three Crosses Square).   23

1.6 "Señora de la chalupa," symbolizing street vendors' dilemmas in Puebla.   24

1.7 The nine study sites (*centros históricos*).   36

2.1a–2.1d Sketches by Le Corbusier for modernizing Buenos Aires, c. 1925.   42

2.2 Layout of Tarifa, Spain (Andalusia).   44

2.3 Urban morphology, nine centros históricos.   46

2.4 Trinidad, street design and individual lots, 2001.   47

2.5 "Layering" of street names in historic Puebla.   48

2.6 Barrio La Candelaria, Bogotá, urban morphology.   58

2.7 Topographic map of Bogotá: 1891, revised 1894.   60

2.8 Supreme Court Palace in Plaza Bolívar, under construction.   62

2.9 Habana Vieja, urban morphology.   63

2.10 *Bohemia* magazine cover promoting steamship travel to Havana.   66

2.11 Image of "gut-and-preserve" facade and restoration, Old Havana.   68

2.12 Trinidad, urban morphology.   69

2.13 Puebla, urban morphology.   72

2.14 Boulevard Cinco de Mayo running through the historic district in Puebla.   76

2.15   Cartagena, Ciudad Amurallada, urban morphology.   78

2.16   Quito, urban morphology.   80

2.17a Bus, truck, and automobile traffic surging through Quito, mid-1990s.   82

2.17b Electric buses introduced in Quito, mid-1990s.   83

2.18   Cuenca, urban morphology.   84

2.19   Municipal offices built in the 1960s and 1970s in Cuenca.   85

2.20   San Telmo barrio, Buenos Aires, urban morphology.   86

2.21   Braided cobblestone streets from the nineteenth century in the San Telmo barrio, Buenos Aires.   87

2.22   Ciudad Vieja, Montevideo, urban morphology.   89

2.23   View of Montevideo from working-class neighborhood of Cerro.   90

2.24   Palacio Salvo, Montevideo's first skyscraper.   92

3.1   Makeshift loft (barbacoa) in an Habana Vieja residence.   106

3.2   Residential café in San Telmo frequented by retirees as well as tourists and artists.   107

3.3   Typical mom-and-pop type retailing in Cartagena.   110

3.4   Building quality, selected centros históricos.   113

3.5   Mean number of floors per building, selected centros históricos.   114

3.6   Rooftop view of Cuenca.   115

4.1   Parking posts in Barrio La Candelaria, Santa Fé de Bogotá.   122

4.2a   Imploded underground parking garage at Habana Vieja's Plaza Vieja.   124

4.2b   The restored Plaza Vieja.   125

4.3   Manuel Copado's Solimar building, Havana, 1942.   126

4.4a   Spanish-operated Parque Central at edge of Habana Vieja.   130

4.4b   Corner facade from 1920s of present Hotel Parque Central, before renovation.   131

4.5   Establishments in Cuenca's historic district receiving or delivering overseas remittances, 1976–97.   134

4.6   New banks with neocolonial design in Cuenca's historic district.   135

4.7   Artisan and Indian residential quarters at the edge of Cuenca's financial district.   136

5.1   Private residence, San Diego neighborhood, Cartagena.   149

5.2 Construction permits in historic district of Cartagena, 1992–2000. 152

5.3 Schematic representation of Colombia's housing dilemma. 154

5.4 Cartagena's historic neighborhoods. 155

5.5 Prominent features of Cartagena's historic neighborhoods. 156

5.6a–5.6e Various perspectives on the remodeled Santa Clara Convent. 158–159

5.7 Getsemaní Carnaval poster, 1999. 162

5.8 Historic Cartagena, land uses, 1992. 163

5.9a Calle de la Iglesia, Cartagena, 1900. 170

5.9b Calle de la Iglesia, Cartagena, 2000. 171

5.10a Calle del Estero, Cartagena, 1900. 172

5.10b Calle del Estero, Cartagena, 2000. 173

5.11a–5.11d Convento de Santa Clara, Cartagena, 1900, 1992, 1997, and 2000. 174–175

5.12 Panza design profile. 176

5.13 Panza and street front, Cartagena. 177

5.14a García Márquez house, Calle del Curato, San Diego neighborhood, 1993. 178

5.14b García Márquez house, Calle del Curato, San Diego neighborhood, 2000. 178

5.15a García Márquez house viewed from Santa Clara Convent. 179

5.15b Renovated warehouse structure as seen in 2000. 179

5.16 García Márquez house viewed from the exterior walls of the old city. 180

6.1 Havana City municipalities. 187

6.2 Master Plan for Old Havana's revitalization. 189

6.3 Sierra Maestra cruise ship terminal, Habana Vieja. 191

6.4a Benetton boutique, Habana Vieja. 192

6.4b Plaza de San Francisco, Habana Vieja. 192

6.5 Streetcar stop at Plaza de Armas Square, Habana Vieja, c. 1950. 197

6.6a Plaza Vieja, in Habana Vieja, under renovation after imploding underground garage. 198

6.6b View of Plaza Vieja, in Habana Vieja, from adjacent building. 198

6.7a Building on northeast corner of Plaza Vieja, Habana Vieja, 1991. 199

6.7b Plaza Vieja, renovated and nearly completed building to be occupied by foreign business community, 1999. 199

7.1   Trinidad's Main Town Square.   207

7.2   Aerial photograph of Ancón Peninsula.   209

7.3   Location map, Trinidad and vicinity.   210

7.4   Entrance to nonmotorized zone in the historic center of Trinidad.   211

7.5   Restoration of an exterior door in the Tres Cruces neighborhood.   213

7.6   Iznaga Tower on the former Manaca Sugar Plantation, Valle de los Ingenios.   214

7.7   Trinidad Restoration Office, organizational chart.   215

7.8   Side view of the landlord's house at the former Guaímaro Plantation.   216

7.9   An abandoned nineteenth-century home, two blocks south of the Plaza Mayor, Trinidad.   217

8.1   Puebla shopping arcade, adjacent to the Main Town Square.   228

8.2   Concrete used to fill in where load-bearing columns and buttresses protrude into sidewalks.   230

8.3   A husband and wife sift through rubble at demolition site in Habana Vieja.   233

8.4   Plaza Santo Domingo, Ciudad Amurallada, Cartagena, July 2000.   234

8.5   Selection of cross-timbers in three Cuban cities reveals variety in design.   235

Tables

1.1   United Nations conference recommendations on heritage tourism   28

1.2   The functions of national heritage legislation   30

1.3   Selected attributes of greater metropolitan areas in study, c. 1990 and 2002   34

2.1   Selected land-use changes in Puebla's centro histórico, mid-1980s– 2002   74

2.2   Strategies of "Plan Montevideo," 2001   93

3.1   Sample sizes (doorways) of nine Spanish American centros históricos, 1990s   99

3.2   Land-use mean percentages, nine centros históricos, 1990s   105

3.3   Building quality percentages and mean scores: Nine historic districts, ranked from highest to lowest quality   112

3.4   Land-use anomalies in historic districts   116

4.1   Selected categories of neighborhood change used in manifest and latent
       content analysis, based on focus groups in three historic districts,
       1997–2000   142

5.1   Tax rates for urban properties according to residential strata and land use,
       2002   167

5.2   Property values and tax payments in Cartagena's historic neighborhoods,
       1999   168

6.1   Social projects funded and organized by Habaguanex in Habana Vieja,
       2003   201

8.1   Selected "best practices" in Spanish American historic district urban design
       and planning   231

Preface

My exposure to the Latin American *centro histórico* dates to my undergraduate days in Guatemala where for six weeks in 1975, I struggled with Spanish classes in Guatemala City's historic core, Zona I. Despite centuries of earthquakes, the heritage of the city's built environment inspired me to read about early Spanish settlements and colonial architecture. The setting, though, was a mere backdrop to my driving interest: understanding subsistence agriculture around Lake Atitlán. Later, while teaching at the Universidad Interamericana de Puerto Rico in 1978–80, visits to Viejo San Juan inspired me to inquire about urban landscapes, history, and land-use changes. Even though our (uninsured) new automobile was stolen from the old city, Viejo San Juan offered respite in a maddening, suburbanizing, and automobile-dependent metropolitan San Juan. Moreover, it had an impressive assortment of old Spanish merchants, artists, boutiques, slums, hide-away bars, and a newly gentrifying quarter. In 1983–84, I left Middle America on a Fulbright award to study health services privatization, which allowed me to visit and conduct archival work in fourteen municipal seats of government in metropolitan Santiago de Chile. During these visits, I deepened my appreciation for the grandeur of old government buildings and reconverted palaces and mansions. In the late 1980s, a National Science Foundation grant led me to neighboring Buenos Aires and Montevideo, where more archival work on privatization and bureaucratic authoritarianism sent me about the older quarters of those Southern Cone capitals. My awe for historic architecture, then, came experientially. These places seemed to be messy, disorderly, but vibrant corners that held a strong sense of community.

I was never able to act professionally on that appreciation until working in the College of Architecture and Urban Studies at Virginia Tech between

1989 and 2003. At that time, I found myself in a college dominated by architects who expressed little interest in the social interpretations of the built environment, especially historic landscapes (theirs was a focus on the Bauhaus school and on the International Style). I was convinced that Latin America had much to offer faculty and students alike. One colleague, Dr. Humberto Rodríguez Camilloni, director of the Henry Wiss Center of Architectural Theory, always had his door open to me and others. He arranged a forum so that I could share my research findings with a small cadre of colleagues over the years. In 1992, I began a study abroad program in Havana, Cuba, at a time when only two other study abroad programs from the United States operated on the island. Today (July 2003), more than one hundred programs operate there, but Virginia Tech's program remains the longest-running U.S. program in Castro's Cuba. While coordinating that program, I tried to speak "architecture" to the social scientists and "social science" to the architects. The result was not always fruitful for the twenty-odd groups that I have taken there, but I have learned a great deal about interpreting the built heritage of the island during my forty-one visits. In the course of the 1990s, my comparative experience was enhanced with periodic trips to Mexico, Colombia, Ecuador, Argentina, and Uruguay.

These collective experiences have informed my research over these past thirteen years. As the reader will discover, this book is a journey through historical corners of the Spanish American city, reflected in the Spanish words *barrio* and *plaza,* which have fortunately become part of North American English. My audience is broad: I hope that both professionals and generalists will take something of value from these pages, set off to walk the streets of these places, and learn from those who live there.

Acknowledgments

Many colleagues, friends, and graduate assistants from around the Americas enhanced this research over the past thirteen years. My graduate students at Virginia Tech — Scott Sincavage, David Zellmer, Nathalie Neaves, Jill Cavanaugh, Wei Huang, Rich Miller, Jason Burdette, Maria Adames, and Vishal Pujal — arranged the data sets, drafted several maps, and conducted bibliographic searches. Jodi Vandervort helped me to get the final manuscript in proper format. Christine Szuter at the University of Arizona Press believed in the project and was patient and supportive as it unfolded.

In Havana, Cuba, Víctor Marín, Mario Coyula, and Orestes del Castillo Sr. listened carefully and offered feedback on parts of the research. Across the Florida Straits, Armando Portella in Miami and Orestes del Castillo Jr. in New York served as "sounding boards" for interpreting trends in urban geography and Latin American architecture. Nancy Benítez, Roberto "Macholo" López, and Marta Castellanos made time to meet with me often and share insights about their restoration efforts in Trinidad, Cuba.

Mexicanist and colleague Nicolás Tamayo allowed me to conduct research in Puebla through a kind invitation for me to take part in a conference held at his university while he was dean of the School of Architecture at the Universidad Benemérita de Puebla. Peter Ward graciously hosted two conferences at The University of Texas and was kind enough to provide financial support. I learned a great deal about the Mexican centro histórico during those Texas-based conferences. Gareth Jones offered helpful updates on the situation in Puebla and commented on chosen portions of this manuscript.

Many functionaries in the Corporación de Barrio La Candelaria provided cartographic and bibliographic help during my work in Bogotá. The U.S. Information Service supported teaching positions in Pereira and Bogotá, which allowed me to conduct fieldwork after those teaching assignments. On the Colombian coast, Nilda Jiménez, Franklin Howard, Gina Silvano, Juan García, Isabel Polo, and Francisco Pacheco steered me toward valuable resources and contacts. The Department of Architecture at Jorge Tadeo University (then found in the historic district but now, sadly, suburbanized outside the walls) was kind to invite me to lecture there in 1997. The Lincoln Institute for Land Policy in Cambridge, Massachusetts, supported my field research twice in Cartagena (1997 and 2000) and once in Cuenca (1999). I am especially grateful to Martim Smolka, Jim Brown, and Laura Mullahaly at Lincoln for their encouragement and feedback. Herman Afiune at the Cartagenan Chamber of

Commerce shared local economic development and census data with me, and Rosa Díaz de Paniagua and Raúl Paniagua were generous with their own publications and sociological insights about gentrification in Cartagena.

In Cuenca, Diego Jaramillo of the University of Cuenca made time (always on short notice) to assist me, and the administration of the University of Cuenca was gracious to host a series of lectures that I delivered back in 1997 with my colleague Roberto Segre. Then mayor of Cuenca, Francisco Cordero, allowed me to work with his planning department in compiling data to present to the United Nations Educational, Scientific, and Cultural Organization (UNESCO) — both my land-use survey results and that of the planning department — in their preliminary study. These data led to placing the historic district on UNESCO's World Heritage List. In this small way, the connection between basic and applied research was extremely rewarding. Victoria Lawson took time off from her National Science Foundation grant while in Quito in 1995 to listen to how my field research was unfolding there. She provided a broader national context for understanding changes in two Ecuadorian cities.

Colleagues in the Southern Cone were no less generous. Argentine scholars and friends José Antonio Borello and Roberto Segre commented on selected versions of chapter 2 and provided insight into the Argentine mindset. Jorge Hardoy and Margarita Gutman were helpful in discussing some larger ideas that set the stage for this book, and their research on Buenos Aires and centros históricos has blazed a path for many Latin American urbanists to follow. In Montevideo, Armando Barbieri and Milton Gutiérrez Mastrogiovanni suggested useful literature on transformations in Ciudad Vieja. Both provided good cheer and support while I worked there.

An earlier version of chapter 6 originally appeared in *Urban Geography* (21:724–44) and is used here with the kind permission of W. H. Winston and Son, Inc.

Last, my son Michael Joseph spent his first eleven years watching his father trek to faraway places, never quite sure what my work entailed, but forgiving me nevertheless. Cristina Alessandra, my daughter, has grown accustomed to these excursions, and has begun to show an appreciation for field research. Their mother, Gilda de los Angeles Machín, balanced career demands and parenting throughout all of this. Her unwavering support is priceless.

Joseph L. Scarpaci
Blacksburg, Virginia
Santiago de Cuba

Plazas and Barrios

1   Approaching Latin America's Built Heritage

Ongoing Globalization

In 1885, Eduardo de Amici visited Paris after a long absence. The surge in "private" advertising that covered his beloved "City of Lights" astounded him. Commercial ads appeared on almost every conceivable corner of the plazas of Paris: taverns, cafés, restaurants, and billboards. Posters were especially popular, as they had become the rising art and communications medium of the day. At his usual table in a café on a major boulevard, he was startled to find brand names of wines, spirits, and tobacco products on napkins, on tabletops, on the parasol at his table, and even on the pavement. The owner of the café explained this was the new form of commercial promotion (what Karl Marx described decades earlier as a manifestation of industrial capitalism), and although it was unattractive, it helped to subsidize his business and keep costs down (Girourard 1985). What de Amici had originally considered to be "charming" facets of Paris — or what James Howard Kunstler (1996) refers to as the public realm where all citizens are invited to participate and share — were no longer there. De Amici's nostalgic recollection of Parisian streets was so bizarre that he remained convinced it was a tragic hoax. Alas, tourists, vendors, and marketers had discovered Paris, much to the chagrin of a few.

The Paris of 1885 had become increasingly accessible to other Europeans because of better steamers across the English Channel, and a network of rail lines fanning out across Europe. International travelers used telegraphs — the budding technology of the era — to book hotel reservations and seats on trains and ships, and to issue bank drafts for transferring money (Noin and White 1997). Bed-and-breakfasts, souvenir shops, jitney services, and more cafés and restaurants sprang up as the city re-sponded to the market demands of industrial capitalism and international travel. Free time and disposable income registered first with the elite classes and gradually became available to the European bourgeoisie (Lash and Urry 1994). Paris in the 1880s was flaunting the achievements of Prefect Baron Haussmann, who had embarked on the most aggressive urban renewal venture of any city in the world a few decades before. Advertising, to de Amici's dismay, merely responded to the new demand that a nascent, international tourist industry had produced.

Fast-forward (a term that did not exist in de Amici's era) a century ahead and cross the Atlantic to the New World. I am seated in a small restaurant with Artemio Lázaro Valdivieso in Cuenca, Ecuador. The establishment is not far from the traditional produce market in the historic district. We munch on *frituras* (fritters) served by his son, a waiter there. The name of the restaurant, McDeli's, is a not-so-veiled reference to the international fast-food chain McDonald's and the English-language term for *fiam-braría:* delicatessen. Like much of contemporary Cuenca, the term reflects the long reach of globalization and modernity into this quaint and distant city in Andean South America. Although McDeli's would close two years later (figure 1.1) and be sold as a historic property, a vibrant real-estate market highlights the contemporary transformation of the Latin Ameri-can *centro histórico* (historic district)[1] (figure 1.2).

Since the early 1980s, tens of thousands of *cuencanos* (Cuencans) have left the city and surrounding Azuay Province to head for the United States in search of work. Their route is circuitous. They often buy a "vacation package" that brings them to Mexico, paying a bit more for the trip than just a roundtrip airline ticket, to avoid raising suspicion with Mexican immigration authorities. The tourist visa issued by the Mexican consulate was easy to secure until the late 1990s. Once in Mexico, the "tour opera-tor" (a *coyote,* or trafficker of illegal immigrants), issues the Ecuadorians bus tickets to a northern Mexican border town along one of the longest international frontiers in the world. Matamoros, Nuevo Laredo, Nogales, Tijuana, and Ciudad Juárez all serve as "jumping-off points" (*trampo-lines*) to cross the border illegally. Once across (the odds vary greatly as to

Figure 1.1   McDeli's, Cuenca, Ecuador. The building is up for sale (1997) and is promoted as a potential site for "luxurious offices" and an upscale "shopping gallery." These and related transformations are the topic of chapters 3 and 4.

whether U.S. Border Patrol or Naturalization and Immigration agents will pick them up in the desert or whether they will die there), many Ecuadorians head for the metropolitan New York area. Whether in the city's five boroughs, northern New Jersey, or Connecticut, Artemio observes wryly, "Almost everyone from Cuenca has an uncle or cousin there." Blood relative or not, there is a thick social network of friends and family (fictive kinship, or *compadrazgo*) that this migration stream has produced. It helps the "Ecuadorian tourists in Mexico" find employment in New York, New Jersey, and Connecticut (Borrero 1992).

Artemio has worked in Queens, New York, for ten years. This city's borough is home to thousands of Ecuadorians such as Artemio, who began in menial trades. His first job was as a busboy, then as a short-order cook, and later (1995) as a restaurant manager. Like others from Cuenca and Azuay, he has sent home thousands of dollars during his fifteen years in the United States. At first, sending money home was difficult; most

JAIME A. BORDA MART LO

CENTRO COMERCIAL BOCAGRANDE OF. 313
P. O. BOX 15361 - FAX (90-575) 6654079
TELS: (90-575) 6653348 - 6655377 - 6658241
CARTAGENA - COLOMBIA

¡ DE OPORTUNIDAD !
EN *CARTAGENA*, OFRECEMOS ESTA CASA

CASA MAGALI PARIS

UBICADA EN LA PLAZA DE LOS COCHES, FRENTE A LA PUERTA DEL
RELOJ. ESPECIAL PARA BANCO, CORPORACION FINANCIERA O PARA
NEGOCIO CON SERVICIO AL PUBLICO.

CASA CON MAS DE 100 AÑOS DE ANTIGÜEDAD, CON TRES (3) NIVELES EN
1.822 Mts². DE CONSTRUCCION, Y LOTE DE **649.34 Mts².**, DOTADA CON
AIRE ACONDICIONADO. CUBIERTA EN TEJA DE BARRO COCIDO,
ESTRUCTURA PARA ALTAS CARGAS. TIENE ENTRADAS POR LA PLAZA
DE LOS COCHES Y POR LA CALLE DEL CANDILEJO.

ESTA PROPIEDAD TIENE UNA UBICACIÓN PRIVILEGIADA DENTRO DEL
SECTOR AMURALLADO DE CARTAGENA, EN UNA CONDICION
PERMANENTE DE VALORIZACION. **SU PRECIO ESTA EN US$ 3.6
MILLONES. CITA PREVIA, JAIME BORDA - CELULAR 93-7310789.**

ASESORIAS DE AVIACION · MERCADEO · TURISMO Y EDITORIAL · REPRESENTACIONES · RELACIONES PUBLICAS · FOTOGRAFIA AEREA

Figure 1.2   Real-estate advertisement for a historic property near the main
entrance to the walled city of Cartagena de Indias in Cartagena, Colombia.
The building trades and renovation activity in the centro histórico have been
relatively depressed, as discussed in chapter 5.

cuencanos relied on friends traveling back to Ecuador to carry rolls of cash or thick envelopes for friends and family. With cash in hand, they started new businesses back home, upgraded their houses, and bought consumer durables. Gradually, couriers, Western Union offices, DHL, Federal Express, and a host of travel agencies have opened their doors in Cuenca's centro histórico. This area has always been the traditional banking center, and with Ecuador's generally lax policy of permitting the remittance of foreign currency (Ecuador officially adopted the U.S. dollar in 2000 as its official currency), capital is now transferred electronically or via courier as cashier's checks or money orders.

Artemio's home and neighborhood in the centro histórico have changed. "No tourists ever visited Cuenca when I was a boy. And the only art available was the Panama hats made by the *cholas* [Indian women] and sold at the market. Cuenca has been discovered!" he says laughing and gesturing. What outsiders find charming about Artemio's hometown is lost on him. "What we have here are old buildings and old ways; what's so special about that?" Our chat ends because Mr. Valdivieso, ever the entrepreneur, is late for an appointment. He will meet with a prospective buyer of his single-story boyhood home. A restaurateur from the Ecuadorian coastal city of Guayaquil is thinking about opening a seafood restaurant there, and the house's colonial patio — with a little fixing up — would be a perfect setting. As long as the buyer leaves the building facade in nearly original condition, the structural changes to the patio and interior rooms will likely not be monitored by the two building inspectors from the Municipal Planning Department.

These tales of two cities — Paris in the 1880s and Cuenca in the 1990s — underscore globalization and heritage tourism. By globalization I refer to an increasingly shrinking world where information, commodities, people, and capital are transferred quickly, and where the traditional domain of government becomes less important in the daily lives of citizens. I use heritage tourism to include the industry of travel that promotes cultural landscapes that hold great historical and symbolic landmarks, monuments, and neighborhoods. The cultural value or heritage of de Amici's Paris and Valdivieso's Cuenca, however, are different. Both cities are socially constructed images created in different times, different places, and different worlds. But were they?

De Amici recognized the artistic and cultural value of the French capital, even though he was saddened by its plunge into consumerism during the Industrial Revolution. Valdivieso reflects a long-standing Latin American Creole tradition that often derides aspects of popular culture and vernacular architecture. When local Latin American culture is portrayed in the region, it is often vulgarized or else it is "intended to please and reassure the elite" (Foster 1993, 5). Artemio Valdivieso's social construction of historic Cuenca is both a product of information technology (at the "high" end of the economic ladder) and the demand for unskilled labor in a postindustrial U.S. economy (at the lower rungs of the labor force). It is ironic that "locals" do not always appreciate the "local" and choose foreign models of lifestyle, architecture, and tastes over their own cities and culture. In the new millennium, Valdivieso's disdaining view of local heritage is ironic because there is money to be made from exploiting the allures of historic churches, tiled roofs, and cobblestone streets. In other words, he may not fully appreciate the historic built environment of his youth, but at least he can "make a buck" from it. As this book makes clear, the same pressures for advertising and promoting tourism in nineteenth-century Paris and twentieth-century Cuenca often mean the distinction between economic survival, on the one hand, or unemployment, on the other, especially in the Latin American centro histórico (figure 1.3).

On Defining the Centro Histórico

Historic centers in Latin American towns and cities are anything but isolated from the forces of change. Property owners and governments change buildings, destroy them, and dictate which social classes shall use them. There is a consensus that the major changes evident in these neighborhoods today began in the latter part of the nineteenth century, and accelerated in the middle of the twentieth. Between 1930 and 1960, most Latin American historic preservationists addressed single public and private buildings, or an occasional town square. Rarely did they focus on a multiblock segment of the original colonial core. While today there is general accord among municipal, national, and international entities that these valuable places should be restored (Tung 2001; Hardoy 1983; Gutman 1992; Hardoy and Gutman 1992), the pace of change and the quality of

Figure 1.3   Neighborhood district sign in Cartagena de Indias, Cartagena, Colombia, an UNESCO-declared World Heritage Site. The signs, paid for by a credit card company, have dotted the historic district since 1997. Here it tells visitors they are in the antique furniture zone.

historic preservation remain uneven. What we ascertain from novels, photographs, art, land-use studies, and ethnographic accounts of residents are just a "snapshot" of the evolution of these districts.

If Latin American architectural historians have elevated the discussion of heritage sites, land-use and zoning enforcement has lagged behind. The 1960s witnessed considerable interest in Spanish American historic districts (the Brazilians began well before World War II in selected towns and cities). Thought of largely as a dilemma of architectural preservation, the decade saw legislative reform that set out clear guidelines for urban renewal, building codes, and preservation efforts. In 1964, protecting the isolated national monument expanded to include "modest works that have, through time, acquired cultural significance" (*Carta Internacional . . .* 1964). By 1967, a conference held in Quito by the Organization of American States had issued a document (often called the *Carta de Quito,* or *Quito Letter*) that moved to link these ideas more closely with legislation and urban planning. This produced a spate of research on the widely acclaimed historic centers of Antigua, Guatemala, Cuzco, Peru, and Moquegua, Peru. The pivotal *Quito Letter* strengthened historic preservation throughout Latin America. It sent a message to all nations to address planning concerns of historic districts, and to capture the social histories of these places. United Nations Educational, Scientific, and Cultural Organization (UNESCO), foreign governments (mostly Spain, Italy, Holland and Canada), and philanthropic agencies helped to publicize World Heritage Sites in the 1980s. However, the economic downturn in the late 1970s and 1980s (known in Latin America as the "lost decade") made governments hard pressed to allocate money to historic preservation, when other more "immediate" needs such as schooling, water, and health care required attention (Weil and Scarpaci 1992).

The Quito Colloquium defined historic districts as "those living settlements that are strongly conditioned by a physical structure stemming from the past, and recognizable as being representative of the evolution of a people" (PNUD/UNESCO 1977, n.p.). This is a useful beginning, and it frames the choice of the study sites in this book. Primarily, people live in historic districts today, rather than in the archaeological ruins of such pre-Colombian settlements as Machu Picchu, Peru, Tikal, Guatemala, or Tulum, Mexico. Also inherent in this definition is the idea that historic districts are not limited to the stock of their built environments: buildings, town squares, fountains, colonnaded galleries, sculptures, filigree ironwork, streetlamps, and arches. Rather, historic districts include non-material culture such as the people, their lifestyles and traditions, productive activities, beliefs, and urban rituals (saints' days, founder's days, pre-Lenten carnivals).

Perhaps the most controversial point of the *Carta de Quito* declaration is interpreting which aspect of a city's past gets included within district boundaries. Although I discuss this below, I note here that such a determination is polemical and ridden with tension. No site choice can be entirely faithful to one particular period in time, architectural style, or social class (Barthel 1996). Unlike rock strata of cliffs that a historical geologist might examine, the urban geographer has no systematic way of interpreting the layers of past cityscapes with great precision.

A critical dimension in defining the centro histórico rests with setting its geographic boundaries. Generally, capturing the largest uniform area guides national and international commissions that identify these districts. Occasionally, nature and cultural criteria are useful for drawing boundaries. Bodies of water (such as in Buenos Aires, Cartagena, Montevideo, and Havana) and walls and fortresses (such as in Havana and Cartagena) set limits on urban growth, or at least they did in a bygone era. Chapter 2 addresses the role of colonial laws that standardized the platting of these Latin American cities. This regimented and standardized carving up of settlements made it easier to identify the spread of the colonial core before the modern era (early twentieth century) than would have been true had each town been established without normative criteria from Spain.

Political decisions, bulldozers, and private land-uses are not the only factors that complicate the look and cartographic representation of centros históricos. Natural forces have lent a hand by shaking buildings to the ground. In recent times, earthquakes have wreaked destruction on Cuzco (1950, 1987) and Puebla (1985) while heavy tropical downpours constantly menace Trinidad, Havana, and Cartagena (Pérez 2001).

A widely accepted paradigm among scholars of historic preservation and historic districts is that the best preservation efforts are those that remain constant over time (Carbonell 1990). As various United Nations Habitat conferences have concluded, the owners and occupants of buildings and private residences serve themselves best by regularly maintaining their homes and neighborhoods. In the study sites reviewed in this book, the traditional elite residences began moving out of these colonial cores into the suburbs during the late nineteenth and early twentieth centuries. Gradually, a new class of residents occupied the old quarters of Latin American towns and cities, and many among them are the urban poor. Urban impoverishment (*tugurización*) means that food, clothing, and other bare necessities get top priority in allocating household income, instead of spending on building maintenance. Because renting in Latin American inner cities has been on the rise since the middle of the last century (Gilbert 1994), property maintenance and upgrading are deferred and fall mainly to absentee owners, corporate landlords, or the state. Insisting that residents of historic districts remain faithful to architectural codes and designs is often costly and even elitist (Barthel 1996; King

1990). Thus, it is unrealistic and utopian to expect residents of historic districts to pay for all restoration costs; economic realities dictate otherwise. Furthermore, accusing the urban poor of neglecting the facades of their houses smacks of victim blaming.

Finally, the Latin American centro histórico largely reflects a low population density when compared to the metropolitan area. Its skyline, discussed in detail in chapter 3, is lower than the modern central business district (CBD) and its accompanying skyscrapers. Fernando Carrión (1992) points out that the skyscraper-endowed central business district, unlike the centro histórico, in the Latin American city responded to the late demands of industrialization: "If one reviews the historical processes of other centros históricos in Latin America . . . it is clear that [the historic centers'] demise stemmed from the fast pace of urbanization, from import-substitution industrialization, from the development of banking and commerce as well as strong waves of migration" (59). Clearly, the CBD and the centro histórico are two discrete places and should not be conflated in studying the Latin American city.

Streetscapes of the "typical" historic district are inviting, and both the street width and building height are captivating to the pedestrian (figure 1.4). One can appreciate premodern skilled work in the plasterwork, ironwork, balconies (cantilevered and otherwise), rails, archways, pediments, doorways, columns (Ionic, Doric, Corinthian, and mixtures thereof), and a variety of roof tiles. Architectural historians have written volumes on the origin and modification of each of the elements (Covo 1996), which combine to make the centro histórico aesthetically pleasing.

The Rise of Modernity and Eclipse of the Colonial Past

The fin de siècle and "bridge to the new millennium" metaphors swept through the humanities, arts, and social sciences in the late 1990s and generated a spate of research that reassessed prevailing epistemologies. Perhaps nowhere were new paradigms reconsidered more thoroughly than in assessments of modernity, and its theoretical cousin, postmodernism. Studies of the built environment provide an excellent venue to trace the confluences of these ideas because architecture, design, and planning reflect the interplay of architectural tradition, politics, and the social con-

Figure 1.4   Artist's sketch of colonial-era streetscape, Calle Cuba, Habana Vieja, Cuba, May 1998. *Courtesy of Marissa Masangkay.*

struction of public spaces (FLACSO 2001). And nowhere is this played out more strikingly than in Latin America, the most urban realm of the so-called Third World.

The modern movement in Latin American architecture portended and delivered great projects by the middle of the last century. It promised new mass housing, high-rise buildings on stilts (*pilotis*), and motorway overpasses (mostly along the ideas espoused by the French-Swiss architect, modernist, and visionary extraordinaire Charles-Edouard Jeanneret, better know as Le Corbusier). Modernity in the building trades meant substituting the dense brick of the nineteenth century with the open box and geometrical configuration of the twentieth. New architecture in twentieth-century Latin America entailed rational forms that embodied the spirit of this new image; decoration and ornamentation would become a relic of the "backward" past. Indeed, the term *architecture* would supplant *building,* and some new populist leaders across the political spectrum were eager to adopt the tenets of the modern movement because such codes represented progress, order, and a strong nation-state. Concrete's plasticity, versatility, and relative low cost afforded Latin America a chance to continue forging new designs (made largely of steel, glass, and reinforced concrete) that could keep pace with a rapidly urbanizing region. While most of the tenets of the modern movement originated in Europe, the preindustrial streets and neighborhoods of the Old World could not be razed easily for historical and aesthetic reasons; cultural heritage (*patrimonio*) has long been a badge of distinction in Europe unlike in its American cousins. In Latin America, industry had made only a modest dent in the urban fabric, and new building styles could easily etch out space for new, brazen designs in the early twentieth century (Jones and Varley 1999a).

By the middle of the twentieth century, Latin American architects were advancing rapidly in the areas of public housing, urban design and renewal, and engineering techniques in ways that most U.S. architects had not yet fathomed. Although errors were made, political, pedagogical, economic, and social forces caused a distinctively Latin American modern architecture to emerge. These innovations did not go uncriticized. When historian and critic Sigfried Giedion concluded in a 1958 graduate seminar at Harvard that the plans for Brasília, Brazil, were unsatisfactory and required the help of Le Corbusier, "Brasilia, along with the rest of Latin American modern architecture, more or less disappeared from the English-speaking world's views of the achievements of the twentieth century" (Fraser 2000, 3). While the inference is sweeping, it echoes what *New York Times* journalist Herbert Matthews purportedly said about the "informed" American public: "[North] Americans will do anything for Latin America but read about it."

Despite criticism of or indifference toward Latin American architectural achievements, work continued, with Brazil, Argentina, and Mexico spearheading much of it with the construction of new cities (Brasília); *ciudades universitarias* (college campuses); industrial and housing complexes; and showcase public, commercial, and residential sites. The pavilion of Brazilian architect Oscar Niemeyer designed for the 1939 World's Fair captured the emerging, minimalist vision of architecture — a hallmark of the modern movement — and showed that Latin America was capable of forming its own patterns of design that departed from the North Atlantic nations. As art historian and critic Valerie Fraser (Fraser 2000, 7–8) points out, most Latin American nations could not afford to mass-produce the iron, steel, glass, and prefabricated concrete panels. Housing, work, recreation, and traffic could be (normatively, at least) organized under new town planning, directed by architects (planning as a distinct profession would come later). In 1953, the New York Museum of Modern Art presented a special exhibit, *Brazil Builds,* which underscored the new currents of design afoot in one corner of the Americas. Henry Hitchcock's *Latin American Architecture since 1945* (1955) also registered the evolution of that design trajectory.

International journals such as the *Architectural Review* and the *L'Architecture d'Aujourd'hui* paid special attention to developments in Latin American architecture. Le Courbusier's early visits to Buenos Aires and Brazil in 1929, and later visits to Colombia, launched Latin America's engagement in the modern movement. Latin America was not a tabula rasa for simply importing Beaux Arts, Art Deco, Eclecticism, Brutalism, and other European aesthetics. Latin America's built environments reflect the tenets of regionalism, *hispanidad,* indigenous styles, and other forces. Like Uruguayan poet José Enrique Rodó's 1900 essay *Ariél,* a monumental work that celebrated Latin America's Mediterranean roots and spiritual background (versus the functionalist and cold Anglo-Saxon realm to the north), Latin America's modern movement signaled a new path for architecture, design, and town planning. Modernity, as envisioned by the Latin American "maestros" of the Modern Movement, would humanize the built environment instead of alienating it as has been done in parts of New York, Chicago, London, and Western Europe (Scarpaci 2003). In all of this, however, the centro histórico emerged compromised and neglected.

By the late 1960s, the notion of modern architecture had been stolen from Latin America and Europe by the United States. Interest in preserving colonial architecture or investing in the centro histórico continued to be forgotten (Quantrill 2000). The discourses shaping Latin American modernity took a variety of forms and stemmed from many places. On the one hand, Brasília was used by critics to epitomize the shortcomings of the movement. On the other, those defending the movement opined that "Latin American modernist architecture, having been dismissed as puerile, exotic, irrelevant or simply *wrong,* then simply disappeared off the map of architectural history altogether. If we are to restore it to its rightful place, we need to try out some different adjectives. How about, for starters: innovative, shocking, exciting, diverse, challenging, brave, witty, adventurous?" (original emphasis; Fraser 2000, 255).

Latin American critics also lent a hand — rightly or wrongly — in dismissing some fine modern structures. The Cuban School of Arts located on the former golf links of Havana's western suburbs is an insightful example (Loomis 1999). The art complex was not finished completely and was poorly maintained. Its structures serve as a wonderful display of local (Cuban) designs, native building materials, and tropical sensuality, regardless of whether socialists or capitalists built them. However, ideology in socialist Cuba in the mid-1960s shifted course. Fraser writes:

> The drama school, on the other hand, is a compact, piled-up design, like a cubist drawing of an Italian hill-top town. The architecture throughout is designed to delight, with the constant interplay of open and closed volumes, light and shade, architecture and vegetation. . . . As Cuba moved closer to the Soviet Union, the schools came to be repudiated first by architects and critics, especially the influential Roberto Segre, and then by the government: they were extravagant; they made use of outmoded materials and methods of construction; the vaulting system was unsafe; and in their explicitly programmatic architecture they presented a pre-Revolutionary image of Cuba as sensual and indulgent, an amoral tropical paradise. By 1975 non-Cubans were joining the attack: the Mexican architectural critic López Rangel argued, echoing Segre, that "the works contain a meaning incoherent with the values of the Revolution." (2000, 249)

This assessment exemplifies how the image of the modern movement was critiqued rigorously from within, but in the Cuban arts schools, we find the same ideological arguments used to critique the most abject modern shopping malls and consumption palaces spawned by Western capitalism and sustained by the modern movement.

Toward a Heritage Geography of the Latin American Historic District: Whose Landscape? Whose Memory?

The study of historic landscapes is fundamentally a geographic inquiry because of the concern over location and the milieu of social, economic, and political forces that alter those landscapes. Interest in landscape has risen enormously in recent years (Muir 1999). Historians, archaeologists, landscape architects, and especially geographers help drive this interest. Scholarly approaches to landscape are nearly as varied as the number of studies in the field. Geographers Stephen Daniels and Denis Cosgrove (1988, 8) approach the study from a postmodernist perspective, arguing that "landscape seems less like a palimpsest whose 'real' or 'authentic' meanings can somehow be recovered with the correct techniques . . . [than like the] flickering text displayed on the word-processor screen whose meaning can be created, extended, altered, elaborated and finally obliterated by the nearest touch of a button." Gillian Rose (1992, 10) notes that in human geography, "pleasure in the landscape was often seen as a threat to the scientific gaze." W. J. Thomas Mitchell (1994, 14) reminds us that "landscape is itself a physical and multi-sensory medium (earth, stone, vegetation, water, sky, sound and silence, light and darkness, etc.) in which cultural meanings and values are encoded."

Not all of geography's recent history celebrated the study of landscape. Richard Hartshorne's seminal work, *The Nature of Geography* (1939), rejected landscape as the central feature of geography because it derived from the narrowly defined German term, *Landschaft,* meaning a "restricted piece of land." But since at least the mid-1980s, geographers disillusioned by the positivist movement have found a new theoretical space for the study of landscape: "geographers have sought to reformulate landscape as a concept whose subjective and artistic resonances are to be actively embraced" (Cosgrove 1985, 45). Part of this reformulation stems from the recognition that landscapes are socially constructed, as chapter 4 of this book makes plain. Indeed, "the study of landscapes offers geographers a means of analyzing and organizing the surrounding material environment . . . [and for understanding] the relationship between landscapes and human beings" (Kobayashi 1989, 165). All of these justifications (cf. Hartshorne 1939) underlie my interest in the cultural heritage of specific Spanish American landscapes: centro histórico, plaza, and barrio.

Heritage means using the past as an economic resource for the present. Historic districts and monuments allow countries to create national identity, forge ideologies, and "ground" abstract notions of history and heritage in tangible forms (Hobsbawm 1990; Hall 1995; Woolf 1996). The wish to preserve relics of past environments is often tied to an influential elite. However, the tension created over what is to be preserved, whose collective memory should be celebrated, is often ignored in official public circles. A bewildering array of places and objects determines what gets included in the web of historic preservation projects (Graham, Ashworth, and Turnbridge 2000; Jones and Varley 1999b).

The many forces that create these landscapes are not unique to either market or centrally planned economies. For example, economic-based images of place drive the present construction boom in the United States. Walt Disney Corporation created Celebration, Florida — a planned community — as a theme to embrace the preautomobile era that characterizes Disney's Main Street boulevard at Disney World. Public demand in the United States is strong for neotraditional design structures such as Seaside, Florida, and related projects of Andres Duany and Elizabeth Plater-Zyberk of DPZ Associates (Duany, Plater-Zyberk, and Speck 2000). Not so many years ago, Eastern European, Soviet, and Cuban public housing brandished banal high-rise housing units to impose a stamp of equality on all its citizens. In centrally planned economies, modest shelter, uniformity, and equality often take priority over building aesthetics.

In *From Aztec to High Tech: Architecture and Landscape across the Mexico–United States Border,* Lawrence A. Herzog claims that North Americans could learn much from their Latin American neighbors. While late-night TV comedians in the United States may poke fun at landscape and architecture, Herzog shows that there are common features along both sides of the border despite the homogenizing forces of globalization and the North American Free Trade Agreement (NAFTA).

If the spirit of place is lagging in America, one way to recapture it is by redirecting America's attention to the cultural diversity of its cities and regions. Here, on the Mexico-U.S. border, places like Tucson, San Antonio, El Paso, Albuquerque, Santa Fe, San Diego, and Los Angeles possess rich cultural heritages. . . . The borderlands, therefore, offer an opportunity to use landscape diversity — contrast — as a way of exciting interest in the daily experience of place. (1999, x)

Herzog's portrayal of an almost Mexican Disneyland designed largely as a museum — Mexitlán — highlights the parody of crass cross-cultural borrowings that stem from globalization and embedded in Mexican tourism. "Here in Mexitlán, there will be monuments from all over Mexico, combined with movement, light, and music," notes one tourist brochure (Herzog 1999, 161). This complex at the edge of downtown Tijuana is not unlike other Disneyesque venues in Spain, Denmark, the Netherlands, and Taiwan. Mexitlán, though, is different: "[It] is a meeting of the First and Third Worlds," remarked chief architect Ramírez Vázquez (Herzog 1999, 163). By 1992, the amusement park/cultural showcase was closing early because of low attendance. Designed to attract Anglos as well as Mexican Americans in the largest Mexican border tourist city, consumer surveys revealed that once inside, the tourists were very satisfied. However, most tourists do not set out for the Mexican border to visit museums or to experience heritage tourism. "The problem was getting them inside . . . They come to the border to be tourists, not of the serious museum-going type, but in a way that may have as little to do with experiencing authentic places as our simulated cybernetic suburbs have to do with their earlier inner-city incarnations. For Mexico, a nation wedded to memory, the path to modernity in this hemisphere means coming to terms with this" (Herzog 1999, 164).

Herzog (1999, 165) also describes how the Americanization of the Tijuana plaza "threaten[s] to turn Tijuana into Anywhere, Mexico/U.S.A." Herzog contrasts the traditional Mexican *zócalo* with its U.S. counterpart: the shopping mall. "The loss of traditional spaces is being lamented in cities worldwide," writes Herzog, "but it is particularly noteworthy in the borderlands. . . . Both the erosion of cultural landscapes as a result of tourism development and the privatization of vital public space are examples of the potentially destructive effects of NAFTA on Mexico's built environment." (Herzog 1999, 176).

In an era of rapid and affordable travel for the middle classes, heritage is becoming a driving force in international tourism. Hewison captures this globalizing trend (expressed earlier by Artemio Valdivieso in Cuenca) by arguing that heritage is manufactured like a commodity, "which nobody seems able to define, but which everyone is eager to sell" (Hewison 1987, 9). If heritage tourism is commodified, then, a further layer of tension is grafted onto local communities in developing nations where the need for hard currency conflicts with what locals want. Cheryl Shanks (2002, 17) calls this paradox one of the many quandaries of "artificial authenticity": "commodifying culture simultaneously preserves, transforms, and destroys it."

This is a delicate matter for local planners and politicians because economic development pressures to bring in dollars or euros may distort the authenticity of local culture (Barberia 2002). For instance, Ernest Hemingway's drinking and sleeping habits in Old Havana, or the tango dancing of the San Telmo District in Buenos Aires, receive a disproportionate amount of attention, respectfully, in those tourist markets. Geographer David Lowenthal argues that reconstructing built environments gives familiarity and guidance to present-day generations, even though their historical veracity may be dubious. Simultaneously, heritage as historic preservation can legitimize the history of local people as well as invoke negative images of the past (Lowenthal 1985). Latin America has no shortage of heritage tourism venues; favela (slums) tourism in Brazil (Mahieux 2002), immigrants' heritage tourism in South America (Schlüter 2000), human-rights tourism (Burtner 2002; Haddock 2002), and sexual tourism (Hannum 2002) are just a few new tourism venues developing in the Latin American market. The potential of gastronomic and heritage tours in Mexico is rapidly rising (Scantelbury 2003, 269) and joins the more traditional venues of heritage tours, such as military heritage, "host-guest" relationships, first-person presentations of heritage routes, and stimulating local awareness of local and national heritage (Robinson et al. 2000).

Chapter 5, on Cartagena, and chapter 6, on Havana, give details about how heritage tourism and historic preservation set up a series of problems that include gentrification, residential displacement, and related social difficulties. These problems highlight the "duality of heritage." By the duality of heritage, we can conceptualize the Latin American centros históricos as sources of cultural and economic capital. Within *cultural capi-*

tal, we can differentiate "high" and "low" levels — this is where the "duality" comes in; the former refers to the major public buildings, cathedrals, town halls (*cabildos*), fortresses, jails, hospitals, convents, churches, and chosen monuments. There may also be grand private residences (*casonas* [spacious homes], *mansiones, palacios, casas-almacenes* [warehouse mansions]), usually European imports, but undoubtedly adapted and changed by Creole vernacular tastes (Segre 1981; Weiss 1950; Early 1994). As this book explains, such edifices attract First World tourists to Third World–heritage tourism and proffer postcard backdrops of unique places.

The domain of "low" cultural capital in the Latin American urban core includes a variety of vernacular architecture and public spaces other than principal town squares. It may range from huts and cabins, small houses, medium houses, and even less-than-palatial large houses (Buisseret 1980, chap. 1). It also includes corners of bona fide (nationally recognized as comprising historic districts) houses that are close together, but not as well maintained, promoted, or frequented by tourists. Nonetheless, these secondary "low" culture spaces serve important local functions (see figures 1.5a–1.5b).

We know that the residential composition of most centros históricos shifted from an elite neighborhood to upper-income residents sprinkled with concentrations of poor (Ford and Griffin 1980; Gilbert 1994; Caplow 1949; Stanislawski 1950; London 1982). In the transformation process, abject urban poverty in the Latin American city becomes more "disguised" than it does in North America. Chilean geographers have termed this more subtle urban squalor the *pobreza disfrazada* (disguised poverty) (CED 1990). Behind the tall walls surrounding many lots and city blocks, and within voluminous nineteenth- and twentieth-century structures, lies a disenfranchised class that is out of view, and usually out of the urban policy realm (Scarpaci, Gaete, and Infante 1988). Unlike the ghetto often found next to the central business district in the United States, the penury of the centro histórico cannot always be seen during a cursory stroll through its streets and alleys. "Low" cultural capital rarely makes it into the travel guides, Web sites, and marketing brochures, yet is an important dimension of inner-city life. It is, moreover, on equal footing with the growing number of street vendors who ply their trades on sidewalks, parks, and open spaces.

Figure 1.5a Main Town Square and Plaza de las Tres Cruces (Three Crosses Square) (see figure 1.5b), just four blocks apart, in Trinidad, Cuba, emblematic of the "duality of heritage" concept. The main square of Trinidad preserves a mid- to late-nineteenth-century plaza in very good structural shape. The Palacio Brunet, the Architectural Museum, the Anthropological Museum, and an art gallery flank it. It is one of the main spots to visit in Trinidad because it displays the amenities that make heritage tourism so inviting.

Class conflicts can simmer in historic districts in subtle ways. Authorities in Puebla, Mexico, have determined that ambulant vendors (*ambulantes*) detract from the "dignity" of the centro histórico; the ambulantes may be banned altogether or moved (figure 1.6). "This ideological shift is found in the built environment and the use of public space in Puebla. Asserting the past, drawing parallels with a 'golden age,' serves to elevate Puebla's profile in the national consciousness (note award of UNESCO recognition before Mexico City)" (Jones and Varley 1994, 41; Conner 1999). These tensions point out the potential tax base that historic preservation can build, and the tensions raise questions about whose heritage and whose past are being preserved. These themes, which pervade urban plan-

Figure 1.5b   Four blocks away from the Main Town Square in Trinidad, Cuba, in the Tres Cruces (Three Crosses) neighborhood, there is another town square. For centuries, a Holy Week procession through the town culminated in this unpaved town square (the procession was discontinued during the Cuban Revolution and restarted in 1999). For the locals, this "low" culture public space holds more meaning than the Main Town Square that attracts millions of dollars to Trinidad. Photo 2002.

ning and historic preservation circles in centros históricos, are explored in chapters 4 through 7.

Another dimension of the duality of heritage entails *economic capital.* This refers to the "consumption" of culture through museums, art galleries, and architectural appreciation. Taken at its broadest level, some analysts claim that all buildings are historic and are economic capital until proven otherwise (Morton 1992; Lash and Urry 1994; Douglas and Isherwood 1979; Ewen 1988). In Europe, the task of serving this economic capital to the public falls to ministries of culture or to quasi-nongovernmental organizations (QUANGOS), such as national trusts. Economic capital used in heritage tourism includes reenactments of the past.

Figure 1.6 The "señora de la chalupa" (1999) symbolizes street vendors' dilemmas in Puebla, Mexico, and other historic centers. While many pedestrians want her products (the chalupa, a corn tortilla served with meat or cheese and various chili or chocolate [*poblana*] sauces), others — especially shopkeepers — object to the street vendors' nominal payment of taxes and fees, and their "cluttering up" of sidewalks and parks. Here, this vendor works adjacent to a plaza in Puebla, just off a sidewalk, in the entrance of a building.

These events have become popular on both sides of the North Atlantic, ranging from Colonial Williamsburg (Virginia) showing the life of a daily colonial town, to the operation of feudal and medieval villages of the Old World (Robinson et al. 2000). Because the authenticity is suspect and tends to glorify the past from an elitist standpoint (often giving no indication that slaves and serfs were deprecated, raped, or beaten), reenactments are "largely a pastiche with no higher purpose than popular entertainment" (Graham, Ashworth, and Turnbridge, 2000, 222).

In Havana, Cuba's World Heritage Site of La Cabaña Fortress, one can experience a reenactment of the closing of the gates to the walled city and hear the cannon blast (*el cañonazo*). Soldiers don wigs and colonial garb for the eighteenth-century ceremony as they march from the barracks to the cannon overlooking Habana Vieja (Old Havana). At us$5.00 per person (versus twenty-five cents in U.S. currency or five Cuban pesos for locals), it steadily feeds the public till. La Cabaña, though, was also where the revolutionary tribunals under the charge of Ernesto "Che" Guevara judged the henchmen of Fulgencio Batista (dictator from 1952 through 1959). Many of the accused were jailed and executed there. The same fortress was a jail for homosexuals, "counterrevolutionaries," and other politically incorrect persons as portrayed in the autobiographical book, *Before Night Falls* (*Antes de que Anochezca*) by the late exiled writer Reinaldo Arenas (the basis of the Julian Schnabel–directed film of the same name). However, sorting out historical meanings for a single building or public space is a complex task and is often ill suited to government agencies. It is more remunerative to present "highbrow" aspects of earlier landscapes than plebeian or "dark" venues. While the historical accuracy of these and connected events may be secondary to the scenery, they are visually striking spectacles that attract audiences. Nevertheless, I do not wish to suggest that low economic capital is simply the result of backwardness, underdevelopment, or Latin American culture. For example, Joan Vilagrasa and Peter Larkham (1995) highlight this unease between high and low culture in their study of Worcester, one of Britain's "historic towns." Worcester's "historic core consists of several pseudo-Georgian structures superficially resembling the predominant character . . . but by default rather than by conscious planning decision" (170). Summing up, despite the veracity or debate that determines what is built and what is restored, there is a growing tourism market that promotes these places (Tung 2001; Serageldin, Shluger, and Martin-Brown 2001).

Globalization and Heritage Tourism

The close of the twentieth century quickly secured a place for the term *globalization* in the world's languages. Once an isolated term confined to policy analysts and scholars, the term has practically become a household word, thanks to a dizzying array of "gee whiz!" technologies. One way to gauge its use in academic circles is the number of citations in the Library of Congress card catalog. In 1987, there were no entries with *globalization* as a keyword in the library's database. In 1994, Waters (2000) found thirty-four entries in the card catalog. In August 2000, I found 884, and in

August 2001 there were 1,384 entries: a 57 percent increase in eleven months (excluding the British spelling *globalisation*, $n = 213$, in the 2001 count). While the use of the term is on the rise, its precise meaning is less clear.

Globalization is a slippery concept that has come to mean everything, but also nothing. The World Bank defines it as "the growing interdependence of countries resulting from the integration of trade, finance, people, and ideas in one global marketplace. International trade and cross-border investment flows are the main elements of this integration" (Soubbotina 2000, 66). I use *globalization* mainly to refer to a shrinking of time and space through the rise of information technologies. We can theorize the economic, political, and cultural dimensions of globalization to make our review of world problems more precise (Lerner and Boli 2004).

As firms and individuals exchange information and commodities at a quickening pace, the abilities of the nation-state and its regulatory agencies diminish. That means nations slowly lose control over the flows of information, capital, and technology that pass through their boundaries. Some argue that these "new spaces of globalization" represent a victory of "post-Fordist" capitalism (Cox 1997; Dicken 2003) because new types of investment are no longer based on the traditional components of economic development that included natural resources and cheap labor. Alternatively, others argue that because labor unions and the conventional blocs of voters are made increasingly powerless in a globalized world, transnational capital can more easily circumvent the traditional coalitions who looked to the state for protection and support (Mishra 2000; Afshar and Pezzoli 2001; Korten 1995; Mander and Goldsmith 1996).

These reasons highlight how globalization is inextricably tied to the transformation of the centro histórico. Whether the changes stem from remittances sent by Ecuadorian dishwashers in New York and New Jersey; European jet-setters or "narco" money-launders in Cartagena; or European multinationals in Habana Vieja, the evidence is clear: those who live in the historic quarters must articulate their needs in a policy arena that is increasingly dominated by international capital.

This book argues that the nation-state and municipal governments are, at best, willing accomplices in promoting change in their centros históricos. Simply stated, except for in Trinidad, Cuba, local authorities in the locales I examined do little to enhance residential buildings either through direct repair, subsidies, or tax incentives. Rather, public efforts go to promoting tourism and commercial enterprises of all sizes. Many of these enterprises are internal, and though globalization is somewhat imprecise, it remains a useful conceptual tool in understanding the nuances of the impact transnational processes make at the local level. For example, how does the French hotel chain Sofitel retrofit the Santa Clara Convent in Cartagena and demonstrate its relationship with the centro histórico at the local level, and its allegiance to international capital (chapter 5)? What are the restrictions that international capital indirectly imposes on tourist workers who labor in Habana Vieja's tourist industry (chapter 6)? These tensions highlight the need for a global and theoretically informed perspective that connects the centro histórico to local, municipal, national, and international factors. As cities scramble to promote the unique selling points of buildings, squares, promenades, and other landmarks, they confront the great paradox that by making their geographic and market niches universally accessible, they may render them literally meaningless and placeless. As Ashworth (2003, 9) argues in the case of European cities, when "local heritage is selected, simplified, and sanitised for rapid and easy tourist consumption," the authenticity of place lessens.

Policies for Heritage Tourism

Heritage tourism is a subset of the broader pattern of international tourism. Accordingly, one has to tease out business travelers from the "sun-'n'-surf" crowd and from other kinds of sojourners to get a grasp on the relative or absolute numbers of tourists that visit "heritage sites." Although there is good evidence that this niche tourism is gaining popularity, there are no reliable data for comparative purposes.

Even if the numbers are imprecise, heritage tourism has formed a well-defined subset of policies and recommendations for the tourist industry. International conferences frequently outline policies and coordinate intranational and international agencies. Table 1.1 identifies the kinds of policy, planning, and cultural issues that are almost universal. The policies

Table 1.1 United Nations conference recommendations on heritage tourism

Recommendation
Cooperation among local, national, and international institutions.
Individual and bilateral projects that facilitate personnel exchange and training, and knowledge sharing.
Emphasizing the need to advance knowledge of tourism management in heritage cities through different activities as well as by means of information technology.
Recognizing that in the situation of heritage cities, sustainable tourism development is closely related to the sustainable development of heritage cities, and therefore it becomes a priority for local authorities to formulate and implement proper cultural tourism policy in partnership with the private sector, and with the participation of citizens.
Noting also that the right balance should be struck between the issue of valorizing heritage as a means to generate both welfare opportunities for the host community — which bears the costs of tourist exploitation — and the financial means needed to preserve and promote heritage itself.
Conserving the physical integrity, value, and symbols embodied in the heritage for future generations and collective memory.

Source: Greatly modified from UNESCO, "Cultural heritage cities: Culture, Tourism, and Sustainable Development Revised Plan of Action for International Co-operation on Tourism Management in Heritage Cities," proceedings of a conference held in Israel in 2000 (http://www.unesco.org/culture/development/highlights/decade/tourism/html_eng/nazareth.html; accessed April 2003).

show the need for real interdisciplinary approaches to historic preservation and how the fields of urban planning, museum science, and economic development overlap.

Several important practical and theoretical notions highlight the findings of the United Nations conference cited in table 1.1. First, heritage tourism is inherently local, thereby calling for careful coordination among layers of government agencies. Second, heritage specialists, curators, planners, and administrative and ancillary personnel need to share their knowledge. International agencies (UN), private philanthropic (e.g., Shell, Getty, Ford), and funding agencies (World Bank, Inter-American Development Bank) can coordinate and subsidize these personnel exchanges. Third, heritage tourism complements sustainable development, and the priorities should complement local needs (Sassen and Marcotullio, forthcoming). Last, local residents should prioritize their goals and have a hand in shaping heritage tourism. These are laudable normative goals. As we will see in later chapters, few centros históricos have embraced this approach because either they use top-down plans or the locals are disaffected or apathetic, or they cannot devote time to grassroots community-based planning.

We should remember that not all heritage tourism is widely accepted; nor are all landmarks and monuments always appreciated. In Bamiyan, Afghanistan, in 2001, the Taliban destroyed two priceless, 1,700-year-old Buddhist cliff statues because they found the objects an affront to Islam and the Quran. The Taliban threatened the destruction for weeks, and that provoked international outrage. Japan even offered to remove the statues and bring them to Japan. Officials in UNESCO also pleaded to preserve the monuments because they had earned World Heritage status, but to no avail. Their destruction could be considered a harbinger of the attacks of September 11, 2001, on the World Trade Center and the Pentagon, and the U.S. retaliatory invasion of Afghanistan on October 7, 2001. The United Nations considered rebuilding one of the destroyed Buddhas, at a cost of up to $50 million. While the price tag is great, Afghan archaeologist Zafar Paiman argued that it would be a small price to pay in rebuilding the nation's larger war-shattered culture because "there's a cultural void" (McGirk 2002, 18). Three years after the destruction, UNESCO officials continue to debate whether building a replica might turn an ancient religious site into a Disneyesque, homogenized, and controlled tourist trap. One advocate for leaving the blasted niches empty is Ikuo Hirayama, chair of the Japanese National Commission for UNESCO, who argues that their current condition represents "a symbolic reminder of the barbaric destruction of culture by human beings" (Gall 2003). A related though less egregious war-related travesty was the looting of museums and archives in Baghdad after the U.S.-led occupying forces established control over the city in 2003. Allegedly, priceless books, carvings, and other rare pieces fell into the hands of mobs while U.S. Marines intervened too late. Fortunately, the majority of the missing artifacts were later found secure in a bank vault where they had been placed a decade earlier.

In the Americas, slave quarters in Brazil and Cuba are controversial when preservationists try to restore them. Does restoration herald

Table 1.2   The functions of national heritage legislation

Heritage legislation aims to	Heritage legislation does not aim to
Provide a municipal policy for the protection of historic properties.	Prevent new construction within historic areas.
Establish an objective and fair process for designating historic properties.	Require that historic properties be opened for tours.
Protect the integrity of designated historic properties with a design review requirement, while allowing for and encouraging change.	Restrict the sale of property.
Stabilize declining neighborhoods and protect and enhance property values.	Require approval of interior changes or alterations.
Authorize design guidelines for new development within historic districts to ensure that it is not destructive to the area's historic character.	Require improvements, changes, or alterations

Source: Modified from US/ICOMOS (2000, 64).

the dominant culture, victimize the enslaved people, or faithfully re-create history? In recent decades, we have seen how war destroys heritage sites, especially along the Iranian and Iraqi border during the 1980s even though both nations were Muslim (Broadway 1999) and, arguably, should revere the same sites. Therefore, consensus on identifying and safeguarding heritage sites is problematic, and rife with tensions that defy facile interpretations.

Heritage legislation plays an important role in safeguarding national cultural assets. When passed at the national level, there is a mistaken assumption that it overrides local laws and possibly infringes on individual and property-owner liberties. In its simplest form, heritage legislation controls how people treat buildings, monuments, shrines, prehistoric sites, and designated historic districts. However, legislation alone is not a panacea. In most market economies,[2] heritage legislation maps out clear responsibilities for both public and private actors about what can and cannot be done (table 1.2). As we will see in the case studies in this book, there is much disinformation about the role of policies and laws, and even greater difficulty in implementing and enforcing those laws.

Latin American tourism is increasingly becoming a major source of economic development. It is vying for the nearly us$476 billion spent in 2000 by 689 million international tourists (Jafari 2002). Many nations in the region realize that if cultural and economic needs are taken into account, tourism can contribute substantially toward social and economic development. Over the past five years, a few countries registered higher than annual growth rates of international tourist arrivals. Central American destinations, including Belize and Panama, witnessed a remarkable growth rate of 13 percent between 1995 and 2000, nearly four times the world average. The Dominican Republic and Cuba experienced more than one million arrivals and had growth rates of 18 and 11 percent, respectively. In 2001, the First Ibero-American Tourism Summit in Cuzco, Peru, gave tourism a priority role in economic development programs. A joint declaration, *The Cuzco Commitment,* states that tourism could provide an edge against poverty, especially when indigenous and cultural elements factor into tourist programs (Frangialli 2002, 2). All this bodes well for reexamining the role of heritage tourism in the Spanish American barrio.

Moving Beyond the Urban Grid

Latin Americanist and urban historian Gerald Greenfield (1994) argues that scholars have long ignored urban Latin America because Spanish America had long been considered an agrarian realm. Since the mid-twentieth century, the classic checkerboard layout of its towns, including the large plazas and ceremonial architecture, has been the topic of many works (Theodorson 1982). The state of urban geographical research on the centro histórico enables scholars to move beyond the classic grid pattern and search for institutional and cultural processes that elucidate the urban condition in these places. In other words, what began as a debate over the evolution of urban design is now part of a larger discussion about historical processes. Why was the grid so widespread, and why did the urban imprint of these early colonial centers seem so similar? Three general suppositions stem from these debates.

First, Spanish conquerors might have known little about urban design. Beyond what the Moors taught them in Andalusia, the Spanish were not well versed in Roman, ancient, or medieval design. The grid provided a simple solution that adapted to a variety of settings (mining camps, military towns, ports, and administrative centers). Moreover, it was easy to apply in designating land grants, "sight unseen" (Vilagrasa and Larkham 1995).

Second, the geometric pattern conveyed an imperial will and supported the colonists' need for a standardized townscape in the overseas settlements. The caudillo or military officers in charge, however, had considerable flexibility in deviating from the norm. Usually, the standards included platting out eight streets that were about 8 meters wide (25 feet) and enclosed blocks that were roughly 70 by 80 meters in size, and divided into four equal lots. The cabildo and church had to face the square, while the main officials received lots near the main plaza. Space was then set aside for hospitals, convents, a butcher shop, and a slaughterhouse (*matadero*). Burial sites for Catholics were sited at the edge of the settlement, and non-Catholics were located even farther beyond. Spain mandated the use of Indian or African labor whenever possible.

Third, town planning in Spanish America represented a liturgical act of sanctifying an extension of the church as well as the Royal Crown. More than just a cartographic feature, the grid was a venue for the diffusion of economic, political, and social order. Nearly every centro histórico has identified where Catholic settlers held their first mass, its date, and the clergy performing the act (Morse 1992). All this information forms part of the city's historical legacy, despite the origin of the mythology or the veracity of its claim. The urban historical geography of the Spanish American centro histórico is described in more detail in the next chapter as are historical synopses of the nine study sites.

Scope and Purpose of Book

This book explores how heritage tourism and globalization reshape the Latin American historic district. My goal is to move beyond the building-specific approach that many architects employ in studying colonial architects. I share the approach of Cuban architectural historian and conservationist Víctor Marín to the study of architectural preservation when he states:

> Architecture as part of culture becomes an endurable [enduring] artifact capable of becoming a cultural property by itself, but architecture is also supposed to contain or to generate layers of history and culture across its lifetime. Preservationists try always to consider architecture as patrimony but in some cases it is not viable because in every epoch and site humanity focuses mostly on every day life and events without a historical perspective on the cultural values of architecture and art. (2002, 19)

Overviews of key literature set the stage for exploring urban land-use in nine historic districts (listed in table 1.3), and in-depth reviews of four of them (Havana [chapters 4 and 6], Trinidad [chapter 7], Cuenca [chapter 4], and Cartagena [chapters 4 and 5]). I use a case study approach to understanding the relationships between heritage tourism, globalization, and the Latin American plaza and barrio. Following Robert Yin's (2002) pioneering methodological work, I reason that the case study method is the most appropriate for understanding the "how" and "why" of contemporary events, versus survey, experimental, archival, and purely historical analyses. Only by weaving these various techniques into a single tome can we enhance our understanding of historic places.

This book describes the *contemporary* condition of the Latin American historic center. I ground my research in a part of urban and cultural geography that Cosgrove (1987) calls a "new" cultural geography. By that, he suggests that the study of place should be contemporary as well as historical (although he is not the first to have made that claim). To do this, the study must remain theoretically informed and contextual, as well as social and spatial. Earlier, much urban and cultural geography confined itself to narrowly defined issues of landscape. One way to avoid that pitfall is to draw on aspects of humanistic geography that stress the symbolic qualities of landscape and try to decipher social meanings of urban spaces. By fastening to that approach, human geographers of all stripes (urban, cultural, political, historical, social) can move beyond mere descriptions and can conceptualize landscapes as "text" that can be interpreted as a social document.

Table 1.3 Selected attributes of greater metropolitan areas in study, c. 1990 and 2002

Place	Admin. division	National rank size	1985[a] pop. (millions)	2002 pop. (millions)	Metro. area pop. (millions)	Latitude (°)	Longitude (°)
Bogotá, Colombia	Santa Fé de Bogotá/Distrito Capital	1	5.469 (1993)	6.540	7.594	4.63 N	74.09 W
Buenos Aires, Argentina	Distrito Federal/Buenos Aires	1	11.256	11.624	12.761	34.61 S	58.37 W
Cartagena, Colombia	Bolívar	5	.728 (1993)	.836	—	10.40 N	75.50 W
Cuenca, Ecuador	Azuay Province	3	.204 (1990)	.271	—	2.9 S	79.01 W
Havana, Cuba	Ciudad de La Habana	1	1.925 (1981)	2.312	2.639	23.13 N	82.39 W
Montevideo, Uruguay	Montevideo	1	1.247	1.432	1.701	34.87 S	56.17 W
Puebla, Mexico	Puebla	5	1.007	1.286	2.459	19.05 N	98.22 W
Quito, Ecuador	Pichincha	2	1.187	1.610	1.738	0.31 S	78.46 W
Trinidad, Cuba	Sancti Spiritus	30	.042	.061	—	21.8 N	79.98 W

Source: The World Gazetteer (http://www.gazetteer.de; accessed April 2003).

[a]Exception: populations from other years are given in parentheses.

Note: Data are not available for those cites with a —.

In this study of Latin American plazas and barrios (neighborhoods) that comprise the historic districts, I have tried to work out of this new "cultural geography," and my approach is intentionally broad both in methodological and conceptual respects. Because cities are layered in meaning, my methods are necessarily diverse. I draw on conventional historical and architectural texts to describe the evolution of these landscapes, using a considerable number of photographs. I agree with Rose (2001, 32) and Stuart Hall (1997), who argue that visual images are never innocent and that they always represent some bias in how they are used and how they will be viewed by the reader. That weakness notwithstanding, I try to use images that complement the text in the best way I can.

Understanding the nuances of geographic scale is important in my approach to these historic centers. While I aim to sketch the connections between these small corners of the Latin American city and global processes, the allure of these locales to the international tourist is their small geographic area and quaintness. If "small is beautiful," then these places have much to offer, but the balance between remaining remote and relatively unexplored, on the one hand, and becoming a global landmark, on the other, is a delicate one. These challenges underscore heritage and museum studies almost universally. The words of a director of a small museum in my home state of Virginia expresses this sentiment well:

> Once people see the new [Virginia Museum of Fine Arts], I won't have to stand up and shout that we're a great museum, it'll be pretty obvious. . . . I realize that we can't be the next MOMA [Museum of Modern Art in New York City], and we can't be the next Met [Metropolitan Museum], and we don't want to be. But visitors can have the experiences here that they can't have there. This is a place small enough that someone who comes to see the Art Nouveau will almost always end up stopping by to see the African art across the hall, because it's so reachable. (Goodheart 2003, 8)

The same accessibility and complementarity can be said for the visitor to Habana Vieja who makes a day trip to Viñales in western Cuba, or the cruise ship passenger to Cartagena who stops at the Rosario Islands, and the tourist in San Telmo (Buenos Aires) who decides to take a high-speed ferry across the River Plate to explore Ciudad Vieja in Montevideo.

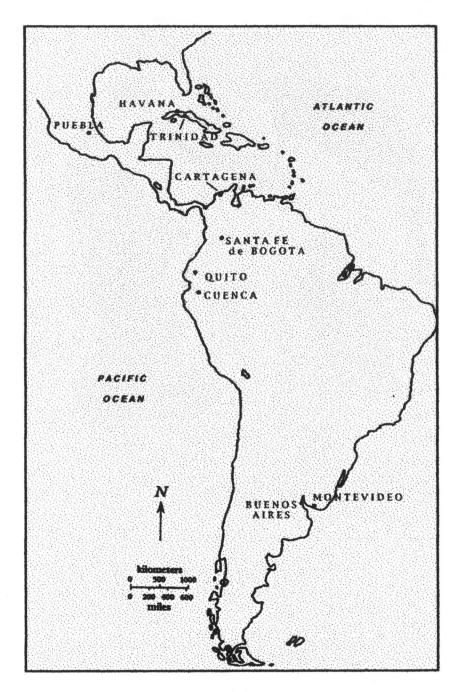

Figure 1.7   The nine study sites (*centros históricos*).

In chapter 2, I turn to urban geographical and urban sociological interpretations of the "shape" of the city to understand the similarities and differences in the nine study sites. I select a few contemporary planning debates that highlight common problems of heritage tourism, planning, and globalization in many centros históricos. The nine study sites that I have chosen (figure 1.7) vary by region (Caribbean, highland Mexico and Andes, and Southern Cone), absolute location (five ports, four inland sites), racial and ethnic profile (Andean and Incan pasts in Puebla and the Ecuadorian sites; African influences or the influence of slavery in Havana, Trinidad, and Cartagena), and other variables. I have tried to enhance archival work and interviews with public officials by conducting focus groups in three locations (Havana, Cartagena, and Cuenca) to capture an ethnographic interpretation of how locals view the transformation of their historic districts (see chapter 4).

Simply stated, I wanted to know how locals felt about the upgrading of their neighborhoods since they had been "discovered" by international tourists. What are their perceptions of local tourism, planners, and politicians? Is tourism good or bad for them? Who were the winners and losers of this new tourism? Did they feel as if they had a voice in the process? In turn, these focus groups allowed me to go back to the literature on social and community organization as well as on political economy. Would locals react more favorably to heritage tourism if the capital transforming their neighborhoods came from family remittances (Cuenca)? Would they be angry if the money were illegal (Cartagena) or came from foreign joint ventures (Havana)? These methods and cross-case approaches will offer the reader a fertile field for understanding the tensions between the modern and traditional aspects of the built environments in each city.

2 The Historical Geography of the Spanish American Centro Histórico

Yeah, buddy, I was born a *porteño*, right here, in the port of Buenos Aires, southwest of the River Plate, that river that separates us from the Uruguayans. I am Roberto Valdés, one of many — one of eight million — who had the good luck of beginning to roam these streets, through the pentagon-shaped city on one side of the river. This is all my nationalism, my "Buenos Aires-ism" [*porteñismo*] to be honest, all within sight.

Pablo Babini, *Buenos Aires con ganas*[1]

This chapter presents my interpretation of the urban historical geography of the Latin American centro histórico. My aim is not to provide a primer for urban geography or to introduce comparative Spanish American histories; vast literatures on those topics already exist (see especially Bromley and Jones 1996b). Rather, I outline selected elements of material culture (i.e., the shape of the neighborhoods, their streets, orthogonality, and the grid) as well as turning points in the urban histories that give these neighborhoods their special character. The shape of these places illustrates common features and highlights subtle discrepancies that lead to the social constructions of the Latin American centro histórico in the age of globalization and international heritage tourism.

For those who are well versed in these perspectives, parts of this chapter may be either skimmed or read selectively. We begin with the imprint and shape of the built environment.

Urban Morphology

A conventional way to study the built environment is to assess the architectural history of a place. In Latin America, colonial architecture is often regarded as a provincial reflection of European art with modest adaptation to the colonial setting. As in most of the world, the type of architecture developed depends largely on three factors: tradition or culture (local or imported), the availability of materials, and climate (Buisseret 1980, xiv; Segre 1995). In recent years, a spate of scholarship has sought to reinterpret the role of tradition, power, and control. Therefore, buildings and public spaces are not merely extensions of a motherland or of a particular style of design but rather project their own identity and symbols. Spanish American architecture was also meant to convey menacing messages to Portuguese, English, French, and Dutch forces. The power of Castile was firmly in place.

Spanish colonizers subjugated the native people by building towering churches, cathedrals, garrisons, bulwarks, and fortresses that served ideological as well as military ends. Unlike the English settlers of Massachusetts, who found only "a hideous and desolate wilderness full of wild beasts and willd [sic] men" (Bradford 1952, 61–62), many of the Spanish conquerors met a populous indigenous civilization, either in the site of a potential settlement or in the vicinity. The intentional display of architectural motifs, as well as labor and building practices, contributed to the religious, political, and economic conquest of Native Americans. Valerie Fraser (1990) and Anthony King (1990) contend that the architectural metaphor is an innate concept in the vocabulary of imperialism. Yet, "imperialism" as such rarely formed part of the language of colonial Spanish America. Instead, writers in colonial Spanish America spoke of the Catholic kings as the first architects of Spain's evangelization campaign. Catholic Spain, unlike Protestant England, could not easily dismiss Spain's victory in 1492 when the Moors were finally driven off the Iberian Peninsula. Castile and Aragon left their mark on the New World at every opportunity, and an aggressive building campaign fulfilled that. Catholic doctrine spurred the Spanish to colonize, build, and evangelize (Early 1994, chap. 1).

The Holy Scripture contributed to that frenzy. References to the *após-toles arquitectónicos* stem directly from the Bible and the history of Christianity. "God the Father" is the great architect, his son Jesus Christ is the foundation or cornerstone, and Peter is the rock or foundation of Christianity and Catholicism. A powerful ideology, this belief system resonated in Spanish America. One of the most extensive building frenzies ensued as churches and garrisons sprang up to secure this new land for the faith.

Fraser contends that "colonial architecture cannot be value-free: its very existence presupposes the suppression of native culture and the exploitation of native labour" (1990, 4). Clearly, Spanish colonial architecture was an architecture of conquest that helped to consolidate the Spanish Empire (Fraser 1990, 167).

If symbolism characterized the first edifices in colonial Latin America, what other factors made the colonizers authoritative? Quite simply, the quality of the public buildings, churches, and elite residences was very high. Leading churchmen and governors wrote to Spain or Italy for the best professionals to direct building projects in the New World. Architects, engineers, and sculptors trained in Europe could make a good living in Spanish America. Designers and builders grafted their projects on to the grid-plan form as stipulated by the *Ordenanzas,* or master plans, which date most consistently from 1573 (Stanislawski 1950; Caplow 1949; Gade 1974; Morse 1992). The result was to bring many classic forms of European design to Spanish America — including Baroque, Neoclassical and Gothic — and to impose a uniform appearance and institute town planning, anchored around the original town squares. The *plaza mayor, plaza de armas, zócalo,* and other names for Spanish American town squares served as important places for ritual promenading (Arreola 1980, 1982; Jackson 1984). In such "proper" public settings, it also became easy to identify "disorderly" conduct by idlers, vagrants, and the unemployed and to display the power of the military and security forces (Brading 1980; Scarpaci and Frazier 1993). What would evolve as the contemporary centro histórico that was anchored by the plaza, then, was imbued with a powerful combination of symbols, prestige, and power (Guillén Martínez 1958). Latin America's centros históricos imposed a stamp of rationality and civility. It was prestigious to live in or near them. Church architecture exhumed symbolism that was important in catechism and in the evangelism of the native population.

Although the forces of modernity, the modern architecture tenets of the Congrès International d'Architecture Moderne (International Congress of Modern Architecture; CIAM), and the rise of the automobile would combine to undermine that sense of prestige in the twentieth century, the pace of that erosion was uneven, as the chapters of this book will attest. The vision of CIAM, molded mostly by the architect and urban planner Le Corbusier (1887–1965), advocated European, North American, and South American cities where people lived in climate-controlled high-rise buildings in high-density suburban bedroom communities. These enclaves were actually "superblocks" surrounded by open spaces. Inhabitants would commute to work in a distant central city by automobile (figures 2.1a–2.1d). Le Corbusier's ideas were shared by other European Modern architects such as Ludwig Hilberseimer and Walter Gropius. The latter group borrowed the traffic-protected superblock notion to establish "machine age" cities on a new scale designed exclusively for the automobile (Southworth and Ben-Joseph 1997, 8). In this vision, imparted to Latin American schools of architecture and planning departments in the twentieth century, the Latin American centro histórico was the antithesis of modernity, a thorn in the side of the modernizing metropolis (Hardoy 1992, 38).

As Spiro Kostof reminds us in his masterpiece, *The City Shaped: Urban Patterns and Meanings through History* (1991), making cities is a universal experience. However, there is no simple answer to the question: "Who makes cities?" The economic and legal history of each city is a complex web of events and land uses. Factors include who owns land, the land market, the practice of compulsory purchase or eminent domain, building codes and taxes, and the role of a master plan in guiding urban design (Kostof 1991, 11). If questions such as these are daunting, so too is identifying the main designers of cities. We know, for example, that the Aztecs carved a complex city in Lake Texcoco where Hernán Cortés and his men grafted their version of a New World city onto the Aztec's plan. Pierre Charles L'Enfant's (1754–1825) work in Washington, D.C., Baron Georges-Eugène Haussmann's (1809–91) leveling and construction of Paris as Napoleon III's appointed prefect of the Department of Seine, or Daniel Burnham's (1846–1912) innovations in Chicago, as well, provide clear-cut examples of associating one designer with a particular city. The truth, though, is that beyond a list of the "big names" in urban design, there are thousands of conscious and subtle actions that shape cities. While the final form may seem to be a neutral pattern of geometry, it is the cultural interpretation and use of those spaces that give those spaces meaning.

The cultural ascription of urban meanings in most Latin American cities was built on "green sites," except in the impressive cases of

a

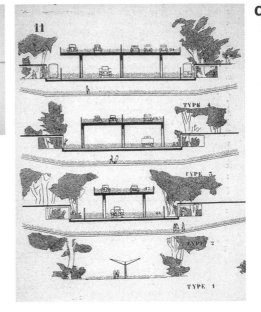

c

b

la ciudad   el río

d

pre-Columbian settlements such as Mexico City or Cuzco, where indigenous urbanization was advanced. Unlike most European cities, Latin American colonial cores (and all nine study sites in our book except Cuenca) were largely "fresh" sites where military engineers, farmers, mariners, and the clergy left their marks on the streets and lots for the "Glory of God" and for the "Honor of Spain."

Colonizers in Spanish America laid out towns according to the requirements set down by the Law of the Indies or in the Ordenanzas, which were part of the Law of the Indies. These formal codes identified sites for major buildings, arranged streets at right angles, and created plazas. Standard practices in laying out the new towns were to intersect two main axes with a large public square. The size of the plaza was the key to the size of the rest of the settlement; it regulated the grid and often varied from one town to another. Santo Domingo (then Hispaniola), the first planned settlement, was laid out in 1493 in a grid pattern. From that time onward, conquistadores and their military engineers clung faithfully to this disciplined spatial order, and only two major exceptions existed. The Jesuits

Figure 2.1a   Figures 2.1a–2.1d contain several sketches by Le Corbusier for modernizing Buenos Aires, c. 1925. Source for all four figures: *Buenos Aires.* Buenos Aires: Hachette, 1925. In this figure, the superblock concept meant leveling several city blocks to construct high-rise apartments that would face an open area in the middle. Roads would be widened to provide easy access into the city. This sketch has lines for roads and buildings superimposed over an aerial photograph of a section of Buenos Aires.

Figure 2.1b   Le Corbusier's global vision entailed densifying the shoreline to denote a stark divide between the sea ("el río," to the right) and land (*la ciudad,* or city, to the left). Building height diminishes moving inland.

Figure 2.1c   Elevated highways increase in size, from bottom of sketch to top. Over- and underpasses were not conceptualized as bringing dead space to a city. Rather, depending on needs and local characteristics, the underpasses could be used to accommodate different roads, pathways, parking facilities, or pedestrian spaces.

Figure 2.1d   Accommodating a "modern" Buenos Aires for Le Corbusier meant widening and limiting access to highways, with service and local roads in the middle. Travel corridors like these would define the new city in which the car would reign supreme.

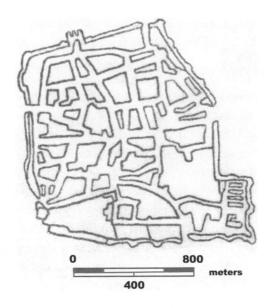

Figure 2.2 Layout of Tarifa, Spain (Andalusian region), reflecting the "organic" style of Moorish and pre-Renaissance cities.

0   800

400   meters

could build their *reducciones* as they saw fit,[2] and the military establishments, or presidios, could adopt different criteria. After 1600, though, the differences between these three types of settlements abated.

Uniformity in Spanish American city-making responded to a broader set of norms that the Renaissance in Europe had unleashed. Its rationality and order, especially as interpreted in Spain, conjured up a disciplined language and contrasted with the more "organic" and free-flowing settlements built during the Moorish occupation of the Iberian Peninsula from 742 to 1492 (figure 2.2). Deviations from the grid plan (*cuadrícula* or *plan en damero*) in colonial Spanish America accommodated existing indigenous buildings, and preexisting Native American streets and canals, as well as the imposition of stubborn topography that interrupted the urban geography of the colonial core (Crain 1994, 29). As Dan Stanislawski (1956, 105–6) argued half a century ago: "The casual assumption that the grid almost automatically becomes the pattern of a new settlement cannot hold up in light of the history of its distribution."

The street grids and block sizes of the nine case studies are presented in figure 2.3 for easy comparison of their sizes and shapes. Each district in the figure corresponds to the national (and, where proper, UNESCO) declared historic district or World Heritage Site (chapter 3 presents the land-use survey of these areas). Two sets of patterns stand out in figure 2.3. One is the more organic and less geometric pattern of Trinidad, Cartagena, and, possibly, Havana. In the former, the heart of the town sits at twenty meters above sea level, in the foothills of the Alturas de Trinidad (Trinidad Highlands, part of the Escambray mountain range). When settled as one of the original *villas* (military outposts, original settlements) in 1514 by Diego de Velázquez, it was set back some eight kilometers from the Caribbean Sea, and it was endowed with a strategic view of ships approaching tiny Casilda Bay. The gentle slope of its site over moderately rolling foothills accounts for its winding look (figure 2.4). Little orthogonality is evident today in the historic quarters of Trinidad.

A second aberration in the strict codes of the Law of the Indies stands out in Cartagena (figure 2.3). The Caribbean Sea and backwater lagoons constrained the islands that created this heavily fortified city and encased its three neighborhoods: Centro, San Diego, and Getsemaní (discussed in chapter 5). One might also be tempted to append a third outlier: Havana. Although the Cuban capital lacks the formal and regimented layout of Cuenca, Bogotá,[3] Puebla, Quito, Buenos Aires, or Montevideo, its north-south axes are straight. A few of the east-west cross streets widen because of the city's piecemeal growth during the sixteenth century. The cape upon which it is located configures Old Havana's spiral shape. In the main, though, the centros históricos in this study convey a sense of order and discipline. Even more remarkable is that Buenos Aires and Quito were platted and laid out before they were actually settled (Fraser 1990, 61–62). This is the urban form set down in the fifteenth century.

Cultural adaptation and change, besides the demolition, birth, and rebirth that city blocks and buildings experience, is also evident in street names. It is common for each street to have at least two or more designations in the historic quarters (Scobie 1974). Usually, the original name corresponded to a military, literary, or biblical note. Then, as local economic geographies developed, names began to reflect institutional or commercial activities such as El Arsenal (shipbuilding activities), Avenida del Puerto (Port Avenue), or Las Minas (the mines, usually because a road

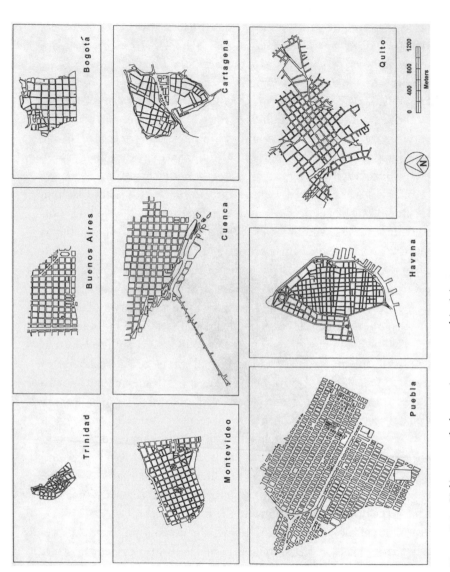

Figure 2.3 Urban morphology, nine centros históricos, 2002.

Figure 2.4 Trinidad, street design and individual lots, 2001.

would lead to a mine or a quarry). Homage to the homeland would reflect a current king, queen, duke, count, or countess. The early Republican era (1825–30, except in Cuba where independence came in 1898) ushered in new street names, and some relabeling occurred to honor national heroes, politicians, soldiers, artists, and local folks (Morse 1992). In the twentieth century, many of those names succumbed to the mandates of a more disciplined scheme and assumed ordinal numbers (First Street, Second Avenue, etc.). Figure 2.5 reflects this "layering of names," which can be an

Figure 2.5   The "layering" of street names in historic Puebla.

important point when asking for instructions; older residents often use older street names that they recall from childhood or from their parents' or grandparents' eras.

Plazas, Culture, and Public Space: Notes from the Field

Plazas are more than just city blocks framed by four sides. They affirm many aspects of public culture, material and nonmaterial. Their functions change over time and during the year. In Latin America, plazas served as places for military training and reenactments, seasonal county fairs, and green markets, as well as places to hold casual conversation. Over time, the local elite anchored important plazas with houses and apartments, though much of that has changed in the twenty-first century. As early as the 1930s, Latin Americanist urbanists began noting that the traditional relationship between elite residences and the center was reversing because of change and population growth. Moreover, the larger the town or city in the Spanish American centro histórico, the quicker the pace of elite out-migration and land-use change was (London 1982, 375–76; Caplow 1949, 132; Schnore 1965; Hansen 1934).

We can interpret the plaza for insights about citizenship, governance, and cultural identity. Vilagrasa and Larkham's (1995) study of urban morphology in Europe, North America, and Latin America revealed that most social scientists fail to consider the role of architecture in urbanization and development. In this book, I approach plazas as if they were mirrors of Latin American culture, class structure, and architectural style. Citizens will become engaged with local authorities over how their town squares are used because those spaces are essential as artistic displays, local historical artifacts, and cultural expressions. For these reasons, their furnishings (benches, playground equipment, light poles) and architectural designs provide the physical settings where informal conversations and other socially meaningful exchanges take place (Low 2000, 30–33).

To crystallize this discussion about the meaning of the Spanish American plaza, I present selections of my field notes from the past fourteen years. I blend my own field observations as well as verbatim (recorded on audiocassette and then transcribed) remarks by local residents and tourists as a way of capturing the social construction of these public places, with an eye toward the impact of heritage tourism. The section that follows is a sampling of field notes that offer insight into this discussion.

HAVANA, PLAZA DE CRISTO, MAY 2, 1992.

6:30 PM   I have been coding [e.g., conducting a land-use survey discussed in chapter 3] all day. This is one of the few benches in the old quarters that is comfortable and is not falling apart. I'm lucky to secure the spot since benches are hard to come by. The view is exceptional, and there are not a lot of tourists here or elsewhere in Habana Vieja. The all-female construction crew has been working on a broken water main for several days now. They proudly display a sign over the manhole that recognizes their quality work. A banner using the red, white, and black colors of the

July 26 Movement reads: "*microbrigada destacada*" (distinguished micro-brigade). Kids are bouncing the ball off the side of the church, and two games of stickball are going on in the space in front of the church. Aside from the church, there is no reason for tourists to visit this square. While the few laurel and fichus trees here are in need of some heavy pruning, they provide much shade and respite from this May heat. Four elderly men have dragged some boxes to use as seats, and an absorbing domino game is under way. No one looks twice at these white-haired men; three of them have their shirts off in this nearly 100 percent relative humidity.

The Vietnamese restaurant on the corner is run by Cubans and sells meals only in dollars. No one is inside. The residential flavor of this square is undeniable; it is a tranquil spot in the midst of Habana Vieja, which, for the most part, seems like parts of bombed-out Beirut [Lebanon]. . . . [Plaza de Cristo] is unceremonious compared to the Plaza de Armas and the Plaza de la Catedral, and has a strong sense of community. I think the planning students in [Virginia Tech's] master's program [Urban and Regional Planning Community] would profit from just observing this scene.

HAVANA, PLAZA DE ARMAS, MARCH 4, 2002.

2:30 PM   There is a "dance" unfolding here between two *jineteras* [prostitutes] and any men in their forties or fifties who look European. The young girls wait in the shade under the Captain's General Palace, glancing every so often at the Italian restaurant that occupies most of the sidewalk leading up to the plaza. A couple of Italian men have gone through several rounds of Cristal [Cuban beer] and definitely eye the young women. The younger of the two women has pink Spandex pants on, and she has caught the eye of one of the men.

2:40 PM   Two men in the beer drinkers' group have paid their tab and start walking toward the port, and the Cuban women follow a few steps behind. The foursome meets in front of the Templete monument at the southern end of the square and greet each other as if they are old friends. Kisses and hands are flying, and they are talking in the sun. The white-haired Italian fellow is turning bright pink. A deep discussion sets in.

2:47 PM   Some agreement has been made. Two couples have been formed. They turn in the opposite direction and head toward San Francisco Square. Three policemen in front of the Santa Isabela Hotel [where Jimmy Carter stayed in May 2002] watch the couples stroll past. About one minute later, the policemen head off in the same direction. It is a cat-and-mouse game, but who is who?

HAVANA, PARQUE CENTRAL, MARCH 3, 1999.

8:30 AM Parque Central is the Republican center of Havana and is flanked by glorious turn-of-the-century [twentieth-century] buildings. Right across from me is a statue of José Martí, erected in 1905 on the tenth anniversary of the death of this liberation fighter, author, and poet. On the southern side of the square the usual "baseball gurus" are meeting. They exchange baseball scores and bet on Cuban as well as on U.S. baseball games. Yesterday I learned that many of these men belong to sports clubs and watch pirated signals from ESPN that cover a wide array of sporting events.

9:00 AM Though it is early, I arranged to meet with an accountant who works at the Parque Central Hotel, gracing the square at the northern end. I want to find out about his work with a joint-venture complex in the old city. Tomás graduated from the José Antonio Echeverría Polytechnic University with a degree in civil engineering in the mid-1980s. After a brief stint with MICONS in the late 1980s, he was laid off in the early years of the Special Period. After several years of un-, under-, and multiple employment in jobs ranging from an illegal auto mechanic, to a taxi driver (*botero*), to a tourist guide, he was hired by the Golden Tulip Management Company [then, administrators of the Parque Central Hotel, but in 2001 the hotel was passed on to a Spanish management firm] in 1997. His familiarity with spreadsheets landed him a job in the accounting department.

Tomás shows up at about 9:15. He tells me that for the first eighteen months he worked as an assistant to the head accountant on the day shift. Then, in late 1998, he had an opportunity to work as an auditor on the night shift; one of several upper-level positions available to Cubans. His task is important, as he must provide a check on eight cash registers from as many departments throughout the hotel (two bars, swimming pool with bar and café, main bar, two restaurants, and two gift shops). Discrepancies between receipts and cash as well as matching charges with the proper guestrooms are his most important responsibility. He is the first line of resolution between any of the eight departments, and the top-line management (Dutch personnel). In the morning, he prepares an Excel spreadsheet file with the previous day's tallies for his European boss.

Half of his $875 monthly salary reaches him in pesos; the other half, of course, is directed to the state. After his third month as the chief night accountant, he began receiving US$80 under the table. As of June 2000, he was receiving an additional $25.

"It is to be expected," he explained. "I've proven my worth and I can weed out any underreporting of low-level petty-cash theft if it continues over time." When asked if he thought that the full US$875 should rightfully come his way, he told me: "Of course. But I cannot complain. Maybe over time things will change." He then proceeded to tell me woeful tales of his siblings and how hard it is for them to eke out a living based on their meager peso salary.

"Golden Tulip knows I am reliable. I clear thousands of dollars for them daily." In addition, he eats breakfasts most every morning in the main tourist restaurant. "With that banquet of a breakfast, I'm good all day, and that helps at home with the *libreta*.[4] Sometimes they have luncheons for us in the back restaurant or in the lobby-bar, and occasionally we can bring our wives." . . . "Joseíto," he laughed, "I really cannot complain! ¡Tú sabes bien que estoy resolviendo! [You know well that I'm just making ends meet!]" He likes that lots of buses and *boteros* (fixed route jitneys) pass right in front of the Parque Central, and allow him to get easily to and from work.

TRINIDAD, PLAZA DE LAS TRES CRUCES, JUNE 11, 1994.
9:15 AM   Last night's rainfall has carved out a small rivulet — about one foot deep — in the middle of the square [also known as Calvary Square (Plaza del Calvario) because the Good Friday procession ends at the foot of the three crosses], which is unpaved and rudimentary. Clay and different-sized stones are piled up around the open space. In some ways, the square looks unfinished and very unkempt, not because it lacks a hard surface, but most of the houses surrounding it are run down, in need of repair and paint. I understand there used to be a Holy Week celebration here [before the Revolution of 1959].
9:50 PM   A white-haired Afro-Cuban woman coming down from the hill

stopped in the narrow shaded sidewalk were I am sitting. We talk about the square, and she tells me that she played here as a child, as did her children, and now her grandkids do the same. She becomes animated speaking about the Holy Week processions. "The little plaza was full of people," she says, and her hand sweeps out from side to side, pointing to where people stood. She then asks me if I'm lost and wants to know what I'm doing here, because tourists never come to this end of town. "The Plaza Mayor is also very nice, very special. But I have no need to go there since the *bodega* [state-run food store] is right here." She takes out a handkerchief, wipes her brow, and moves on, wishing me a good day.

TRINIDAD, PLAZA DE LAS TRES CRUCES, MAY 23, 1999.
8:15 PM   It must be at least 88°F and the sun has only been up for just over an hour. I'm struck by how run down this plaza is; the only one in the many that I've studied that is still not paved. Three self-employed (*cuentapropistas*) vegetable vendors are sharing part of the shaded sidewalk with me. We talk about vegetables, what makes a good mango, and the high price of produce. I turn the conversation to the ceremonial use of the square, and the vendors eagerly tell me about the two processions they joined in.

"After the Pope's visit, they allowed the processions. It was wonderful! My grandmother told me about them when she was young. I've never seen the square so full of life. The [Catholic priest] gave his blessing to everyone that was present."

I ask whether the vendors would like some porticos for shade or some market stalls. "No!" they quickly chime in. The older vendor says: "People from the edge of town come through here; they know we sell our produce here. The square is fine; it's my house that needs the work; it's a real dump."

CARTAGENA, RAMPARTS, NORTHERN WALL, CIUDAD AMURA-LLADA, JUNE 28, 2000.
2:30 PM   This has to be one of the most picturesque baseball diamonds I have seen! The old walls surrounding the city frame a small baseball field that is nestled between the ramparts and the Caribbean Sea, to the north.

There are no dugouts present, but the adolescent boys' teams seem to be part of a league because each side has its own colors. Hard to believe that just a few steps into the walled city are densely stacked homes and apartment complexes. No public toilets are located anywhere in sight, and the boys take turns urinating in the corner base of the rampart. From where I'm seated atop the ramparts, I see an abandoned sentry lookout tower. Yesterday I walked by there and noticed that hideaway also served as a bathroom, and the smell of excrement was strong.

3:15 PM   Cars have pulled off the small road that runs along the shoreline. A few teenagers have their speakers turned up full volume. The salsa blasting from the cars is welcomed by the players. A few minutes later a young women (mother?) pulls up, and one of the ball players runs over to the car and carries back two plastic containers of water for his teammates. It is hot, and it is only the third inning.

The famous Nobel laureate, Gabriel García Márquez, has a house in sight from where I'm perched; I can see his rooftop to my left and the ball game to my right. I wonder if he ever wanders out to watch the game.

3:25 PM   Two young girls, friends of the players, have joined me atop the wall. They want to know what I'm writing. I ask them if Gabriel García Márquez ever watches the game. They've never seen him here. "Gabo? Everyone knows Gabo. But he is sick. My older brother used to see him a lot, but not so much anymore."

CARTAGENA, PARQUE SAN JOSÉ, CIUDAD AMURALLADA, JULY 8, 1999.

9:30 PM   The sausage vendor carts are doing a lot better than the upscale restaurants surrounding the square. It is interesting to see how the locals have not allowed the restaurants that started here—no doubt after the five-star Hotel Santa Clara opened its doors a few years earlier—to stop them from coming to this square. An evening art class from the art school at one corner of the square has let students out. The male students stop at the mom-and-pop grocer to get beer and soft drinks, and the girls are buying sausage sandwiches from the vendor. This vendor has his children working a series of carts near his kiosk that have charcoal, storage bins for buns and relishes, and paper-foil wraps for the hot sandwiches. Small lanterns and soft lights in this small square blend seamlessly into the storefronts of the three restaurants that have pink-colored tablecloths on their tables-for-two.

10:15 PM   A few months ago, a pizzeria (really an Italian restaurant) at one end of the plaza was raided by police, who busted the owner for running a brothel. Very little business is going on on the ground floor, and I'm keeping an eye on the second-story windows (where, I'm told) the brothel operates. One of the art students says that it gets busy over there around 1 AM, and I'm not inclined to wait around. Two art majors talk about the circus and myriad characters [*personajes*] around the plaza. "Hey, this show is free. You've read Gabo's [Gabriel García Márquez's] books, right?" I start to talk about *One Hundred Years of Solitude,* and the older artist cuts me off: "Well, this is it. Right here, this is magical realism! Pimps, prostitutes, artists, families, and, even you, a college professor. This is the show, this is it!"

BUENOS AIRES, PLAZA DORREGO, DECEMBER 23, 1989.

1:30 PM   A fair number of white-collar workers have been walking from the direction of the Plaza de Mayo, which is flanked by large government office buildings. I assume many of them work there and are coming home for lunch. Many of the elder pedestrians that I saw yesterday around 7:30 are gone; they were making their way to neighborhood bakeries. Nor do I see the elderly sitting in the cafés chatting with other seniors or reading the morning paper. Now, there are younger, better-dressed people in there, and more than a few are tourists. Flyers stapled on telephone poles around the square announce the flea market on Sundays.

In front of one bar, a pair of tango dancers has taken to the streets. They are rehearsing, I know, because I've seen them dressed formally for the large weekend shows. A few tourists don't know, and stop to watch.

My first time [in Plaza Dorrego] was in 1983 as a tourist along with a group of Chilean public school teachers. The plaza seems less vibrant now that it did six years before. Now, this square seems to be turning around, though I'm not quite sure how.

It is such a place of contrast: the antiquities stores are full of family china, furniture, paintings, and heirlooms brought to these vendors because hard times have fallen on the nation. People are selling their families' goods just to make ends meet. The shop windows look like something out of London's antiquities shops — a lot of broken memories for sale. I can see three bookstores that were not here six years before. The *bandoleón* [accordion] music in the background really tops off this choreography. I'm concerned that these trappings make this plaza "too easy" to read. Note to self: be more critical, look beyond the obvious. . . .

BUENOS AIRES, PLAZA DORREGO, DECEMBER 15, 1995.
8:10 PM   The value of the peso has fallen off sharply, and that may be why there are fewer locals here and more tourists than in past visits. What is noticeable, though, is the quality of the facades: someone has been painting, plastering, and cleaning. In some ways, this is looking like a more Bohemian version of the park at Recoleta, across town. It also looks like any plaza in southern France or parts of northern Italy. Or a Latinized Greenwich Village? More tables and chairs ring the plaza than before. This is at once familiar (e.g., Mediterranean) but foreign. It has all the allures of a wonderful setting to have a coffee, a glass of wine, an empanada.

PUEBLA, MAY 3, 1997, ZÓCALO (MAIN TOWN SQUARE).
10:40 AM   What a delightful time of the year to be in Puebla! I had forgotten that the Cinco de Mayo holiday originated here, and the town authorities have laced the plaza with ribbons that are the colors of the national flag: red, white, and green. Except for the cathedral at one end of the square, it looks remarkably late nineteenth century: the ironwork, lampposts, and gardens. This is the stateliest of squares, and the tall pine trees provide an unusual amount of cool shade in this normally hot and dry city. The pigeons are unexpected, but there they are, and several clusters of elderly women and nannies with children are feeding them.

There are decidedly very different spaces here. The open light and spaces near the church do not attract many pedestrians; opposite the church is a long stretch of retail stores, set back under shaded porticos [where more pedestrians gather]. No matter how they attempt to disguise it, there is no mistaking the McDonald's there, but at least the plastic signage does not protrude outside the colonnaded gallery's facade. The heart of the square has a deep, "urban garden" feel about it, and the trees muffle the sound of traffic a few blocks away. It is a busy village green, one of the statelier and more sober ones I have seen (certainly in Mexico, and even in Uruguay, Argentina, and Chile).

QUITO, JULY 13, 1998.
I've just fought my way through streets packed with street vendors (ambulantes) and anxious local shoppers. The main town square is refreshingly uncluttered, but a few land uses stand out. First, there are small shops — perhaps a half dozen or so — under the main government building on the square. They look as if they may have been sentry stations for soldiers. Today, though, they are used by shopkeepers who sell small souvenirs, trinkets, Ecuadorian memorabilia, etc. Second, there is a horrible modern building opposite the main government building. Though it respects the skyline somewhat, its modern intrusion cannot be masked. Third, this square slopes gently and is most unusual in that regard. It is probably the noisiest of squares, not from pedestrians, but rather from the buses, trucks, and taxis moving through the lower end of the square. This is not a place to seek solace.

My field notes, then, captured my impressions of the varied nature of the plazas and barrios that make up the centros históricos in Spanish America. This small sampling of observations reflects the background of a white, bilingual, male of forty-odd years from the United States, who is broadly trained as a human geographer. I have reprinted these notes to offer the reader the kinds of events that caught my eye personally and intellectually as I traveled through these barrios. These impressions were, in part, the reason for exploring these places in a more systematic fashion. To do that, though, requires a brief historical introduction of those plazas, barrios, and centros históricos in the following section.

Selected Histories: Plazas and Barrios

Bogotá: Barrio La Candelaria

Brief History, Settlement, and Economy. Bogotá, the capital of Colombia, is the center of the country geographically and economically. It lies in a fertile highland basin at 8,660 feet (2,640 meters) above sea level in the

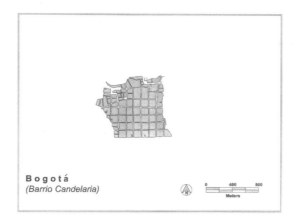

Bogotá
(Barrio Candelaria)

0   400   800
Meters

Figure 2.6   Barrio La Candelaria, Bogotá, urban morphology, 2002.

Cordillera Oriental of the northern Andes. The city occupies a sloping plain (*sabana*) at the base of two mountains, Monserrate and Guadalupe. The oldest neighborhood of the city, Barrio La Candelaria, sits at the bottom of Monserrate. Bogotá was laid out faithfully in a grid pattern that contains modern skyscrapers (comprising the International Center) just beyond the original colonial core (figure 2.6). Road types in Bogotá continue this pattern: *carreras* (avenues) run parallel to the mountains from south to north. Streets (*calles*) align from east to west and cross the avenues perpendicularly.

Gonzalo Jiménez de Quesada founded Bogotá in 1538 after defeating the Chibcha Indians. Originally, the settlement carried the name Santa Fé de Bacatá: *Santa Fé* signified Quesada's birthplace in Spain, while *Bacatá* — an indigenous warrior — was soon changed to Bogotá. As capital of the Viceroyalty of New Granada, the Colombian capital also served as a major center of Spanish colonial power, and Barrio La Candelaria denotes the first platted neighborhood of Bogotá. Twelve *chozas* (shacks) marked the first residences in the neighborhood (Sanz de Santamaría 1989, 26).

Geographic isolation characterized Bogotá because of the many mountain ranges and long valleys that dissect Colombia. Growth in the colonial era, therefore, was modest compared to that of Lima, Mexico City, or Havana. By 1670, for example, the city had only three thousand residents. It lacked the gold that the Spaniards sought, and commerce and manufacturing on the Pacific were concentrated in Medellín, while Cartagena controlled the maritime economy of the Caribbean coast of Colombia. By 1800, the population of Santa Fé de Bogotá had reached just twenty-four thousand residents.

After the Independence Wars that ended around 1825,[5] Bogotá continued as the capital of New Granada, which later became the Republic of Colombia. The balance of the nineteenth century witnessed struggles for political domination in the capital and, along with its geographic isolation, limited Bogotá's prosperity and growth. By 1891, Bogotá had only expanded about a half-dozen blocks to the south of La Candelaria and about a dozen or so to its north (figure 2.7). In 1928, the city claimed just over two hundred thousand residents, but that figure tripled by 1951. After World War II, the northern neighborhood of Chapinero had become the preferred elite quarters of the city, marking steady out-migration of the well-heeled and powerful Colombian families from the colonial center (Greenfield 1994, 147). In the spring of 1948, riots known as the *bogotazo* battered the city. Civic unrest continued in the capital and the rest of the nation for the next decade.

Political violence continues today among factions of the Left and the Right, and the narcoguerilla forces. Historic Barrio La Candelaria has not been the target of this violence. However, in 1985 guerilla forces attacked the Supreme Court Palace found on the main plaza of Bogotá (Plaza Bolívar) next to Barrio La Candelaria. Although over a hundred hostages were killed, the Colombian Army mounted tanks in front of the palace and obliterated it. Seven years later, the palace was still being rebuilt (figures 2.8).

Contemporary Overview and Planning Issues. Colombia's constitutional change in the 1990s to rename Bogotá to Santa Fé de Bogotá bodes well for a new appreciation of the city's colonial past. Contemporary planning (over the past two decades or so) has focused on keeping abreast of new peripheral settlements throughout the valley. Between 1958 and 1972, for instance, the metropolitan area gained one million residents in illegal, "clandestine" settlements (Greenfield 1994, 149). Municipal governments have been hard pressed to supply these settlements with a basic public infrastructure. Consequently, historic preservation by public leaders in Barrio La Candelaria has been assigned a lower priority. In 1982, however, a public-private corporation managed a good bit of

historic preservation, especially the plazas, sidewalks, and other public spaces (Corporación Barrio La Candelaria 1989).

The historic district has been well maintained because of the large number of universities in the centro histórico, as well as a vibrant retailing sector that caters to the universities and related businesses: office supplies, photocopying, and information services (chapter 3 examines its retailing and residential land uses.) Some of South America's oldest universities were founded and still operate in Barrio La Candelaria. These include the Xavier Pontifical University (1622) and the University of Santo Tomás (1580). Barrio La Candelaria serves as one of the main cultural sites of Santa Fé de Bogotá, with its numerous museums, theaters, art galleries, nongovernmental organization, and libraries, many housed in colonial structures from the eighteenth and nineteenth centuries. It receives brisk and steady foot traffic by tourists who stroll uphill from the Plaza Bolívar.

Entering Barrio La Candelaria from the city's main town square, one finds the Iglesia de la Candelaria, just across from the modern Luis Angel Arango Library. Calle 11, or "Calle del Cajoncito" (or "Pigeon-hole Street," because it's so small), houses many *chocolaterías*, serving the famous Bogotá hot chocolate. Unlike some study sites in this book, the old neighborhood is eminently available, enjoys a strong cultural life, and is free of large sections of shanties and squatter settlements.

In 2003, Bogotá mayor Antanas Mockus performed the politically unthinkable task of showcasing his city to more than five hundred leaders at the ninth annual Inter-American Conference of Mayors and Local Authorities, held in Miami. Although much of Colombia's countryside is mired in civil strife, Bogotá is a relative oasis of parks, bicycle and pedestrian paths, and heritage sites. Moreover, Mayor Mockus requested that

Figure 2.7 Topographic map of Bogotá: 1891, revised 1894. The thick, dashed lines identify portions of Barrio La Candelaria. With the north at the left of the image, the southern border of the neighborhood parallels a streambed running in the middle of the picture. The uniform platting of the neighborhood is evident. Bogotá's main town square (Plaza Bolívar) is the lighter shaded block, in the middle of the map, just at the western (bottom) edge of the neighborhood. Original cartographic source taken from a copy at the National Library, Cartographic Section, Bogotá. Dashed lines added by the author.

Figure 2.8 Supreme Court Palace in Plaza Bolívar, under construction, at left, 1992.

the city residents voluntarily pay more taxes — approximately 10 percent — beyond existing levels. To the surprise of many, more than sixty thousand *bogotanos* anted up because they knew the additional revenue would be earmarked for social and cultural projects. This "110 percent" program is heralded as an attempt to show city residents that metropolitan government is not a wastrel when it comes to resources. "To my great pride," remarked Mockus, "the highest percentage of [voluntary tax-paying] participants came from one of the poorest neighborhoods in Bogotá" (Lynch 2003). Such civic engagement bodes well for heritage promotion and cultural showcasing, from which Barrio La Candelaria stands to benefit.

Havana: Habana Vieja

Brief History, Settlement, and Economy. San Cristóbal de La Habana, like Trinidad, Cuba, is one of the island's original seven villas. The settlement's first location, directly south of its present site but on the Caribbean Sea

Figure 2.9   Habana Vieja, Havana, urban morphology, 2002.

(Gulf of Batabanó), was established in 1514, but it was moved to the north shore of the island along the Florida Straits in 1519 (figure 2.9). A complex network of military fortresses appeared by 1540, and by 1590 the city's garrisons — still standing today — were nearly complete. A British incursion in 1762 discovered a weakness in Havana's defenses, an unprotected ridge across Havana Bay, overlooking the city; the British seized it and bombarded the city into surrender. After a yearlong occupation by the British, Spain financed the construction of La Cabaña, which protected the city from the seventeenth through the nineteenth century.

A rudimentary ring of bulwarks, bastions, turrets, and garrisons surrounded the city. Their function was to prevent non-Spanish forces (mainly buccaneers and corsairs) from pillaging the port's Spanish riches shipped in from South America (Colón and Cartagena) and Mexico (Veracruz). Havana Bay provided a natural, deepwater port that filled with ships at the end of hurricane season, before they sailed back to Cádiz and Seville.

Despite the military network, the Spanish Crown did not always consider Havana its most important villa. The island's first government seat was in Santiago de Cuba, at the opposite end of the island, and on the

Caribbean Sea. Yet, because West Indian resources (gold, silver, and native woods) paled in comparison to those of the mainland, the colonial powers shifted the administration to the western end of the island, closer to Mexico and Veracruz. Havana was primed to become the island's center of colonial rule, and with the completion of an important aqueduct running from the Almendares River to the west, Philip II granted Havana its official title as a "city" in 1592. It adopted a coat of arms that defined important elements of the city's geography and history. The symbol denotes the great fortresses and garrisons (Fuerza, Morro, and Punta) and a key that represents Havana's ability to "unlock" the lands and seas of the Caribbean and beyond. Positioned at a crucial juncture between the Gulf of Mexico and the Atlantic Ocean, the city's maritime importance grew despite the absence of weighty mineral or agricultural resources in the fifteenth and sixteenth centuries (Aguilar 1993).

Colonial life in Habana Vieja—Havana's colonial core—evolved around four major plazas. Administrative and government affairs clustered around the cabildo at the Plaza de Armas. Two blocks away lay Plaza de la Catedral, where the city's sober baroque cathedral was completed in the early 1800s. Maritime commerce entered Havana through San Francisco Square (Segre 1994), which today receives a new brand of seafarers: cruise line passengers sailing out of Jamaica who pass through an Italian-financed $11 million air-conditioned cruise-ship terminal (Scarpaci, Segre, and Coyula 2002). Wholesaling and retail functions developed around Plaza Vieja, which is undergoing major renovation and is detailed in chapter 6.

The colonial architecture in Old Havana was modest compared to the ornate edifices found in Mexico City, Cuzco, or Lima (Alvarez Tabío 1994). A natural endowment of good hardwoods allowed the construction of impressive, if modest, homes, government buildings, religious architecture, and military installations. Shipbuilding and certain residential construction used designs comparable with the ceilings of many structures still standing today (such as the Santa Clara Convent) resembling inverted ship hulls (*Urban Design and Planning in Havana, Cuba: An Historical Perspective* 2001). Commercial demand for wood depleted the forests around Havana by the late eighteenth century. However, the sugar plant-ings saved the economy and created a dense network of railroads in the first half of the nineteenth century.

When the slave revolts in colonial Haiti broke out in 1791, Cuba benefited from the migration of French sugar planters who brought their knowledge to nearby Cuba (Zanetti and García 1998). Wealth from this prosperity enhanced the look of Habana Vieja, as did the rise of coffee production. Mansions and palaces built during the sugar boom reflect that prosperity, and the sugar and coffee passing through Havana to the U.S. eastern seaboard added to the city's coffers. Elite structures in Habana Vieja were mixed in among huts (*bohíos*) made of wattle, guano, and wood. Broken plaster, crushed stone, and rubble (*mampostería*) improved some of these flimsy structures.

The public defense relied on the systematic construction of the walls around the city, begun in 1663, but already outdated before 1740. Ship artillery could easily shoot over the top of the sea-fronting bastions and strike targets. Moreover, overcrowding within the walled city (called *intramuros*) was becoming unbearable. Therefore, in 1861, the colonial administration began tearing down the walls, and the suburbanization of farmlands, pastures, and clusters of homes accelerated outside the walls (*extramuros*) in such places as Cerro (to the south) and Vedado (west).

The latter part of the nineteenth century interrupted a steady flow of urbanization and prosperity for the colonial capital city. Although most of Spanish America was liberated by 1830, Spain—a fading European power—clung steadfastly to the island of Cuba. Independence Wars, beginning with the Ten Years' Wars (1868–78) and culminating three decades later with the 1898 Spanish America War, left Havana drab and unkempt (Scarpaci, Segre, and Coyula 2002, chap. 2). The U.S. occupation of the island (1898–1902) enhanced the city's infrastructure in Havana, especially Habana Vieja. Engineers from the United States improved electrical, telegraph, telephone, public water, waste removal, port facilities, and road systems. Habana Vieja, the seat of the commercial and banking operations, underwent a building boom that lasted well into the 1930s.

The advent of the automobile and the streetcar eased suburbanization to points south and west, but not to the east. The bay had not been forded,

Figure 2.10   *Bohemia* magazine cover promoting steamship travel to Havana.

and a tunnel to the eastern side would not be built until 1957. Habana Vieja retained its traditional financial and administrative functions during the Republican era (1898–1958). A growing steamship industry brought affordable, mass tourism to the island, benefiting Habana Vieja and the rest of the city during the first half of the twentieth century (figure 2.10). Unfortunately, an inordinate amount of public money went to beautifying the cityscape as seen from the rails of steamers entering the port from Galveston, New Orleans, Tampa, Key West, Miami, Jacksonville, Savannah, Baltimore, New York, and Boston (Schwartz 1997). Corruption in the post–World War II era led to a growing presence of organized crime figures from the United States. Although their investments were not concentrated in Habana Vieja, U.S. influence was widely felt in the customhouses, banks, and import-export businesses in the old city.

In the first three decades of the Revolution, the socialist government (1959–89) paid little attention to the city of Havana, and even less to Habana Vieja. Housing authorities converted commercial storefronts into housing in the old quarters to hold the roughly one in twenty Havanans who lived in shanties in 1959. The socialist government did build large-scale public housing projects in Habana Vieja, thanks to a large development in eastern Havana that had become open with the tunnel completion of 1957. The revolution foiled plans proposed by José Luis Sert and his team from Harvard to demolish several city blocks of Habana Vieja to house high-rise modern apartment complexes in the middle of the colonial core. The revolution's antiurban biases would change after the collapse of the Soviet Union in 1989, and Habana Vieja would be recognized as an asset in heritage tourism.

Contemporary Overview and Planning Issues. If necessity is the mother of invention, then Cuba's economic free fall in the first half of the 1990s proved to be a redeeming feature for Old Havana. The selection of Habana Vieja by UNESCO as a World Heritage Site in 1982 had not led to major improvements of the heritage sites within it. The municipal and national governments directed few resources to Habana Vieja at the time. On nearly every corner of the old city are the state-subsidized grocers (*bodegas*) and doctors' offices are located on practically every block of the old city. These social badges of honor received government attention; less care was given to the built fabric (Violetta and Scarpaci 1999). In 1993, the Office of the City Historian created a semiautonomous firm that began revamping Habana Vieja. Joint-venture partners have been sought out to upgrade old hotels (figure 2.11). This new firm (called Habaguanex and reviewed in detail in chapter 6) also created a chain of dollar-only stores that have been open since 1993 to all Cubans who manage to get dollars (not just diplomats). Old Havana today is rife with two types of activities. One type is domestic and peso-run companies confined to low-end goods and merchandise. A second type is the part of the dollar economy that is closely tied to the tourist trade (Peters and Scarpaci 1998; Scarpaci 1998). In 2002, nearly two million tourists visited Cuba, and most of them walked the streets of Habana Vieja. Nowhere in the Americas has heritage tourism created such potential conflict as in the colonial quarters of

Figure 2.11   Image of "gut-and-preserve" facade and restoration in Old Havana's many "renovated" hotels, 2002.

Havana, where the ideals of socialism collide with the demands of the marketplace (Scarpaci 2000c).

Trinidad

Brief History, Settlement, and Economy. The first accounts of Trinidad date back to 1494 when a seaman in Columbus's crew noted hunters and gatherers in the region. They described a landscape with "fruits and bread and water and cotton, and rabbits and doves of the most different species, unknown in our lands, and [the indigenous people] sang joyfully believing that people had come from heaven" (Gutiérrez n.d., 3). Settled in 1514 by Diego Velázquez, Trinidad lost the attention of the conquistadores when Hernán Cortés, who had stopped there briefly, headed off to the Central Valley of Mexico.

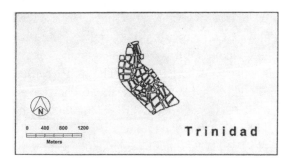

Figure 2.12 Trinidad, urban morphology, 2002.

During the sixteenth and seventeenth centuries, the settlement remained distant and hard to reach. As a result, contraband flourished. As noted earlier, its street layout ran somewhat organically along the side of a hill and deviated from the geometry of a formal grid plan (figure 2.12). The reasons used for deviating from the grid pattern seem as logical as they were in medieval Europe: "With local control each unit used its topography as individuals saw fit. There was no necessity for following the rigorous grid plan. Indeed for many topographic situations it would have been costly and excessively difficult" (Stanislawski 1956, 118).

Because Trinidad was out of the oversight of Santiago de Cuba to the east, and Havana to the west, pirates and corsairs from England, France, and Holland took advantage of Spain's frequent wars in Europe. Smuggling in Trinidad provided some income, even though dealing in contraband was illegal and restricted under Spanish monopoly. Trinidad's economy benefited from reforms enacted during the reign of Charles III (1759–88), which broke the privileges and monopolies enjoyed by Havana. Trinidad took advantage of these Bourbon reforms and expanded trade, especially with other Caribbean islands and the ports of Cartagena and Veracruz. In the nearby island of Saint Dominique (Haiti), the 1791 slave revolt sent sugar planters to Trinidad. The adjacent Sugar Mill Valley (Valle de los Ingenios) had fertile soil and came to house more than fifty sugar mills by the early nineteenth century. By 1825, Trinidad was producing 10 percent of the island's sugar from this single valley (Venegas 1973). Trinidad and its vicinity became one of the world's leading sugar producers. Landed aristocrats usually spent the sugar harvest season in country palaces, and the remainder of the year in Trinidad. Several

restored palaces that are now museums show the opulence of the era
(Núñez Jiménez, Zerquera, and de Lara, 1986). Elite families from that
era—Brunet, Becquer, Cantero, Iznaga, and Borello—constructed elaborate residences that are national landmarks today. The 1827 census
showed twenty-nine thousand residents, twelve thousand of whom lived
in the urban core, with the remainder scattered throughout the countryside in sugar mills and small hamlets (Gutiérrez n.d., 29).

By the mid-1800s, however, Trinidad's slave-based sugar production
method could not keep pace with the newly introduced mills. The traditional *trapiche,* consisting of oxen-driven millstones for crushing the cane,
could not compete with modern mills (Marrero 1983). Since slavery was
not abolished officially until 1878, the landed aristocracy was loath to
abandon the system and modernize sugar production. At the same time,
other parts of Cuba and Louisiana competed with the sugar production in
Trinidad. European beet-sugar production also undercut the world price
of sugarcane. In the 1820s and 1830s, investment opportunities lured
local capitalists to railroad construction between Villa Clara and Cienfuegos, and between Puerto Principe and Nuevitas. Moreover, Trinidad
experienced stop-and-go railroad construction, and its network was not
fully developed. Instead, plantation owners had their slaves float cane
down rivers, but when the rivers filled in from siltation, the logistics involved in getting cane to the trapiche became complicated. Cienfuegos,
founded late (1819) in Cuban history, had opened its new deepwater
seaport and drew traffic away from Casilda, Trinidad's port. For these
reasons, the town and region fell into a deep recession by 1860. While
other sugar-growing regions of Cuba—especially parts of Matanzas and
Havana Provinces—were connected by rail lines to sugar mills for pro-
cessing, and ports for export, Trinidad remained isolated and stagnant.
The Cuban Independence Wars of the late nineteenth centuries reduced
cattle production in the valleys and coffee cultivation in the foothills and
mountains around Trinidad. When American investors entered the region
after the war of 1898, they bought large tracts of land cheaply and replaced some forty-eight smaller sugar mills (*ingenios*) with a single, central modern facility (Marín 1945).

Economic recession and geographic isolation combined to leave important sections of the historic core of Trinidad in place. It was not until 1919

that a rail line made its way into Trinidad and connected the town with the national network. A paved road to the provincial capital, Sancti Spiritus to the east, was completed in 1950, and two years later another road was paved to Cienfuegos, to the west. All these factors — history, geography, transportation, and technology — kept Trinidad out of step with modernity and, in turn, preserved the antiquity of its built environment.

Contemporary Overview and Planning Issues. In the 1980s, Trinidad's municipal government began to capitalize on architectural resources for heritage tourism. In 1988, UNESCO declared the old quarters of the city a World Heritage Site. Other than tourism in the historic core, the regional economy consists of sugar refineries; sawmills; dairies; fisheries; and cigar, cattle-processing, and cigarette factories. A small airport brings in several flights daily from the "tourist poles" of Santiago de Cuba, Camagüey, Varadero, and Havana.

The first hotel with modern tourist facilities in Trinidad was erected in 1957. Hotel Las Cuevas sits on a hillside just above the colonial core and beyond the historic limits. Within the historic district there are no hotels, and the larger facilities are a twenty-minute drive away at Ancón Beach, on the Caribbean Sea. Fortunately, no modern structures disrupt the colonial skyline of Trinidad's centro histórico. However, in 2002, scores of legal and illegal bed-and-breakfast facilities operated, and they put serious strains on the city's water and waste system.

Chapter 7 discusses the Ministry of Tourism's 1999 plan to add more than four thousand additional hotel beds (units) to the Ancón Peninsula on the Caribbean, and the implications this holds for the World Heritage Sites of Trinidad and Valle de los Ingenios.

Puebla: Centro Histórico

Brief History, Settlement, and Economy. Puebla was founded in 1532 as Puebla de los Angeles for the express purpose of producing agricultural products for New Spain. Situated on a broad plain 7,093 feet (2,162 meters) above sea level in the foothills of the Sierra Madre Oriental, it is also on a strategic route between Mexico City, 80 miles (130 kilometers) northwest, and coastal Veracruz, 140 miles (225 kilometers) east. Puebla

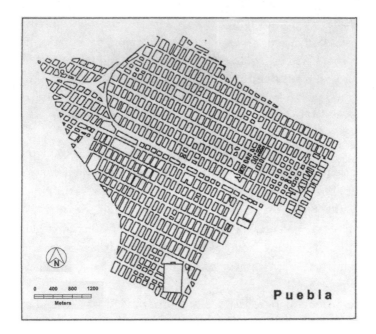

Figure 2.13   Puebla, urban morphology, 2002.

was allegedly home to Mexico's first textile factory and developed a colored tile and ceramics industry whose splendor can be seen today on practically every building facade in the historic district.

In the colonial era, Puebla was the most important city in Mexico. Besides closeness to Veracruz (Mexico's most important port), the city boasts significant architecture of interest to historians and tourists. Puebla has the most European appearance of all Mexican cities because it was planned from the ground up by Spanish designers instead of built from an Aztec town (figure 2.13). The cathedral was built between 1552 and 1649 and is considered one of the finest in Mexico (Early 1994). Its colonial theater erected in 1790 claims to be the oldest on the continent. Its university was established in 1539, also making it one of the oldest in the Americas.

Puebla was considered a strategic military point in Mexico in the eighteenth and nineteenth centuries. The United States occupied the city in 1847 during the Mexican-American War, but the *poblanos* successfully fended off the French in 1862, only to succumb to them the next year (Sánchez 1991; Perry 1997). Fortunately, none of the important buildings were lost during the city's occupation by foreign powers.

In the late nineteenth century and early twentieth, Mexico's industrialization took off in many central parts of the nation, but spared Puebla from the problems of urban primacy and hyperurbanization afflicting Mexico City, which got priority and investment. However, like all Mexican cities in the central region, Puebla is often rocked by tremors and earthquakes. In 1973, it suffered a major earthquake that caused considerable damage, especially in the centro histórico.

Contemporary Overview and Planning Issues. The center of important agricultural and industrial production today, Puebla is known for its onyx elaboration, glazed ceramic tiles, cotton and woolen textiles, glass, and pottery. Its industrial prowess was cemented with the opening of a plant for the assembly of Volkswagen cars in 1970 (Sánchez 1991). The State of Puebla's highway system permitted the spread of industry beyond the historic core toward the metropolitan edge and elsewhere in the state.

Modernity and the need for integrated planning strategies may work at cross-purposes, as Puebla's planning record in the 1990s shows. One study on the effect of a tourist project canvased neighborhoods at the edge of and just beyond the district's limits. The neighborhoods surveyed— Analco, La Luz and El Alto—include some fourteen blocks that were slated to improve infrastructure (waste, sewage, parking, public lighting), and tilt the proportion of residential land uses to commercial ones.

A research team at the Universidad Benemérita Autonóma de Puebla surveyed residents to assess their attitudes toward the project. The researchers found that seven out of ten residents were tenants. All residents valued the relative location of these neighborhoods because of easy walking distance to work and services in the historic center. Four out of five residents were averse to the state government's determination to convert the area into an international tourist spot. Instead, they viewed their neighborhoods as residential areas with an artisanal flavor (food preparation, pottery, bakeries, leather goods, glassware, furniture making, and confectionery). Their preference was to see the state grant credits for home repair, restrict the encroachment of space-consuming chain

Table 2.1   Selected land-use changes in Puebla's centro histórico, mid-1980s– 2002

Structure of area	Change
La Victoria Market	Converted from a large covered public market catering to low-end retailing, to a VIP department store and small shops.
Los Sapos Market	Modernized collection of small kiosks to attract related upper-end artisanal goods, art galleries, restaurants, bars, and cafés.
La Fábrica de los Francés	French-designed and French-manufactured building from the porfiriato era (1890s) that was turned into VIPs (a national department store chain).
Bus terminals	Several were closed or forced to relocate outside the historic district to reduce congestion and impede petty merchants from selling in the La Victoria vicinity.
Boulevard Cinco de Mayo	Multilane highway continues to cover up San Francisco River, runs through the middle of the historic district (see figure 2.14), and divides Analco from the rest of the historic district.
Paseo del Río de San Francisco	An archaeological site linking parts of the old town with the William O. Jenkins Convention Center.

Source: Author's field research, 1995, 1997, and 1999.

supermarkets, and enhance the pedestrian networks linking the series of public gardens, plazas, residences, churches, and small shopping districts in historic Puebla (González 1995).

Urban geographer Guadalupe Millán has analyzed the transformation of Puebla's historic center as "systemic modernization." Drawing on the works of Jürgen Habermas, Millán shows how the commercial deconcentration of colonial Puebla is a response to local elites and municipal leaders attempting to rid the center of petty vendors (*ambulantismo*) and low-end retailers (Irragori 1980). Planning officials conjectured that the petty vendors who used to concentrate around La Victoria Market (which was closed in 1986 and served as the major traditional produce and retailing market) were local. However, about one-quarter of the kiosk vendors at La Victoria came from outside Puebla's city limits (27.3 percent) but still from the State of Puebla, one-third were from the State of Puebla, and just over one-quarter (28 percent) came for Tlaxcala, Veracruz, Oaxaca, and the Federal District (Mexico City) (Millán 1995, 204). Officials failed to appreciate that by "cleaning up" this low-end retailing, they disrupted one of the largest national retail markets in Mexico (Conner 2001b).

Millán argues that the exclusion of working-class vendors and the transformation of certain classic buildings confirm "the elite-centric project of the historic center" (Millán 1995, 208). Indeed, several prominent land-use changes have taken place and have continued into the new century. While these land-use changes bode well for a "sanitized" and upscale historic district geared to tourism (table 2.1), they may fail to favor the needs of local residents (figure 2.14).

Despite the problems of land use and change in Puebla's centro histórico, Puebla's regional planning is well developed within Latin America (though it is not always community based). In July 1993, Puebla teamed up with thirteen other towns in the metropolitan area to create an administrative and planning zone called Angelópolis. Using GIS (geographic information system), land-use maps, and land records, the Angelópolis project aims to coordinate the planning challenges of the metropolitan area. Revitalizing the historic center is one of many projects that the state, municipal, and town-planning agencies address. Historic preservation competes for public resources with scores of shantytowns (*colonias*) throughout the region — all in need of potable water supplies and distribution, road construction, solid waste removal, water treatment, and affordable housing (*Angelópolis: Programa de Desarrollo Regional Angelópolis* 1997).

While Angelópolis is an ambitious plan, it has not always been well received. Nancy Churchill Conner (2001a) describes the controversial effort to implement the Paseo del Río de San Francisco project in the northeastern corner of the centro histórico. The project included a convention

Figure 2.14 Boulevard Cinco de Mayo runs through the historic district in Puebla forcing pedestrians on this sidewalk to step into ongoing traffic on this limited-access primary road, 1999.

center, museum, hotels, restaurants, movie theaters, and retail outlets. In 1993, 18.9 hectares, occupying twenty-six blocks became the site for the San Francisco project, where 70 percent of the residents were renters who worked mainly within one kilometer of their neighborhood. Conner (1999, 2000) argues that the official state discourse on the project is hegemonic because it is undemocratic and uses terms such as *rescue, revive,* and *recover* to mask the residential displacement caused by the project.

Former president Ernesto Zedillo declared on January 6, 1999, at the opening ceremony of the new William O. Jenkins Convention Center — built as part of the San Francisco project — that the facility was "without a doubt, a great project, a project of enormous vision, because it coincides on the one hand with the need to give a modern development to that which is the old heart of Puebla, but without forgetting about Puebla's deep roots" (*Palabras del presidente Ernesto Zedillo . . .*).

Clearly, President Zedillo's vision of modernity includes a standard economic-development tool: a convention center. The way in which the center cuts into the historic district highlights the conflict between economic growth and historic preservation. The promenade that forms the main axis of the Paseo del San Francisco is described by one prominent urbanist, Gareth Jones, as "a bizarre garden with bits of industrial brickwork jutting out from the ground, beautiful in a way and frequented by courting couples. . . . This is where the old houses from which people evicted by [then State of Puebla Governor) Bartlett once stood. [Residents] were never compensated" (personal communication, Gareth Jones, July 24, 2002).

Because of the San Francisco project, many residents of the adjacent barrio of Analco began moving out in 1993, an out-migration that has left parts of the barrio empty. Conner (2001b) says that religiosity and traditional practices — especially Analco's celebrated religious procession held on the fourth Friday of Lent — are important to residents. The Puebla experience shows that "modernity" can nibble away at the corners of *centros históricos* and that capital often "dictate[s] what . . . transformations occur and why" (Harvey 1996, 401).

Cartagena: *Ciudad Amurallada* (Walled City)

Brief History, Settlement, and Economy. Founded in 1533, Cartagena de Indias is located on the Caribbean coast of Colombia, at the northern end of Cartagena Bay. The original urban design of streets and blocks evolved unevenly because of the constraints of small islands and marshes dotting the bay (figure 2.15). Cartagena de Indias was eminent from the mid-sixteenth century onward when Spanish fleets annually docked there to load gold, silver, and other products extracted from northern South America. In convoy, they continued to Portobelo, Panama; Veracruz, Mexico; and Havana, Cuba; and on to Cádiz and Seville, Spain. Cartagena also served as a center for the Inquisition and a major slave market (Greenfield 1994, 139).

An ardently independent city, Cartagena de Indias, along with the surrounding province of Cartagena, declared its independence from Spain in 1811. Although it reverted to Spanish control from 1815 to 1821, it was recaptured by rebel forces. Spain called the region surrounding Cartagena Nueva Granada. Poor roads and rail connections made the port difficult

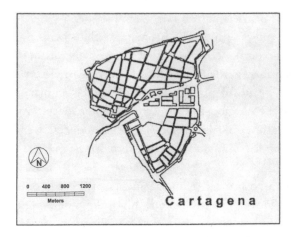

Figure 2.15 Cartagena, Ciudad Amurallada, urban morphology.

to reach from other parts of the colony. In 1831, Gran Colombia was divided into three sovereign nations (Venezuela, Ecuador, and Colombia), with Colombia using Barranquilla on the Caribbean coast as its preferred port (Lemaitre 1994). By the 1840s, population and commerce had plummeted, and it was not until the twentieth century that Cartagena began to revive.

A key factor in the city's renewed prosperity was the opening of petroleum fields in the Magdalena River valley after 1917. A completed pipeline from Barrancabermeja to Cartagena Bay in 1926, and the construction of an oil refinery, made Cartagena the country's chief oil port. Tourism has played a major role in the past twenty years, and is discussed in chapter 5.

Contemporary Overview and Planning Issues. The colonial quarters include the walled sections of the historic district (Ciudad Amurallada) and the seventeenth-century fortress of San Felípe de Barajas, which lies outside the walled city. (The three neighborhoods comprising the historic district receive more attention in chapter 5.) Metropolitan Cartagena encompasses the islands of Manga and Manzanillo, the latter serving as the home to the international airport. Shantytowns ring the city, the result of massive migration to Cartagena triggered by guerilla warfare in the highlands and Amazon River Basin. Rightist and leftist guerillas, as well as cocaine producers and smugglers remain committed to their ideologies, their multibillion dollar illegal trade, or a combination of both, but Cartagena increasingly relies on tourism. With monuments (San Felípe de Barajas Castle) and nearly 70 percent of its original colonial walls still intact, the city boasts vast amounts of colonial architecture. These include the Church of San Pedro Claver (1603), the Palace of the Inquisition (1706), several major plazas, Jorge Tadeo University, and the University of Cartagena (1827). Aware of the importance of a captivating world image, Cartagena promotes itself as a Caribbean tourist center, far from the highland wars or Amazon basin conflicts elsewhere in the nation. Chapter 5 explores in considerable detail the relationships there between heritage tourism, property taxes, and contemporary planning issues.

Quito: Centro Histórico

Brief History, Settlement, and Economy. Sebastián de Benalcázar and two hundred Spanish soldiers founded San Francisco de Quito in 1534. Settlement of the valley came slowly because of the more than seventy ravines and volcanoes surrounding it. A rumor circulated among the conquistadores that there was considerable mineral wealth in the region that the indigenous people knew about. However, compared to Potosí, Bolivia, or to parts of Mexico in the sixteenth and seventeenth centuries, settlers found only trivial amounts of minerals for metals. Quito's relative location became a central point for administering the mining operations of the Spanish colonists and for subduing the Incan settlements in the surrounding highlands.

Quito is as an equatorial Andean word referring to a kingdom broken into chiefdoms called *cacicazgos*. The Spanish founders imposed their own kingdom with the usual gridiron system (figure 2.16), defining the elongated settlement through the long, slender valley. In 1534, the settled parts of the city contained 175 hectares, while by 1888 the figure had risen to only 238 hectares (Fernández 1994, 240–41). Quito's historic core rests at the foot of a prominent hill, Pichincha, and the suburban areas — not growing much until the twentieth century — spread out along the valley floor.

Seventeenth-century Quito suffered when a royal decree closed the textile workshops (*obrajes*), which had been a specialty of the region.

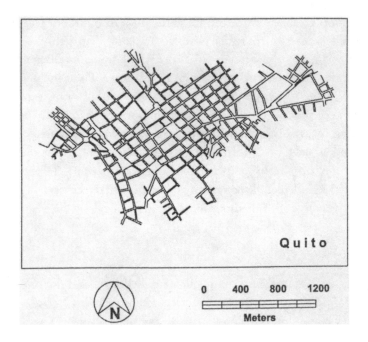

Figure 2.16   Quito, urban morphology.

Disease (a plague in 1759 killed eleven thousand Indians; smallpox in 1784 claimed the lives of about twenty-five thousand) and the Independence Wars with Spain deterred any substantial population and economic growth until the nineteenth century. When growth did take off—owing largely to a rail line linking the highland city with coastal Guayaquil—the municipal government used detailed zoning regulations (*planos reguladores*). Urbanization in Ecuador is a new phenomenon, with just over half the nation (55.4 percent) urban in 1990 (Fernández 1994, 218). By 1950, the population of Quito had exceeded two hundred thousand residents, and by 1990 it had reached the one million mark.

Urbanization delayed until the twentieth century spared much leveling in the centro histórico. New retailing and elite residences sought the open sites of the suburbs, leaving intact a large collection of historical buildings from the independence and republican eras. These historical and architectural attributes of Quito were recognized by UNESCO, and in 1979 the organization added two hundred hectares containing buildings from the sixteenth century to the eighteenth century to its World Heritage List. Over a thousand of these buildings have been inventoried. With so many historic buildings, the historic district might seem a "living museum," but in reality it is a dynamic retailing hub and is examined in the next chapter.

Contemporary Overview and Planning Issues. In the 1990s Quito's mayoral office entered into a new relationship with a private firm, Empresa del Centro Histórico, to provide services and programs to complement municipal planning. This public/private partnership, unusual among Latin American cities, works to provide affordable housing and promote small business growth within the historic district. Its goals are to "generate more adequate conditions to reactivate the economy in the 72-block core of the Historic Center" and to promote "urban renewal of the Historic Center with a human dimension in order to achieve a better quality of life that will benefit all residents and users involved in the process" (ECH 1998, n.p.).

Public transportation is especially important for bringing the masses into the centro histórico for shopping. In the early 1990s, some two hundred thousand buses, trucks, and cars circulated daily through the historic center. Not only was air and noise pollution great, but the snail-paced traffic created low-level vibrations threatening older buildings (figure 2.17a). Just as in many other Latin American cities, streetcars ran through early twentieth-century downtown Quito, but city authorities removed them after World War II to make way for more bus routes. In the mid-1990s, the municipality reintroduced electric trolley buses connected to an overhead guide rail (figure 2.17b). As riders get used to the new mode of transportation, city planners hope to lessen the environmental and seismic pressures on the centro histórico.

Cuenca: Centro Histórico

Brief History, Settlement, and Economy. The Spanish found Cuenca, like Quito, attractive because of its relative location in a highland valley and its proximity to Incan settlements. The Tomebamba River in the heart of the contemporary city provided an adequate supply of water and a defensible location. The Cañari people occupied Cuenca (known as

Figure 2.17a   Bus, truck, and automobile traffic surging through Quito's centro histórico in the mid-1990s. An estimated two hundred thousand vehicles daily passed through the district. Photo 1997.

"Tomebamba") before the Spaniards arrived and were skilled builders with established military quarters, homes, and temples around a square of forty by five hundred meters. An Incan civil war destroyed much of Tomebamba between 1525 and 1530. In 1537, the Spanish founded Santa Ana de los Ríos de Cuenca (Caprio 1979) and closely grafted a grid settlement patterned loosely after the original Tomebamba site (figure 2.18).

True to their traditional goal of seeking quick riches, the Spanish spent the early years searching for gold and, when they did not find large amounts, set off to farm the surrounding countryside. Subsistence-level production kept population growth low, and the city and region hobbled through the sixteenth and seventeenth centuries. Population growth in Cuenca actually declined from 18,919 in 1778 to about 13,500 in 1838 (Palomeque 1990).

Figure 2.17b   In the mid-1990s, the municipal government introduced electric buses into the city of Quito to cut down on air pollution and reduce vibrations of vehicle motors idling in the historic district. Photo 1997.

The inclusion of Quito and the surrounding area as part of Gran Colombia after independence was short lived. When the federation dissolved in 1830, Quito became part of the new nation of Ecuador. Although agriculture remained Cuenca's main activity, *cascarilla* (quinine) exports boosted the city and region's economy in the mid-nineteenth century. By 1862, cultivation of palmetto fiber (*paja toquillo*) supported a hat industry that shipped the finished products from Panama. When the hats reached markets in the North Atlantic, vendors called the finished products "Panama hats" after the last port of customs clearance before entering the haberdasheries of New York, London, and Paris (T. Miller 2001). In the 1860s the Panama hat industry became one of Ecuador's largest, second only to cacao (Caprio 1979). While the rail line between Guayaquil and Quito benefited those cities greatly, Cuenca was marginalized.

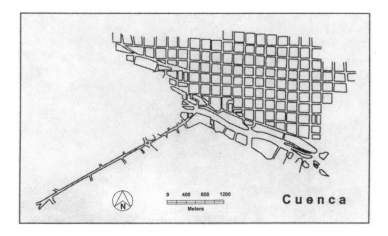

Figure 2.18   Cuenca, urban morphology, 2002.

Twentieth-century Cuenca had changed little from the fifty previous years. When the demand for men's hats ended in the United States and Europe after World War II, a basic sector of the city's industry went into crisis. For the hatmakers in the historic center, transitioning from a "light" industry to a "heavy" industry was not easy. The city and provincial governments embarked on a program of import-substitution industrialization that was much in vogue throughout Latin America during the 1950s and 1960s (Gwynne 1986). Government and private agencies built new factories at the city edge, while the historic quarters were spared major disruptions. Emphasis on industrial revitalization allowed the city to change from traditional artisanal production of roof tiles, plates, pitchers, and jars, to a modern ceramics and refractory center (Fernández 1994, 226). The city sought out "smokeless industries," and tourism fit the bill. Except for a few modern buildings built to house public offices in the 1960s and 1970s (figure 2.19), the urban fabric remains uniformly colonial in Cuenca's historic district.

Contemporary Overview and Planning Issues. Tourism promotion during the past two decades rose out of private, not public initiatives, and Cuenca remains one of the most popular destinations in Ecuador. Like many colonial towns in the central Andes, especially from Quito south-

Figure 2.19 Municipal offices built in the 1960s and 1970s in the heart of the historic zone of Cuenca. Photo 1997.

ward to Arequipa (Peru) and Potosí (Bolivia), the churches of Cuenca are ornate, with deeply cut stone facades and a flat ornamentation resembling woodcarving or embroidery (Blakewell 1997, 251). Modernization spared the traditional colonial grid, and the original pattern radiating out in all directions was undisturbed. In 1982, Cuenca was listed as a national historic district. Seventeen years later, on December 4, 1999, UNESCO added the historic district to its list of World Heritage Sites. As the opening vignette to this book illustrates, out-migration and dollar remittances have transformed the colonial core, a topic covered in chapter 4.

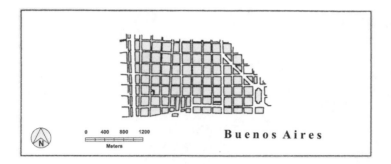

Figure 2.20   San Telmo barrio, Buenos Aires, urban morphology, 2002.

Buenos Aires: San Telmo

Brief History, Settlement, and Economy. Juan Díaz de Solís visited the site of present-day Buenos Aires in 1516, but it was not until 1536 that Pedro de Mendoza established a small settlement. That settlement was short lived, and after five years it succumbed to hostile indigenous tribes. The colonists moved upriver to Asunción, Paraguay, and left two legacies on the banks of the River Plate (Río de la Plata). One was a name: Nuestra Señora de Santa María de Buen Aire (a tribute to an Italian patron saint popular among mariners). The second was horses and cows that later multiplied to become a pillar of the Argentine economy in the eighteenth and nineteenth centuries.

Buenos Aires was the last of a string of settlements that extended from Paraguay to the Río de la Plata. An expedition from Paraguay returned to the site in 1586 and erected a permanent settlement that was little more than a backwater village. The Spanish built a fortress fronting the river and carved out the main civic space, the Plaza de Mayo, directly behind the fortress. Buenos Aires was platted in striking uniformity, with streets running at perpendicular angles every 137 meters, causing such world travelers as Charles Darwin to remark on its "perfect regularity," while others complained that it was monotonous and dull. The original platting (figure 2.20) includes the neighborhood of San Telmo — south of the Plaza de Mayo — and it became part of the city's fifth and sixth wards by 1855 (Moya 1998, 128–31).

Figure 2.21 Braided cobblestone streets dating from the nineteenth century in the San Telmo barrio, Buenos Aires. Photo 1999.

Demand for Argentinean beef and a growing industrial network in the late 1800s transformed the city. Buenos Aires quickly evolved from a "big village" (*gran aldea*) in 1870 to a metropolis in just forty years (Scobie 1974, 13–14). A white-collar service economy did not fuel that growth. Instead, the city's first skyscrapers and major industries in the twentieth century were the *frigoríficos* (meatpacking houses) and grain silos stacked along the banks of the Riachuelo River in La Boca (meaning the "mouth" of a main river), just south of San Telmo (Rottin 1949, 84). Considerable British capital financed the rail, meatpacking, shipping, and related industries — all evident along the Buenos Aires port areas, but also intricately tied to production from the pampas hinterland surrounding Greater Buenos Aires.

Contemporary Overview and Planning Issues. Today, the barrio of San Telmo is distinctive because it retains some of the "big village" elements of the past (Borges 1969). Nineteenth-century mansions, cafés, antique shops, theaters, cobblestone streets (figure 2.21), and an outdoor antique flea market in Plaza Dorrego every Sunday make it alluring. For local residents, many of them elderly, affordable housing is a major concern. Pressures for rent control have conflicted with Argentina's broader policies of liberalizing its markets and removing public subsidies. The housing market is demographically skewed. At one end are young people attracted by the art, music, dancing, and nightlife. At the other, is a veteran San Telmo population now in retirement (or who took early retirement on their labor union's once generous benefit packages). The bohemian ambiance and urban diversity add to the tourist appeal of the neighborhood, though the conflicting interests can cause planning conundrums.

Montevideo: Ciudad Vieja

Brief History, Settlement, and Economy. Montevideo, the capital of Uruguay, opens to the sea from its location on a rocky cape along the Río de la Plata estuary. Mauricio de Zabala settled Montevideo between 1724 and 1730, where it served as a fortification for thirteen families from the Canary Islands (*isleños*). Spanish settlement replaced a short-lived Portuguese camp begun in 1723. Walls enclosed the colonial center as a Spanish garrison (*ciudad fortaleza*), and today they constitute the historic district known as Ciudad Vieja.

Colonial duties tied Montevideo to the government in Buenos Aires. Because these two cities flanked both sides of the Río de la Plata estuary, they were in a prime position to defend access up the Plate-Paraná-Paraguay River networks leading into the heart of South America. They were also poised to run contraband trade to complement the wealth from the rich mines of Potosí located upstream. Trade from Andean South America was to pass through Lima, but the Atlantic ports of Montevideo and Buenos Aires had evident comparative advantages (e.g., greater proximity to Spain). When the Royal Crown proclaimed a "free-trade" status in 1778 as part of the Bourbon reforms, Montevideo prospered by exporting hides, tallow, and salted beef to Havana.

The rocky peninsula of Ciudad Vieja framed the colony's original six blocks (figure 2.22) that have spread to include 5,270 hectares inhabited by 1.3 million residents. Its beginnings, however, were modest. In 1725, just six blocks had extended along the bay respecting the template im-

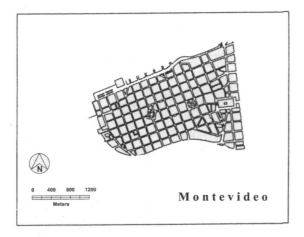

Figure 2.22   Ciudad Vieja, Montevideo, urban morphology, 2002.

posed by the Law of the Indies. Colonial administrators added twenty-six blocks to the settlement in 1726. Unlike Buenos Aires, whose main plaza (Plaza de Mayo) lies next to the shore, Montevideo's principal plaza lies in the middle of the grid at a small crest along its cape.

Montevideo's early economic geography made a lasting impression on the city's land use. Financial activities and shipping offices clustered along the port side of the peninsula, while government offices and commercial activities located around the Plaza de la Constitución where the town hall (cabildo) and cathedral stand. It was not until independence in 1828 that city government drafted plans for a "new city" (literally, *ciudad nueva*) beyond the old walls. Houses and retailing would shift to public lands called *ejidos*. Although the new city was home to mostly well-off Uruguayans, working-class neighborhoods such as Cerro (originally Villa Cosmopolis) were created for the European immigrants who in the late nineteenth century and early twentieth labored in the emerging hide and meat-salting industries (Pendle 1950) (figure 2.23).

New technology and planning regulations changed the colonial geography of the place. The horse-drawn tram or streetcar in 1868 allowed the first wave of elite out-migration from Ciudad Vieja and some commuting to the old quarters. Just as is common in the suburbanization of the Latin American center, this out-migration allowed larger homes in the centro

Figure 2.23 View of Montevideo from the working-class neighborhood of Cerro, which dates back to the 1830s as a site for immigrant labor who worked in the hide and meat-salting industries. Photo 1995.

histórico to be carved up into smaller units. Many of those residential subdivisions eventually became *conventillos* (tenement houses). Dockworkers and others working in the port and fishing trades established residences there as well. Legislation trying to check the spread of conventillos in Ciudad Vieja dates from 1871.

Related progressive social legislation in the late nineteenth and early twentieth centuries helped create one of the most complex welfare states in the Americas (Finch 1981). Progressive ideas carried by immigrants from across the Atlantic inspired Uruguayan urban social policies (Scarpaci 1990). By 1910, Uruguay ranked in the top ten of nations with the highest standard of living (Finch 1981).

European immigrants furthered Montevideo's urban primacy (a condition whereby the capital city is much larger than a nation's second-largest city) and the municipal census of 1889 reported mostly foreign-born folks in Montevideo. Specifically, just under half (47 percent) of the city's population were Italian, followed by Spanish (one-third), French (8 percent), and Argentine (5 percent) (Sargent 1994, 481).

European influences in Ciudad Vieja and the "new city" came in the form of British investment as well. Montevideo's belle epoque period extended from the 1880s until at least World War I (Artucio 1971). Aside from a scattered and eclectic collection of belle epoque and Beaux Arts buildings in the old and new quarters of the city, Montevideo's infrastructure was not up to date. British capital financed waterworks, sewers, and port facilities. Electricity came in 1886 and represented the continent's first utility plant. In 1898, twenty years after the telephone was introduced, the city boasted the highest per capita telephone usage in South America. In addition, British influence contributed to the spread of soccer (*fútbol*) and golf. Modernity crowned the old city in 1922 with the nation's first skyscraper (figure 2.24), the twenty-six-story Palacio Salvo, at the edge of Plaza Independencia (Castellanos 1971). That same decade marked the founding of the master plan and city planning, as well as a Faculty of Architecture (Rial Roade and Klaczko 1981). As late as 1997, large British buses (Leylands) circulated through the streets of Ciudad Vieja, highlighting Britain's role in Montevideo's impressive urbanization.

The centro histórico retains some colonial (pre-1830) buildings and private residences whose high open doors reveal antique Spanish patios. Although few sections of the walls remain, a gate has been preserved and marks the entrance of Ciudad Vieja at one end of Independence Square. This square, the most symbolic of Uruguayan history, displays an equestrian statue of General José Artigas, a national hero.

Like its sister city across the estuary, Buenos Aires, Montevideo exudes a European atmosphere, though it also contains a significant black population relative to other Southern Cone nations. During the colonial period, black slaves performed West African dances and songs next to the walls of the city. When the city pulled down the defensive walls and abolished slavery, blacks mainly settled on the coast and kept their rituals, folklore, and music. Today, black folklore in Montevideo is strong, and the drum roll (*candombe*) forms a type of South American black dance in this nation of mostly Italian and Spanish immigrants. Black culture is celebrated

Figure 2.24   Palacio Salvo, Montevideo's first skyscraper, at the edge of Plaza Independencia, in Ciudad Vieja. Photo 1995.

especially during the carnival processions of performing groups, and today it is part of heritage tourism in Ciudad Vieja.

Contemporary Overview and Planning Issues. Planners in the old city of Montevideo face an urban fabric unlike any other in these case studies except, perhaps, Buenos Aires' San Telmo neighborhood. Even though little colonial building stock remains, the old quarters are rich with belle epoque structures and their striking mansard roofs. The colonial concentration of commerce around the main town square has continued, especially since the period of authoritarian military dictatorships between 1973 and 1985. The generals in control aimed to restructure the national economy and to convert Uruguay into the "Singapore of South America." Besides restructuring the economy along neoliberal development principles (tax shelters for foreign investors, minimal capital-accountability

Table 2.2 Strategies of "Plan Montevideo," 2001

Approach
Strong commitment to reviving the central areas, including the main downtown areas, as a way of consolidating its essentially democratic nature.
Prioritization of the Bay of Montevideo, which will become the new neighborhood center of the city, making best use of all adjacent urban areas and facilities and contributing in this way to the westward extension of the city.
Major boost to help preserve the city's historical and cultural heritage, and to preserving the rural and urban protected areas including beauty spots and conservation areas.
Commitment to promoting investment in real estate and in productive activities by encouraging services, and residential and industrial activities, and by protecting the productive rural area and the rural area in general.
Adequate structuring of peripheral parts of the city with the aim of maintaining them as residential areas for diverse sectors of society while discouraging their indiscriminate spread into rural and agricultural lands.
Strong commitment to improving the environment and water courses (recuperation of streams and riverbanks), as well as coastal areas, public spaces, and green areas.

Source: Intendencia Municipal de Montevideo (translated by the author) (http://www.monte video.gub.uy/pl-seve.htm; accessed April 2003).

requirements, government assurances, investment protection), the city's banking district needed to project an image of modernity. Translating this symbolism into "bricks and mortar" meant modernizing sections of the nation's "Wall Street" (*bolsa*) in Ciudad Vieja. Shiny new hotels, glass-wrapped and spiral-ramped shopping galleries (*caracoles*), and office complexes are on the rise. Slum eradication and street upgrading have also been part of this new "urban face" in Ciudad Vieja. These and other planning strategies form part of Plan Montevideo, a comprehensive zoning and master plan (table 2.2).

The development scheme is very different from the welfare state of a century ago. To achieve these goals, the Montevideo Plan seeks both public and private investors. Mario Arano, the mayor of Montevideo in the late 1990s, intended to bring a degree of sensitivity to urban revitalization as well as encourage community participation in the planning process. Montevideo, however, entered the new millennium with severe budget constraints, reflecting broader structural problems with the Uruguayan economy.

Conclusions: On Becoming "Historic," Yesterday, Today, and *Mañana*

This chapter has provided a historical context for exploring the nine centros históricos discussed in this book. It also summarized some of the key ways the historic quarters have changed over time, with special attention given to events that have left their mark on these old places. Most of the study sites have clung faithfully to the geometric template laid down by the urban design laws of the sixteenth century. Only Trinidad and Cartagena depart from the classic grid pattern. These Spanish American plazas and barrios have etched an indelible mark in their cities and towns. If Latin American cities are the most complicated of artifacts, and if they harbor the values of centuries of growth and change, then they merit an appreciation of their built environment in guiding their future design.

I offered a portion of my field notes to suggest some of the attributes of these plazas and barrios, at least as I have perceived them over the past two decades. My impressions were not meant to fully document a particular participant-observation task but were rather aimed at highlighting what I perceive to be defining features of these plazas and barrios compared to other ones in Spanish America.

The cities in which these nine case studies lie are highly varied: they represent ports versus inland locations, agricultural versus mining and manufacturing economies, and small versus large cities. Each historical profile of the study sites shows irregular economic and demographic growth during the colonial period. Stages of prosperity ended with economic stagnation because of war, political fighting, and downturns in regional and global economies. While Havana, Bogotá, Quito, Puebla, Cartagena, and Buenos Aires performed main administrative tasks under Spanish rule, Trinidad, Cuenca, and the others tended toward more regional economic tasks. Bourbon reforms of the late eighteenth centuries and liberalization of trade benefited these centers in different ways.

Local geographies and accessibility to the broader national and international arenas varied too. Bogotá, Cuenca, Cartagena, and Trinidad, for example, had modest rail, canal, and road connections with their hinterlands, and it was not until the twentieth century that those places were fully integrated into the national networks. Others (Havana, Buenos Aires, Puebla, Montevideo, and Quito) became the transportation and economic hubs of their nations. While British capital spearheaded modernization in the Southern Cone cities, U.S. capital was more important in Cuba. Indeed, it was not until the advent of industrialization that transformations occurred in land use and the urban fabric of their historic neighborhoods started to change. Such geographic isolation was generally conducive to preserving the original platting of the city. In addition, helping the conservation of buildings and public spaces was the differentiation between the centro histórico and the CBD. Even tiny Trinidad has placed its twentieth-century commercial center beyond the limits of the UNESCO-framed historic quarters.

Despite historical forces that promoted preservation, modernity scratched away at the colonial fabric of the centros históricos in the late nineteenth and early twentieth centuries. Traffic congestion, old infrastructures, and the advent of a new labor class were often the "push" factors in sending the elites to the suburbs. Over the course of the last century, new residents — often European or rural immigrants — began occupying the colonial vestiges of the historic districts. Appreciation for the quality of these built landscapes did not keep pace with the change in the residential composition of these places, and many barrios slipped into decline. To be sure, the Spanish American plaza and barrio remain unique in the Western Hemisphere. As early as 1944, town-planning experts from the United States observed there are "two divergent types of cities in the Western Hemisphere; those of the United States, impressive but ungracious; and those of the Latin American countries, historic and old-world like, but thoroughly delightful and human" (Violich 1944, 34–35).

Not until the post–World War II era did politicians, planners, architects, and civic activists raise public interest about preserving these "delightful and human" places. The 1967 *Carta de Quito*, coupled with UNESCO's designation of World Heritage Sites, helped to focus national and international attention on historic preservation. Historic districts today represent a pedestrian-friendly lifestyle — recast as the New Urbanism or neotraditional design — and this has placed them on the international tourist's destination map. However, heritage tourism is not conflict free. Cultivating and defining authenticity, heritage, and historic periods are difficult tasks. The later chapters will show that ascribing a UNESCO or national landmark label is no promise for high-quality historic districts. The labels *socialist* and *capitalist* begin to blur as the case studies describe the transformations of the centros históricos and the forces behind them.

Maintaining viable historic districts in the twentieth and twenty-first centuries is rife with tension. The balance of this book offers insights into how historic preservation, gentrification, and urban renewal unfold in these neighborhoods, and how the past might inform the present. Their contemporary land-uses provide an empirical and comparative basis to chart that course, as the next chapter shows.

3 Land Use, Building Quality, and Skylines in the Centro Histórico

Toward the Measurement and Comparison of Old Places

Without entering the debate about whether any analysis can be completely impartial, this chapter aims to present the findings of a street-level assessment of land uses in these nine places. The term *land use* is employed here in the conventional sense of urban and regional planning, urban geography, and urban economics. That is, how are buildings and open spaces occupied? Before I describe the methodology, it will be immediately clear that buildings have multiple land uses. Moreover, not all land uses can be fully documented because some will be unknown, illegal, transient, or a combination of all the above.

In the first two chapters I identified a few ways of conceptualizing and describing centros históricos. Thematic aspects of the Latin America historic district's makeup often include race, class, gender, nationality (foreign tourists or locals), language, local economy, governance, and other variables. Although these variables are insightful, I sought out a common empirical metric to compare the street-level aspects of these places. I needed to develop a methodology that was flexible, easy to administer, low in cost, and relatively objective. My goal was to be able to compare general land uses, building quality, and building height dimensions in these myriad places. Therefore, I used a straightforward way of getting an empirical handle on the economic and social "land" uses of Latin American centro histórico. In the section that follows, I explain the methodology I developed for surveying nearly thirty thousand doorways in the nine study sites.

Method: Measuring Antiquity and Form

My first sustained contact with a Latin American centro histórico happened in Habana Vieja, in May 1992. Architectural writings on the historical periods and styles of the old city shaped my first impressions, especially Joaquín Weiss's (1978) *Techos coloniales cubanos* (Cuban Colonial Roofs). He approaches buildings in Habana Vieja by classifying them as colonial (pre-1898, but the colonial period in Cuba extended beyond the 1830 mark that characterizes the end of Spanish colonialism in most of Latin America). Other buildings are classified as Republican (1898 and beyond, marking the end of the Spanish-American-Cuban War), or modern (1925–65) (see also Rodríguez 2000).

Like other architectural historians, Weiss provides a finer scheme of interpretation based on styles such as Art Deco, Art Nouveau, minimalist, Brutalist, Neoclassical, Baroque, Eclectic, Italianesque, and so forth. While I found the language, vocabulary, and historical periods useful, they failed to identify contemporary building uses. I wanted to know how nonarchitects might describe Habana Vieja (or any other historic place) at the level of the entire historic district, versus a selection of buildings. How might social scientists or an interested reader (unfamiliar with the facade-oriented language of the architect) come to appreciate what happens inside those buildings? Would it be useful as well to calculate an aggregate assessment of how land uses in one Latin American centro histórico differ from another? The late Jorge Enrique Hardoy (1983) often summarized census data from all over Latin America to do just that. However, the different variables, methodologies, and years of the censuses made comparisons difficult at times. His pioneering work did help me craft general questions that framed the land-use survey. The results of this survey form the basis of this chapter.

I used a curbside approach in establishing a land-use profile of each centro histórico. The unit of analysis for coding each land use was not, as some often suspect, the entire building, but the doorway. Every building within the designated limits of the historic district was surveyed. Therefore, there was no sample of buildings; rather, I surveyed the entire universe of structures. Because buildings often have several land uses, each doorway at the ground level that led to a different land use at the ground level and subsequent floors was coded accordingly. Thus, a single doorway could be coded several times. For example, a main entrance into a building might lead to retailing at the ground floor and government offices on a second floor, while apartments (residences) occupy the upper floors.

Table 3.1 Sample sizes (doorways) of nine Spanish American centros históricos, 1990s

City	Doorway (N)
Buenos Aires	1,294
Bogotá	1,329
Cartagena	2,142
Cuenca	4,054
Havana	4,747
Montevideo	2,611
Puebla	7,899
Quito	3,894
Trinidad	1,902
Total	29,872
Minimum	1,294
Maximum	7,899
Mean	3,319

Source: Author's field research, 1992, 1995, 1996.

Since most buildings were coded during working hours, it was easy to ask locals what kinds of businesses or activities took place in other parts of the buildings or to enter the buildings myself and verify the land use. Building directories were useful, as were posted signs that promoted businesses, public agencies, or church groups (informal activities could not be determined readily). On occasion, I had to make a second visit to the building to confirm a land use if it were not immediately apparent, or if I could not speak with residents in the barrio. The final sample size of just under 30,000 ranged from 7,899 in Puebla to 1,294 in Buenos Aires, with a mean sample for all nine cities of just under 4,000 (table 3.1). Each district sampled included the nationally or internationally recognized historic district of each city.

Three variables constitute the survey: land use, quality of the facade, and number of stories (a surrogate measure for building height).

The first variable, *land use,* was carved up into a manageable set of seven attributes, loosely ranging from the most "benign" to the most "noxious." The variable attributes are as follows:

— Residential. Are people living in the structure as tenants, owner-occupiers, or squatters? Any of these housing tenures counted as "residential."

— Restaurant or small grocer. The first city to be surveyed was Habana Vieja, where state-run bodegas (small grocers) are found on nearly every block. In the market economies outside Havana, the local coffee shop, small restaurant, café, or mom-and-pop style grocer performed the same function. Urban economists and urban geographers call this a low-order function because the product or service offered is inexpensive, procured often, and needs a small consumer population (threshold) to sustain it (Losch 1954). Restaurants or small grocers add vibrancy to a neighborhood because they prompt a small but steady amount of pedestrian traffic. If a larger, more modern supermarket existed, it was coded as "commercial" (discussed below). The presence of restaurants, small grocers, and cafés form what Jane Jacobs, Elizabeth Plater-Zyberk, Andres Duany, Peter Calthorpe, Larry Ford, and other neotraditional proponents or designers consider important dimensions, which add to the livability of a place. James Howard Kunstler (1996) calls these livability attributes the "charm" of a place, or those allures that engage us in city life. Significantly, this pedestrian focus is largely free of the automobile, recalling what Francis Violich (1944) referred to as "delightful and human." A lower skyline and a less dense population usually mean that Latin American centros históricos can be pedestrian friendly while the automobile is kept in check.

— Institutional. This attribute described most nonprofit and civic activities. The lion's share included government buildings and offices, nongovernmental organizations (NGOs), churches, synagogues, schools, political-party headquarters, and both public and private universities. More "benign" than retailing, institutional land uses were common in the centro histórico because the first seats of government in the colony were established there. Many of those government buildings continue to function today, although other public administration centers have dispersed throughout the city in each study site.

Some of the first churches, convents, chapels, and schools were also built in the centro histórico, as reviewed in earlier chapters. A classic land-use pattern in the centro histórico was to anchor the town hall (cabildo) at one end of the place and build the church at the opposite end of the square (Stanislawski 1950; Ford and Griffin 1980). Because of the civic nature of the colonial city center throughout Latin America, primary and secondary schools as well as universities have concentrated in the old quarters. Some of the first national universities opened their doors here as a testimony to the rich tradition of the city center as well as proximity to other institutions such as libraries, government archives, post offices, bookstores, publishing houses, and museums.

— Commercial. As much as 99 percent of this attribute reflected general retailing (clothiers, hardware stores, pharmacies, newspaper stands, and kiosks). In a few instances, some light industrial production would be under way. This included newspapers and printing (on heavy, older printing and lithography machines, particularly in Habana Vieja and Barrio La Candelaria in Bogotá), or small manufacturing (toy assembly; plastics melting and molding; piecemeal textile work). However, these light industrial activities were minor. Generally, the commercial activity bestows some sign of the retailing "vibrancy" of a place, and it is a good attribute for discerning the "residential" nature of centros históricos (Trinidad, Habana Vieja) from retailing (Cartagena, Quito).

— Park, open space, plaza, or plazuela. Open spaces are the exception in the tightly packed centros históricos. Their presence provides a major amenity for obvious reasons. They are places for children to play, the retired to sit and watch, and neighbors and tourists to congregate. Although a few "green parks" formed part of the study sites (the waterfront perimeter of Ciudad Vieja in Montevideo; Habana Vieja along Avenida Paula and Avenida del Puerto; the Tomebamba riverfront in Cuenca; Centennial Park in Cartagena's Getsemaní neighborhood), green parks were uncommon. Instead, hard surface town squares with benches and playground equipment, plazas, or tiny plazas (*plazuelas*) constituted most of these land uses. Regrettably, I did not incorporate any quantitative measure of the surface area of a park, open space, plaza, or plazuela into the research design. Thus, a property or lot (not a doorway) was simply coded as an open space if it met these criteria. A half-acre green park received the same statistical weighting as a slightly widened sidewalk, if it was set back several meters from the curb and dotted with a few benches.

— Parking. The conventional large parking lots dotting North American and European cities were rare in the Latin American centro histórico. Instead, street-level lots were usually cleared areas with some custodian or chain guarding the entrance. In addition, small-scale parking was shown by the numerous wide gates and doors leading into driveways or courtyards. I could determine this by noting whether (a) the door was wide enough to accommodate a car and (b) if a street curb was lowered or recessed as an "apron" to allow motor vehicle access through a door. This attribute, then, could be coded as a lot (parking garage, parking lot), or a doorway.

— Abandoned, under construction, or in demolition. This final attribute was the most noxious and visually disruptive feature of the historic district. Because construction projects did not always have building permits posted, were not carried out quickly, and included much self-help activity, it was difficult to determine whether a site was actively under construction, in demolition, or abandoned. Therefore, these conditions were combined under a single measure. Like the park, plaza, and open space variable above, it was not possible to calculate what percentage of all buildings or lots (in cubic meters or otherwise) was devoted to this land use. Still, it provided a general index to the disturbance of the urban fabric and distortion of the streetscape.

The second variable was the *quality of the facade*. I wanted to rapidly assess an important aesthetic of the exteriors of buildings in the study sites. My interest in this variable stems from the importance that the "visual" plays in the consumer's aesthetic. As Rose (2001, 1) argues, "There's an awful lot of hype around 'the visual' these days. We're often told that we now live in a world where knowledge as well as many forms of entertainment are visually constructed, and where what we see is important, if not more so, than what we hear or read." In this spirit, I coded building attributes as poor, fair, and good. I realize that building cycles pass through neighborhoods unevenly, and that at the time of the surveys, there was no guarantee that I was observing any fixed point of neighborhood revival, zenith, or decline (Jones 1994; Bromley and Jones 1995, 1996a; Jones and Bromley 1999; Jones and Varley 1999a). If timing is considered methodologically as a "sampling error" (i.e., assessing facade quality of these nine barrios at different parts of their building cycles), then the error should cancel itself out because it is a random process carried out over ten years.

— "Poor" buildings displayed unquestionable structural weaknesses such as missing balconies, exposed beams and rebar, cracked support columns, wide cracks, abandoned rooms or floors, and a considerable amount of flaking plaster and paint.

— "Fair" buildings showed no major structural flaws. In need of some minor repairs, the buildings' exteriors revealed paint flaking and some missing plaster or whitewash. However, the facades suffered no apparent weaknesses.

— "Good" facades were in solid physical condition and were generally well maintained. They often had been recently painted or else were built with modern building materials (wrapped glass, concrete panels) that gave them an edge against weathering, neglect, or both.

Except for matters of instrumental validity that I note below, it is important to underscore that since the variable was to assess the complete "appeal" of the streetscapes comparatively (e.g., compare San Telmo with Puebla), the overall statistical average was the result of this measure. Thus, while two reasonable surveyors might disagree over whether a structure was in good or fair shape, in the long run, we can assume that such error will cancel itself out over the 29,872 units classified.

The last variable served as a simple measure of the skyline of the centro histórico and, in turn, as a surrogate measure of modernity. Building height was based on the usual North American measure (unlike the Latin American one) that counts the ground floor as the first floor, the second as the second, and so forth. In other words, every building that had a facade (including abandoned buildings whose shells remained but were hollow inside) was coded as having at least one floor. Only the parking or open spaces surveyed were coded as zero.

Validity, it will be recalled, posits whether a variable that a researcher sets out to measure is actually assessed. Qualitative research tends to be more valid (accurate) in its assessment of variables and their attributes than large-sample surveys and studies. In the latter, although many more people and units of analysis may be reached, it is not always apparent that the variables are precise. However, quantitative research tends to be more reliable (e.g., it can be replicated fairly easily and yield consistent results) than does qualitative work (Babbie 1999). For instance, a survey on urban crime might posit the question "Do you feel safe in your city?" followed by standard Likert-scale responses (never, hardly ever, sometimes, mostly, and always). In turn, each response could be assigned a measure of 1 through 5, and a statistical mean, standard deviation, and other central tendency measures could be calculated. However, the researcher would need to assume that everyone would interpret the question similarly. In a qualitative research design venue, though, the researcher would be able to explain to the respondent the precise meaning of "in your city" (Scarpaci 1993). Some might interpret it to signify "in the metropolitan area." Others might refer to "downtown," while a few might think that it includes "in their neighborhood." Thus, the particular question about public safety could be considered to be quite reliable (everyone answers) but not a valid measure (different interpretations and therefore less valid). I avoided the dilemmas posed by trying to make a study both valid and reliable in several ways.

First, in order to maintain validity, I based most of the observations on the built environment; only an occasional neighbor was interviewed to confirm a land use when I was unsure about the land use of a particular site.

Second, instrumental validity was high because there was a single researcher for about 97 percent of the land-use study; only in the case of Havana did I enlist a few students to assist me in the survey. I trained the students in Havana in May 1992 and then checked their field observations to ensure the group was coding the variables and attributes as I would.

In the most subjective variable — quality of facade — I was quickly able to discern (in my own mind, at least) what I meant by poor, fair, or good.

Table 3.2 Land-use mean percentages, nine centros históricos, 1990s

City	Residen-tial (%)	Park (%)	Restaurants (%)	Institu-tional (%)	Commercial (%)	Parking (%)	Aban-doned
Buenos Aires	33.00	1.00	**12.98**	6.96	36.01	**5.02**	5.02
Bogotá	62.98	1.05	7.98	10.01	13.02	3.01	1.96
Cartagena	37.02	0.70	8.03	5.00	47.01	0.23	2.01
Cuenca	34.88	0.74	1.78	2.81	56.09	3.28	0.42
Havana	73.65	0.86	4.17	**11.71**	4.82	1.31	3.48
Montevideo	42.13	0.92	6.59	3.41	38.64	2.80	**5.52**
Puebla	36.80	1.10	4.04	4.27	49.16	3.13	1.51
Quito	19.69	0.81	5.69	3.77	**66.69**	2.57	0.78
Trinidad	**93.01**	**2.00**	0.89	2.00	0.47	0.68	0.95
Mean	48.1	1.02	5.7	5.5	34.6	2.4	2.3

Source: Author's field research, 1992, 1995, 1996.
Note: The barrio with the highest percentage in each land-use category is in boldface type.

In the end, the aesthetic judgment was mine in all nine cities. The final stage of assessing the facade quality was to provide an ordinal ranking and basis of comparison, addressed in the balance of this chapter.

Land-Use Patterns

Five of the seven attributes that define land use are worthy of review. Of those five attributes, land-use patterns emerge that allow us to character-ize the salient features of each centro histórico (table 3.2).

Residential Housing

Residential housing dominates about half (48.1 percent) of the land uses. Socialist Cuba in the early to mid-1990s allocated the greatest number of their historic districts to housing. While the percentage of street-level

Figure 3.1 Makeshift loft (barbacoa) in an Habana Vieja, Havana, residence, 1999.

entrances leading to commercial ventures has increased since the 1993 opening of the market, Habana Vieja is still predominantly residential. Overcrowding is endemic, as an estimated eighty-five thousand residents live in an area that should house about half that amount (Scarpaci, Segre, and Coyula 2002). Consequently, *habaneros* (residents of Havana) have introduced lofts called *barbacoas* (literally, "barbecue grills") to increase interior space. Taking advantage of the high ceilings on the ground floors, these lofts usually afford one couple the privacy of a makeshift bedroom (figure 3.1). Although Trinidad's UNESCO World Heritage District forms the second of two cities in Cuba's heritage tourism circuit (Havana is the other), it too remains largely residential (93 percent); it is discussed thoroughly in chapter 7.

Figure 3.2   A residential café frequented by a large retired clientele as well as tourists and artists. San Telmo is in many ways a sort of "Greenwich Village" of Buenos Aires, 1995.

Restaurants

"Restaurants" (including small grocers, and state-run food distribution centers, bodegas, in Cuba) form the second attribute of the land-use variable. Three historic districts reveal above-average concentrations of restaurants: Buenos Aires, Bogotá, and Montevideo. Buenos Aires (13.0 percent) has more than double the mean percentage (5.7 percent) of food establishments. Not only is Buenos Aires renowned for its Europeanlike cafés, but also for a particularly large number of restaurants, cafés, and bars that cater to both the tourists who seek the famous tango music and dancing and to the retirees, artists, other workers, and professionals who live there. Until the fiscally austere policies of *menemismo* (policies of President Carlos Menem) changed the Peronist course of state-welfare provision (Scarpaci 1991), many Argentines could retire at an early age, and they concentrated in what used to be the low-rent district of San Telmo (figure 3.2). Since the mid-1990s, the district has attracted even

more coffeehouses, bars, after-hours clubs, and a variety of live performing arts venues (ranging from the bandoleón and guitar, to folk, underground, punk, and hard-rock shows). Argentina's fiscal crises in the early
2000s, coupled with its rapid-fire succession of presidents and high inflation in 2002, brought new investment in building repair and real estate to
a grinding halt.

Institutional

Institutional land uses, it will be recalled, include government buildings
and offices, churches, synagogues, schools, and universities (both public
and private). Here again, the data show three pronounced concentrations
of institutional land uses. First, Havana leads with 11.7 percent, well
above the sample mean of 5.5 percent. Habana Vieja, like Trinidad, has no
private property, but this does not account for this concentration. Rather,
several national, provincial, and government offices are clustered in the
old quarters. Many government offices connected to port activities such as
customs, the naval headquarters, the coast guard, shipping offices, and
analogous activities are located in Habana Vieja. Second, and not far
behind (at 10 percent) is Bogotá (Barrio La Candelaria), which is home to
half a dozen public and private universities. Third, Buenos Aires registers
an above-average concentration (nearly 7 percent) of public offices, labor
union headquarters, NGOs, mutual-aid societies (*sociedades mutualistas*),
and political party headquarters.

Commercial

Commercial activity is vital to all neighborhoods, especially in historic
districts. The degree to which retailing caters to local needs (e.g., daily
goods) versus higher-priced tourist facilities (art galleries, high-amenity
hotels, upscale restaurants) is often a surrogate measure of residential
displacement or gentrification (Smith 1979). It also shapes whether a historic district becomes a "ghost town" in the evening, inhabited only by
tourists who stroll the streets in search of an authentic, local experience
(Barthel 1996), or whether local residents mingle with heritage tourists. In

the latter, few local residents sit on their doorsteps, porches, and balconies, or chat on street corners.

On average, commercial activity occupies about one-third (34.6 percent) of land uses. At the low end, not surprisingly, are socialist Havana
and Trinidad with just 5 percent and 0.5 percent, respectively. At the other
extreme are Quito (with nearly double the sample average), Cuenca (67
percent), Puebla (49 percent), and Cartagena (47 percent). Historic Quito
swells with low-end retailing of a general nature (Bromley and Jones
1995). Hardware stores, shoe stories, clothiers, and automotive stores
dominate storefronts. In addition, there are clusters of kiosks set up in the
streets of historic Quito (not counted in the survey because they are not
permanent structures), which add to the bustle of retailing the neighborhood conveys. Indeed, Quito's centro histórico is the retail capital of most
of highland Ecuador and is frequented daily by hundreds of buses from
both highland and coastal cities.

Puebla's historic district is also a major retailing center for metropolitan
Puebla, Mexico's fifth-largest city. Like Quito, it showcases a broad array
of commercial activities. Cartagena's historic district (Ciudad Amurallada) has maintained low-end, traditional mom-and-pop retailing while
larger, modern shopping complexes are beyond the walls. A common
building land use is retailing at the street level, with shopkeepers who live
above their businesses (figure 3.3). The effect is a balance between important retailing and private housing that bestows a vibrant sense to the street
life of these places twenty-four hours a day.

Abandoned

Abandoned is the fifth variable attribute of land use warranting review
here. Most of the unoccupied sites classified as abandoned were not under
construction. Instead, there were clear signs that the rubble and other
physical deterioration were not by-products of repair. In general, the survey found that the more "developed" and populous a city, the greater
amount of abandonment. Montevideo and Buenos Aires registered over
5 percent abandonment versus half that as the survey average. Parts
of Ciudad Vieja and San Telmo reflect in many ways the low-income

Figure 3.3   Typical mom-and-pop type retailing in Cartagena at street level with residences on the second floor, 1995.

"ghetto" aspect associated with the conventional urban morphological models described by the Chicago urban ecologists in the 1920s and 1930s who studied U.S. central cities (i.e., downtowns) (Park, McKenzie, and Burgess 1967). When I surveyed San Telmo and Ciudad Vieja, a deep economic recession had gripped Argentina and Uruguay. That may account for the lack of real-estate investment in the potential real-estate markets of historic districts. Moreover, the structures on abandoned lots were late nineteenth- or early twentieth-century building stock. With the exception of a few public buildings and churches, little "colonial" architecture remained in San Telmo (Buenos Aires) and Ciudad Vieja (Montevideo) (Amaral 1994; Waisman 1994).

Facade Quality: The Sidewalk Aesthetic

One does not need to be an architect to glean impressions of the built environment's quality in the Latin American historic district. A simple stroll through its streets is an effective way to determine neighborhood appeal (Gutiérrez 1990). Along with public spaces such as sidewalks, parks, plazas, and open spaces, and the cleanliness of a setting, building facades leave a strong impression on residents and tourists. In this section, I provide a cursory summary of the second variable of the survey: facade quality.

Several patterns are striking about those centros históricos. Historic districts in Cuba and the Southern Cone cities dominate the low-quality end of the survey (table 3.3). Cuba has only begun aggressively restoring its historic districts since the demise of the former Soviet Union, and since the disruption of its traditional trading partners and commodities (Scarpaci 2000a). The Southern Cone nations, however, have traditionally had the strongest Latin American economies, suggesting that the poor condition of the buildings reflects little public or private investment or a combination of the two.

At the other extreme, the Mexican and Ecuadorian case studies show the highest percentages of good-condition buildings, at 79 percent (Puebla), 72 percent (Cuenca), and 69 percent (Quito).

What explains the quality of these facades? While I can advance no concise explanation, it is noteworthy that Mexico and Ecuador are pioneers in the historic preservation realm (Hardoy and Gutman 1992). There is relatively smooth coordination among municipal, provincial, national, and international agencies concerned with historic preservation. Unlike Colombia (where the private sector prevails in historic preservation), Cuba (a latecomer to proactive conservation), and Argentina and Uruguay (where the relative lack of extant colonial architecture has evoked a passive policy response to historic preservation in the capital cities), the Mexican and Ecuadorian governments have steadily supported heritage preservation.

In Buenos Aires, Graciela Viñuales (1990, 264) argues, San Telmo remained a European immigrant neighborhood (mainly Spanish and Italian)

Table 3.3 Building quality percentages and mean scores: Nine historic districts, ranked from highest to lowest quality

City	Poor	Fair	Good	Totals
Buenos Aires	**16**	38	46	100
Bogotá	12	48	40	100
Cartagena	10	52	38	100
Cuenca	6	22	**72**	100
Havana	**23**	**65**	12	100
Montevideo	**16**	36	48	100
Puebla	5	16	**79**	100
Quito	3	28	69	100
Trinidad	15	**54**	31	100
Mean	11.8	39.9	48.3	100

Source: Author's field research, 1992, 1995, and 1996.
Note: Two highest percentages of each column are in bold.

well into the 1940s. In the following decade, the modernist ideas of Le Corbusier and CIAM led planners to condone demolitions to facilitate construction of modern infrastructures such as interstate highways and modern buildings. Except for a few major civic buildings near the Plaza de Mayo, many nineteenth-century structures fell to the bulldozer. In their wake stand high-rise apartment buildings that accord San Telmo the highest population density of all the study sites.

Across the River Plate, Mariano Arana and Andrés Mazzini (1990) note, Montevideo's historic district began losing population in the second quarter of the twentieth century. Elite families began moving out to new suburbs such as Carrasco, and the population of Ciudad Vieja fell from about twenty thousand in 1936 to about seventeen thousand by the late 1980s. Laura Benton (1985) documents the impoverishment of the old city during the military rule of the early 1980s, which added to the deterioration of the district. A strong ethos of neglecting the traditional and embracing the modern characterized the military governments of Uruguay in the 1970s and 1980s. It was not until the late 1980s that the Banco

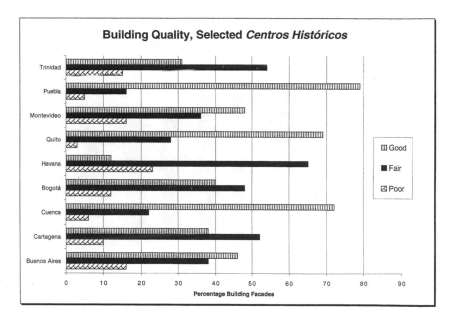

Figure 3.4 Building quality, selected centros históricos, 1990s.

Hipotecario (Mortgage Bank) in Uruguay began low-credit loans for up-grading and "recycling" older residences in Ciudad Vieja (Arana and Mazzini, 1990, 280–81). While many buildings had clearly benefited from these improvements to low-income apartments, Ciudad Vieja still looked "run down" in the mid-1990s.

To summarize, there is little correlation between the wealth of a nation and the age of the housing stock. Building quality in chosen centros históricos reveals considerable disparity (figure 3.4) that defies a simple explanation. Chapters 5, 6, and 7 offer more insight into the transformations of three of these districts.

Building Height: Measuring the Skyline

The previous two chapters outlined how traditional colonial settlements began as rudimentary sites, often nothing more than distant military out-posts between the sixteenth and eighteenth centuries. Over time, a few government buildings, church steeples, and bell towers raised the skylines

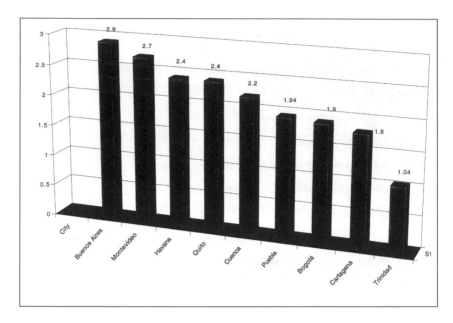

Figure 3.5 Mean number of floors per building, selected centros históricos, 1990s.

over these sleepy villages. Wattle, mud, straw, and crude stone structures gave way to wooden, crushed stone (molded with egg white and ox blood, called mampostería in the Caribbean basin), and brick office buildings, factories, and homes. Until the advent in the late nineteenth century of load-bearing columns — columns that could support multiple floors beyond just a few stories — the Latin American centro histórico exhibited a low-lying, gentle skyline. Although the Modern Movement left its mark throughout the world, the average number of stories surveyed in the centros históricos in this study was just 2.26. Figure 3.5 displays the range of building heights, with the Southern Cone port cities — Buenos Aires (2.9) and Montevideo (2.7) — at the high end and Puebla (1.94), Bogotá (1.9), Cartagena (1.8), and Trinidad (1.04) at the low end.

Builders placed most of the skyscrapers and modern buildings of the twentieth century outside the Latin American centro histórico (Carrión 1992). These decisions had less to do with respect for a colonial architectural aesthetic, and more with the ease of building in new parts of the city,

Figure 3.6 Rooftop view of Cuenca, 1997.

where it was convenient to install newer infrastructure (water, sewage, telephone) and build parking lots. For these reasons, parts of the colonial quarters still stand (Ford and Griffin 1980). In Havana during the last century, Centro Habana and Vedado took on higher skylines than Habana Vieja did. Carrasco and districts near Montevideo's airport acquired buildings that would have changed the look of Ciudad Vieja, while the suburbs of Palermo, Flores, Caballito, and the Costanera received much of Buenos Aires' towering buildings. The skylines of these Latin American historic districts stand as testimonies to landscapes of the past and decisions about urbanization and development (figure 3.6).

Beyond the Surveys: Regularities and Anomalies in the Centro Histórico

Thus far, this chapter has presented the aggregate findings of a land-use survey of nearly thirty thousand doorways in nine historic districts. For comparative purposes, I used statistical means to show general trends in these unique corners of the Latin American city. However, statistical

Table 3.4 Land-use anomalies in historic districts

City	Anomaly
Bogotá	Eight buildings greater than nine stories high.
Buenos Aires	Sixteen buildings greater than nine stories high.
Cartagena	A wooden bullring built in the 1930s that functioned until the 1970s. From that time until the 1980s, it was occasionally used to show outdoor movies. It has not yet been demolished, but there are no laws preventing its demolition.
Cuenca	Airport runway within ten meters of historic district limits.
Havana	Modern $11 million air-conditioned ocean terminal built in mid-1990s at the Plaza de San Francisco taps into potentially lucrative Caribbean cruise ship market.
Montevideo	Six-story parking garage; numerous corkscrew ramped (*caracoles*) multilevel shopping malls; glass and steel skyscrapers, all as part of Uruguay's efforts to become the "Singapore of South America."
Puebla	A faux colonial facade on McDonald's off the main town square (zócalo) in the heart of the historic district.
Quito	Kiosks and souvenir shops located in the stone foundations under the Government House (Gobernación) on Plaza Grande.
Trinidad	Not a single hotel in the historic district, but more than a hundred legally registered bed-and-breakfast establishments, and a comparable number of unlicensed ones.

Source: Author's field research, 1992–2003.

averages cannot capture unique land uses. To illustrate this, I will draw on Cartagena de Indias to show the vibrant civic and the cultural land uses that characterize these places.

Behind the ramparts and walls of colonial Cartagena are a variety of functions that typify the centros históricos. A dense network of educational facilities is common in such places, and Cartagena is no exception.

I found four public schools, seventeen private schools, two technical schools, and three universities (Bolívar, Jorge Tadeo, and Cartagena). There were also twenty-three small hotels (guesthouses, pensions, and bed-and-breakfasts). However, since the survey, two five-star hotels have been added: Santa Teresa and Santa Clara, both housed within the facades of convents that carried the same names. Cultural, religious, and diplomatic centers are located in historic Cartagena because of the symbolism these neighborhoods hold. At the time of the survey, Cartagena boasted six churches, five museums, four union headquarters, two consulates, and one functioning convent. Similar civic and cultural endowments characterize most of the other study sites.

If centros históricos are emblematic of anything, it is that they are "old" Latin American spaces, steeped in antiquity and tradition as shown by the *plazas* in this book title. However, nearly eight months of field research in these places turned up another dimension: the imprint of modernity (table 3.4).

Conclusions: Interpreting the Empirical "Snapshot"

This chapter has identified basic features of land use and building profiles in nine historic Latin American central districts. As of this writing, no research I've encountered to date has sought to sketch the empirical and aesthetic dimensions of these architecturally rich places, known variously in Spanish America as *centros históricos, cascos históricos, cascos antiguos,* or *ciudades viejas*. Steeped in history and rich in cultural patrimony, these neighborhoods have survived centuries despite their proximity to central business districts. While the Latin American city core has largely been spared the massive leveling that accompanied North American urbanization, the pace of urbanization and historic preservation has been uneven throughout the Americas (Ward 1993).

A spate of research to date on the centro histórico has either been building specific or has included "neighborhoods" whose social and economic histories have been reassembled solely through secondary data such as census materials, published reports, books, and articles. In this chapter, I have tried to move beyond that methodological bent by combining quantitative and qualitative approaches, and by blending primary and secondary data sources. My goal has been to complement other chapters and not to present empirical aspects of the centro histórico that portray it as a sterile, lifeless place. In searching out common features, a land-use survey provided a "snapshot" of these barrios, and it has allowed me to compare segments of their economic and social geography.

The land-use patterns of these nine neighborhoods defy easy interpretation and cannot be divorced from other chapters. Nonetheless, several patterns emerge. Cuban cities exhibit the highest percentage of residential land uses and display the poorest condition of the built environment. Retailing also varies. Montevideo's Ciudad Vieja, for instance, functions mainly in the banking and financial sector, as does Cuenca's (discussed in more detail in chapter 4). These "banking" and commercial activities are markedly different from the "mom-and-pop" retailing found in Cartagena and Quito, but the survey instrument did not differentiate between the two.

Regarding the general quality of building facades, the chapter revealed several paradoxes. While San Telmo and Ciudad Vieja are arguably part of the most modern metropolitan areas of all the cities studied, nearly one in six dwellings is in "poor" shape. This finding suggests that if modernity and urbanization help to ensure high-quality building stock, they also produce great extremes. No amount of "romanticism" can ignore the fact that the quality of these buildings runs the gamut from having nearly seven out of ten structures in "good" condition (Puebla, Cuenca, and Quito), to having only one in eight (12 percent) buildings in "good" condition (Havana). It must be noted that in the late 1990s, however, both Havana and Trinidad had embarked on broadscale renovations, and the land-use surveys predate urban revitalization there.

Last, I gauged the skyline of the centro histórico by measuring floors in buildings. An imprecise measure because of different ceiling heights — especially on the ground floor, where, in the tropics, ceilings are high to cool the buildings, whereas in the highlands (Puebla, Quito, Bogotá, and Cuenca) the first-floor ceilings are lower — it does serve as a surrogate measure of the "look" of the cityscape. Three clusters of building heights emerge. Buenos Aires and Montevideo have averages that exceed two floors; Trinidad, Bogotá, Puebla, and Cartagena registered less than two stories; and the balance of the study sites was closer to the sample mean

(2.26). No longer do just national monuments, statues, hills, crucifixes, or church steeples loom over certain corners of these neighborhoods. Demand for central locations and port warehouses, admiration for the tenets of the Modern Movement and the dictums of the CIAM, and disdain for the colonial aesthetic have permitted the encroachment of high-rises. No doubt preservation and zoning ordinances will wrestle with special interest requests to waive building-height restrictions and further distort the character of these barrios.

4 The Social Construction of Latin American Historic Districts

How Neighborhoods are Tethered to the Global Scene

Local communities face a local-global dilemma in resolving neighborhood problems. When global forces rock local economies because of price increases, commodity shortages, and terrorism, locals are not always helpless victims without viable coping strategies. Frequently unaware that the causes of their problems originate outside their neighborhoods, they often identify local actors who appear to be responsible for their troubles (Klosterman 1990; Miller 2000). Understanding how local residents conceptualize these problems is an important first step in learning how they socially construct their neighborhoods and in interpreting the public discourses that give meaning to these places (Calhoun 1996, 456).

Geographers approach this global-local continuum cautiously, and methodological and conceptual challenges confront them as they frame their research questions (Johnston, Taylor, and Watts 1995, 9). Space reflects the power of social domination from both the past and present in Latin American historic districts. Left alone, space has no influence over the lives of local residents. Therefore, the rational and empirical approach espoused by the spatial organization school that for so long dominated urban geography may not be effective in understanding local planning conflicts. This is because space—especially urban spaces in Latin America, where the gaps between rich and poor are great—embraces the intangible elements of ideology and cultural symbolism (Jones 1994). These spaces of representation include the "lived" or "experienced" worlds and are difficult to measure. How citizens contest space forms part of local politics and ideology, whether locals believe these contestations are imagined or real. The study of contested spaces is now the hallmark of much cultural and urban geography.

Municipal governments usually spearhead preservation and conservation efforts in the Latin American inner city, but they do not always consult residents. These governments, in turn, interface with national governments and international agencies. Increasingly, international aid comes from for-profit investors who target specific buildings and projects that have little to do with enhancing the housing of locals. These activities include intervention in large colonial structures such as warehouses, fortresses, convents, jails, hospitals, port facilities, and an assortment of public buildings. There is also a gradual cycle of phasing in historic preservation work as buildings and public spaces deteriorate and require intervention. Rosemary Bromley and Gareth Jones (1996b) argue that upgrading the built environment in Third World cities diminishes the traditional heterogeneity of social groups and their lifestyles in historic districts. Latin American municipal governments, hard pressed for funds to cover anything more than essential services, often have no recourse but to secure funding from for-profit investors (Irarrázaval and Scarpaci 1994).

While national governments or international agencies such as UNESCO focus international attention on heritage sites, these "badges of honor" rarely carry large sums of money. As neoliberal policies take hold in Latin America, investment in historic districts may be discouraged because lenders do not consider them to be "productive" investments, despite the potential for heritage tourism income. National political economies rupture in devastating ways due to the social effects of these neoliberal policies and to other sociopolitical struggles: post-Soviet Cuba; warfare (Colombia's Revolutionary Armed Forces, or FARC); narcotics traders, or right-wing militias (Argentina's political and economic woes that escalate inflation and unemployment). Under these difficult economic circumstances, funding heritage projects is especially difficult (Tung 2001).

If securing investment in these built environments is difficult and controversial, the ways local residents confront urban revitalization pose even greater challenges. Gareth Jones and Ann Varley (1994) differentiate between pragmatic and imagined contests for the historic district. There are practical concessions that locals seek in their neighborhoods when governments cannot provide basic housing, health care, or police and fire protection. Local residents can see with their own eyes subsidized building materials, increased staffing at public clinics, and more police officers

Figure 4.1   Parking posts in Barrio La Candelaria, Santa Fé de Bogotá, designed to keep cars from parking on the sidewalks, 1995.

walking the beat (Scarpaci 1991). Symbolic goals in historic districts, though, are more difficult to quantify (Ward 1993). Reappraising the built environment may stem partly from a need to "morally" clean up the city center, a paradigm associated with the Department of Sociology at the University of Chicago and their human ecology studies on such sites as "skid row" as a place of ill repute and urban social deviance (Park, McKenzie, and Burgess 1967). Moral contestations about parts of the city change over time, as Puebla reveals (see table 2.1). The town's Plaza de los Sapos serves as the traditional center for mariachis and other musicians as well as bawdy cantinas and houses of ill repute. On the weekends, however, it has become the antique market for the local gentry and international tourists. Changing land uses reveals both different classes and diurnal uses of this part of historic Puebla.

Pragmatic contested spaces, seemingly benign, also contribute to the social construction of historic districts. Clearing out automobile congestion is a common urban planning strategy. Many residents in the historic district cannot afford automobiles, and those living outside the historic district usually park on the street. Simple barriers, such as mounting concrete posts on sidewalks in historic Bogotá (figure 4.1), blocking automobile access to the old quarters of Trinidad (Cuba), or removing underground parking garages in Habana Vieja (figures 4.2a–4.2b), contribute to the "pedestrianization" of the historic districts in direct ways. These are just a few of the ways urban design, modernity, and architecture collide in the centro histórico.

How local residents, journalists, politicians, and scholars frame contested spaces in the Latin American city must, I believe, be traced back to the arrival of the Modern Movement in the early twentieth century. Here, we observe how the Modern Movement conditioned historic districts and, in some instances, left them tattered, neglected, leveled, and then "revived." Habana Vieja is illustrative in showing the interplay of these forces.

Luis Rodríguez offers an interesting assessment of the meaning of the word *modern* in his recent book on Havana's modern architecture. He suggests that the discourse on the "modern architectural movement" in Cuba was derived from successive interpretations of this design period and that the term *modern* took on a conceptual connotation in Cuban urban design and planning for the first time in the early twentieth century.

> The word represented the epitome of a series of assumptions that over time, and filtered through subsequent controversies, would culminate in the clamor for renewal, which by the late fifties, allowed Cuban architecture to join the vanguard in the Americas.
>
> Various factors encouraged the assimilation of the groundbreaking rationalist ideas that had sprung up around Europe after World War I. But the most important role was undoubtedly played by the architecture journals, which succeeded in maintaining a high monthly circulation for many years, despite countless changes of name, format, and editorial boards [and led to] . . . heated debates conducted in their pages from the mid-twenties onward [that] testify to the sophisticated theoretical levels already attained by young Cuban architects of the day. (Rodríguez 2000, viii–ix)

Architectural modernity in Havana evolved from an uncritical adoption of European and U.S. interpretations of "good" design in the early

Figure 4.2a   The imploded underground parking garage at Habana Vieja's Plaza Vieja, 1995.

twentieth century, to one of *creolization*. It meant adapting design to a particular urban culture and climate. Cuban architecture in the mid-twentieth century searched out the local, the authentic, or *lo cubano* (figure 4.3). As early as 1926, the journal *El Arquitecto* had argued that there were acceptable forms of architecture that could be termed "aerodynamic architecture": the great ocean liners with their graceful and thrusting curves, formidable battleships, enormous airplanes, and huge locomotives (Rodríguez 2000, ix). Yet, in the 1920s in Cuba, most new designs did not adapt themselves to the broad-minded aesthetics of the machine, opting instead for Art Deco.

Neocolonial revivalism had taken hold in Cuba by the end of the 1920s. This, curiously, was the same time that the Modern Movement was mov-

Figure 4.2b   The restored Plaza Vieja, in Habana Vieja, with a fenced-off half million dollar Italian marble fountain, 1999.

ing through the island. Alejo Carpentier (1977) argued that vanguardism deprecated the past and that it was nationalist by tradition. The dialectical tensions of backward-looking and forward-looking approaches to urban design surfaced in Mexico, Colombia, Cuba, Chile, Argentina, Uruguay, and Brazil in the pre–World War II era (Segre 1981). The Modern Movement lacked adequate planning to accommodate this new type of built environment. Modernist pieces, often isolated from the urban fabric, were showcased for their own merits at the exclusion of the existing urban fabric. More important, they transformed the historic district. Yet, these changes would not leave as deep an impact on local culture, economy, and architecture as would international tourism focused on Spanish colonial charm.

Globalization, Heritage Tourism, and Local Spaces in the Centro Histórico

Over the past three decades, transformations in the industrial organization of advanced societies have been accompanied by the acceptance of the ideas of postmodernity and postindustrialism. Geographers, sociologists, and planners seek an understanding of how the urban world has evolved. Facile interpretations often examine this phenomenon at the

Figure 4.3 Manuel Copado's Solimar (Sun and Sea) building, Havana, 1942. The building displays the Cuban Modern Movement's faith in the plasticity of poured concrete, and the repetition of balconies as a tenet of modernity but with the sensuousness of the sea waves. Photo 2000.

global level and point to general conclusions about uneven urban development as the result of capitalism (see Clark 1996).

Put another way, there are two notions that underlie much debate on globalization. One contends that it is a zero-sum game: whenever the global economy gains, the nation-state loses. The second position claims that events happening in a national territory (a judicial decision or a business transaction) are simply a "national" event. As Saskia Sassen (1999, 17) contends, "to posit, as is so often done, that economic globalization simply has brought with it a declining significance of the national state is inadequate. . . . Most global processes materialize in national territories and do so largely through national institutional arrangements, from legislative acts to firms, an [*sic*] hereby are not necessarily counted as 'foreign.'" Painting the world with such "broad strokes" as Sassen has runs the risk of pushing the inference ratio between local empirical work and global processes. My approach here and throughout this book is to focus specifically on one dimension of international tourism, and then to identify the way in which the Spanish American barrio is tethered to broader processes.

Tourism incorporates the interplay of globalization, culture, and locality, and it shifts the problem setting for analyzing communities to include various geographic scales of analysis.[1] Theories of globalization bring issues of space, time, and territorial organization into the center of this analysis. This means that a predominant paradigm of political sociology — the role of the nation-state as the catalysis of change — has been retheorized and recast into a secondary role. In its place are the many actors ushering in globalization. Following M. Albrow (2000, 119), I identify several core propositions about how heritage tourism relates to globalization in the Spanish American centro histórico.

1. Disembedding. International institutional arrangements enable people to cross national boundaries with the assurance that lifestyles can be maintained regardless of place.
2. Time-space compression. Communication and information technologies now allow one to maintain social relationships as direct interaction across any distance around the globe.
3. Globality. Commodities, images, and information from any corner of the world can be available at any time to increasing numbers of people. Simultaneously, the results of worldwide forces and events impose on local lives at any moment.
4. Globalism. Values shaping daily behavior for many people relate to imagined or real material states.

In earlier chapters, I suggested that one of the globalized dimensions of international tourism in Spanish American historic districts is that consumers (tourists) can now conceptualize far-off places as not being geographically discrete from their own daily spaces, but as a single generic place. Central to the "rediscovery" of these historic places is what Pico Iyer (2000) calls *Homo turisticos:* one who searches for new and exotic places. The ensemble of the elements of historic districts — castles, cathedrals, cobblestone streets, courtyards, galleries, grilles, louvered doors, and colonial lore—are the props that make this exotic stage possible throughout Latin America (Llanes 2001). These common objects of gaze vary only slightly across the Americas, at least in the eyes of the average tourist. Homogenizing these places in reality or in the minds of tourists contributes to Arjun Appadurai's (1986) argument about the gradual decline of the unique "leisurescape." If Appadurai is correct, then, leisurescapes might signal the end of tourism, since homogenization erases the idiographic, the unique, and the local.

Latin American historic districts also form part of what Louis Turner and John Ash (1975) call the "pleasure periphery." Most North American travelers frequent the Caribbean, South America, and Central America for leisure excursions. Of the four S's of "tropical" tourism—sun, sea, sand, and sex—we can state that Cuba offers another letter and dimension: socialism. A post-Soviet Cuban economy has created a pronounced hustler class (*jineteros*) in Habana Vieja that services tourists seeking prostitutes, home restaurants, drugs, cheap (and often counterfeit) cigars, and other wares and services (Elinson 1999; Trumball 2001). The Cuban leadership considers such illegality a by-product of capitalism and globalization, which contrasts with the "law-and-order" approach of the socialist state, an assumption rife with contradictions (Pérez-López 1995).

We can conceptualize the heritage etched into Latin American historic districts as a duality anchored by economic factors at one end, and cultural capital at the other. Urban heritage remains a commodity widely sold in differentiated markets (Graham, Ashworth, and Turnbridge 2000, 22). As David Brett (1996) argues, overperfecting built heritage can trivialize it, which makes it become either shallow, contrived, or both. Heritage situates itself within geography's concern of the representation and meaning of place. Geographers have examined the dichotomy of landscapes as physical representations as well as the socially constructed interpretations of the same. There is interplay of knowledge about heritage: its physical, economic, cultural, class, racial, and political aspects each provide frameworks for interpreting how identities are constructed. Central to the debate about place identity is the question: Whose heritage is represented? The discord that results reflects a broader set of power struggles in cities and nations. If power structures legitimate landscapes, nowhere is this more pronounced than in historic districts. One consensus is that constructions of "otherness" help to set apart the modern inventions of "universal" traditions and values (Donald and Rattansi 1992).

Cynical views hold that the end of tourism is imminent because travel is so commonplace and has become a regular chore that must be faced with stoicism (Lash and Urry 1994). Writer Walter Kirn (2001) captures the demands (and absurdity) of some kinds of air travel through his fictional character, Ryan Bingham, in *Up in the Air*. The protagonist strives to accumulate one million airline miles in his job as a software executive. In his travels, he seeks comfort in the ubiquitous spaces of airplane cabins, airports, newspapers, cable television news, and hotels. Homogenization and standardization of space and travel bring comfort and order. In a similar vein, Virilio (1997) observes that because places can be easily and quickly represented on a video screen or through a computer monitor, the unique features of historic districts become blurred. If, as Virilio argues, "the screen has become the city square," then the "colonialscape" of the casco histórico becomes a visual morsel made generic and disseminated easily through tourist promotion literature.

Although transnational service, especially in tourism, has lagged behind the manufacturing sector in the realm of globalization, there are telltale signs of its reach. Transnational service conglomerates maximize their ability to provide onstream production and onstream parallel services (Dicken 2003, 390). This service provision is evident in how transnational hotel chains operate in the centro histórico. For example, the French chain Sofitel administers the Hotel Santa Clara in Cartagena's walled city (reviewed in chapter 5) and the Dutch firm, Golden Tulip, managed the Parque Central in Habana Vieja until 2001, when it came under Spanish management (figures 4.4a–4.4b). In the former, the French hotel chain transformed a 250-year-old convent from an abandoned city block to an upscale hotel (Scarpaci 2000a). In the latter, a Dutch consortium kept only the corner facade in Havana's historic district, and it mounted a garish hotel that hardly resembles the surrounding built fabric (Scarpaci 2000b, 2000c). Authenticity — unlike beauty — is not in the eyes of the beholder, but is shaped by international investors who have the economic muscle to alter the built environment as they wish.

The "crumbling of walls," as Frederick Clairmonte and John Cavanaugh (1981) argue, is an apt metaphor for the erosion of a state's ability

Figure 4.4a Spanish-operated (Novo Hotel) Parque Central at the edge of Habana Vieja, within the UNESCO-declared World Heritage Site, 2000. *Photograph courtesy of Mario Coyula.*

to regulate its own affairs. Clearly, deregulation has aided capital's ability to move; nowhere is its arrival more welcome (or so it would seem) than in the Latin American historic district. Cuba remains cash starved yet requires investment for tourism. Colombia is cash strapped because it must fend off the guerillas of the Left and the militias of the Right in a terrifying war within its own boundaries. Ecuador is so vulnerable to the vicissitudes of the world market that in 2001 it adopted the dollar as its legal tender. How this private-public relationship, remittances, and the dollarization of Latin American economies affect historic districts is essential in understanding the context of contested urban spaces.

Public-Private Partnerships, Remittances, and Historic District Change

The lines drawn in the public-private debate — that is, which mode of finance and revenue generation is more suitable — have been blurred in the new millennium. Multinational companies buy and sell commodities at a

Figure 4.4b Corner facade from 1920s of present Hotel Parque Central, before renovation, at corner of Neptuno and Prado Streets. Photo 1994.

dizzying pace, often making it difficult to trace these transactions. Witness, for example, fugitive U.S. millionaire Marc Rich who allegedly violated U.S. law by trading with Iran (for purchasing and reselling oil), Libya (for buying oil in the late 1980s and 1990s and for shipping agricultural goods to Libya in 1999–2000), South Africa (for selling oil to South Africa in 1979–90), and Cuba. In each instance, the United States had an enforced embargo or sanction against the "pariah" nation. In the last case, Rich traded oil with Cuba and then purchased and resold Cuban sugar despite a long-standing U.S. embargo ("Open for Business . . ."). Although he renounced his U.S. citizenship after fleeing to Switzerland in 1982 because of tax evasion charges, Bill Clinton granted him a presidential pardon in January 2001. Part of his dealing with Cuban sugar entailed swapping and reselling Russian oil. Before the collapse of the Soviet

Union, Russia often exchanged one ton of oil for the same weight of Cuban sugar.

Remittances

Globalization facilitates the international travel of documented and undocumented workers. The process eases the flow of capital, perhaps the most defining feature of economic globalization. As the Rich incident shows, the "money trail" in international business is hard to trace even in formal financial markets. Barbara Garson's (2001) recent review of how investment patterns become entangled, disappear, and then reappear is insightful. She demonstrates the considerable discrepancy between what regulators and creditors claim about "transparency" in financial markets. Her call for a re-regulation of capital flows by imposing taxes on currency transactions to limit speculation may be a harbinger of banking changes to come (Harris 2001). In 2002, scandals, accusations, and illegal conduct rocked the U.S. business community. Wall Street reacted unkindly to the practices of such widely recognized companies as Adelphia, Arthur Andersen, Enron, Halliburton, JP Morgan-Chase, WorldCom, and Xerox, all of whom found themselves facing prosecution for violating commerce and banking regulations.

International migrants and their remittances form just one part of this globalization chain. Like formal multinational companies, some of their activities are legal and others are not. In time-honored fashion, migrants send portions of their incomes from the United States to Latin America. In Mexico, the Dominican Republic, El Salvador, and Colombia, remittances have increased 26 percent annually since the 1980s — to the tune of some $8 billion. At one end of these capital flows are hometown associations (HTAS) in the United States, while at the other end we find millions of households and businesses strengthened by the infusion of capital. Briant Lindsay Lowell and Rodolfo de la Garza (2000) estimated that the average amount of money transferred to Latin America from the United States is $320. Commission fees at origin and destination approach 5 percent to 15 percent, and occasionally they reach 20 percent of the transaction amount (Lowell and de la Garza 2000). The Mexican government has long been a leader in leveraging a percentage of these remittances by earmarking part of these funds for development projects. Government agencies in all remittance settings serve as the highest level of actors, followed by, in descending order, nongovernmental agencies in Latin America, HTAS, and the individual households at the base of the hierarchy. Remittances, then, involve a significant number of businesses and households.

In the late 1990s, remittances to Ecuador approached US$500 million annually, making them the fourth-largest source of national income. In 1999, the national currency, the sucre, fell from seven thousand to the dollar to nearly thirty thousand. President Gustavo Noboa implemented a far-reaching reform package in March of that year to correct economic disorder and stem rising corruption. With annual inflation hovering at around 80 percent, the government formally adopted the dollar as the official currency in an attempt to stabilize the economy and promote investment. By the middle of 2000, though, only 2 percent of the sidewalk merchants knew how to use dollars, make change in coins, and convert sucres into dollars. Ecuador's currency dilemma is ironic given the formidable role the dollar plays in bolstering its national economy. The number of counterfeit dollars manufactured in nearby Colombia has risen because of Ecuador's new currency. By June 2000, all banking operations were carried out entirely in dollars ("Ecuador's Switch to the U.S. Dollar Is in Full Swing").

Dollars are not new in Cuenca and surrounding Azuay Province. Many immigrants who leave Ecuador to work in the United States hail from the region. A common way to obtain informal and petty-formal employment in the United States is through illegal "coyotes,"[2] who smuggle immigrants into Mexico or else arrange tourist excursions into Mexico (see chapter 1). From there, the coyotes funnel the Ecuadorians into illegal immigrant streams that cross the border. A large percentage makes their way to the New York City metropolitan area, with a pronounced concentration in the borough of Queens.

Property owners and businesses modified the banking districts to capture remittances sent back to the Azuay and Cuenca region. As in many centros históricos in Spanish America, banking institutions cluster in the old quarters of Cuenca. Over the past three decades, Cuenca's historic neighborhood has expanded its array of banks, courier services, and travel

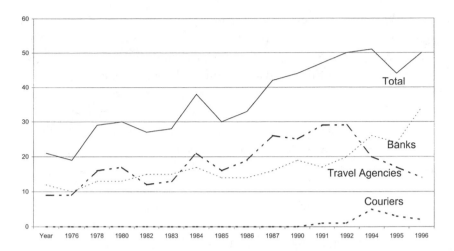

Figure 4.5 Formal establishments in Cuenca's historic district receiving or delivering overseas remittances, 1976–97. Data sources: City telephone directories of Cuenca. Time-series calculated by the author.

agencies. I documented the rise in the formal establishments receipts of wired money orders, cashiers' checks, or couriered cash shipments between 1976 and 1997. Figure 4.5 shows a 250 percent increase in businesses locating in Cuenca's UNESCO-acclaimed World Heritage Site. However, this only captures one "formal" dimension of remittances; it cannot measure cash carried by *cuencanos* who return permanently to the city and region after working in the United States, or by those who return to Ecuador to visit.

The remittances have important consequences in the historic district of Cuenca. Property values and rents have risen. A small banking district nested within the historic district has expanded appreciably. New banks adopt neocolonial designs and attempt to blend seamlessly with the existing buildings (figure 4.6). Nevertheless, the consequences are the same: the traditional centro histórico resident must either pay higher rents, pay higher property taxes, or seek housing elsewhere. In the late 1990s, this corner of the historic district witnessed a rise in art galleries, restaurants, boutiques, and other services. This retailing caters to affluent groups — many of them tourists — instead of the traditional artisan and indigenous population that historically inhabited the district (figure 4.7).

Figure 4.6 New banks with neocolonial design in the banking zone of Cuenca's historic district.

Figure 4.7   Artisan and Indian residential quarters at the edge of the financial district, Cuenca.

Depressed economic conditions in the Azuay region surrounding Cuenca have forced thousands of poor peasants to the United States in search of a better life. That characterization fits the journey of single mother Julia Toledo and her four sons aged 11, 10, 6, and 3. Locals saw her family walking the neighborhood surrounding the Bridgeport, Connecticut, homeless shelter, some neighbors referring to Toledo and her brood as "The Pied Piper." The forty-seven-year-old had migrated to the United States in 1999 because relatives had told her of work and a better life for her boys. After spending several nights in a homeless shelter, she and her children set off down the railroad tracks leading out of Bridgeport. A parish priest where Julia and her family worshiped assumed she chose the cover of night to walk to the next town in search of work because she thought it would be safer than walking the streets of Bridgeport. On May 26, 1999, Amtrak's Twilight Shoreliner caught the family of five crossing a railway trestle where the speeding locomotive could not stop (Lavoie and O'Neill 1999). This family's saga is but a footnote in Cuenca's experience with globalization.

Cuba also relies on remittances from relatives in the United States. The U.S. consulate in Havana estimates that between $1 and $1.5 billion reach the island annually (personal communication, Vicki Huddleston, U.S. Consulate, November 11, 2002, Havana). If these figures are correct, then remittances are the main source of net foreign earnings in Cuba. Although the money circulates through the economy after reaching relatives, its presence is most evident in the state-run dollar stores. Philip Peters and I found that numerous self-employed workers in Habana Vieja rely on remittances to sustain their operations, buy raw materials for production and service, and complement their household income (Peters and Scarpaci 1998).

The Dollarization of the Latin American Economy

It is not surprising that Latin American economies are becoming increasingly dollarized, because two-thirds of all dollars in circulation are outside the United States (Análisis Internacional 2002). One conventional but risky economic and banking solution is to replace local currency with the U.S. dollar when economies become unstable. The year 2001 began in El Salvador with the government's adoption of the U.S. dollar as its currency. For years, the dollar had been the de facto currency used for buying goods, paying salaries, and doing business. El Salvador's Congress approved the measure in 1999 because the nation had faced chronic inflation with the previous national currency — the colón — and because the Congress had hoped it would stabilize and boost the nation's economy. Salvadorans living in the United States send home an average of $4 million a day, making remittances the third-largest source of national income ("El Salvador Will Bank on Dollars 1/1/01"). Panama has used the dollar as legal tender since 1904 (Bogetic 2000). Guatemala incorporated the dollar alongside its currency (quetzal) in 2001, following Argentina, which had pegged its peso to the dollar for several years by then. Even Cuba's centrally planned economy uses dollars mostly for international trade and commerce (including tourism), but in June 2002 it began circulating the Euro at Varadero Beach, a peninsula accessed by a toll road and frequented largely by Europeans vacationing on charter packages.

As Julia Toledo's saga highlights, Ecuador's dollarization and economic woes do not come without human costs. Inflation and devaluation continued into the 2000s, but the government also implemented a series of austerity measures and plans for the privatization of public firms. Officially, the U.S. Treasury warns nations that the dollarization of their economies can only be done at the nations' own risk. Yet at the same time, the International Monetary Fund will lend Ecuador $300 million between 2000 and 2003, the World Bank will contribute $425 million, and the Inter-American Development Bank will extend $620 million in credits; another $700 million in loans will come from the Andean Development Corporation. Opposition to the program in Ecuador stems from the nation's inability to control its own domestic economy. Some outcomes are inevitable: Ecuador will have to accept that interest rates will be set in the United States, even if Ecuador's economy "is moving in the opposite direction of the U.S. economy" (Bussey 2000).

Foreign policy, illegal migration, and regional planning in Ecuador have become embroiled in the ramifications of the United States' Plan Colombia. This $1.3 billion "aid" package is for a counternarcotics development program in Colombia, and it is a point of contention throughout the Americas. In 2001, Ecuadorian President Noboa announced that his nation would remain "neutral" on pronouncing whether or not the Plan Colombia is beneficial. In a related move, the Ecuadorian ambassador to the United Nations abstained from voting on Cuba's human rights record in April 2001, to avoid alienating Hugo Chávez, the president of Colombia's northeastern neighbor, Venezuela, and leftist and admirer of Fidel Castro's Cuba (Guillén 2001). The diplomatic signals also suggest that Ecuador wants to avoid paramilitary wars within its own borders so as not to aggravate its own economic conditions or force northbound cocaine through its territory. This regional posturing reveals how alliances and economic well-being relate to matters outside legal international trade.

Residential Perceptions of Heritage Tourism in Three Centros Históricos

These brief overviews of remittances and the dollarized economy have shown that the study of heritage tourism and Latin American historic districts poses many challenges. I have identified how monetary linkages in the global market have strengthened recently. In the section that follows, I wish to change the geographic scale of analysis from the international to the local level. I wanted to better understand the perceptions of the local residents of the historic neighborhoods of Havana, Cartagena, and Cuenca. To that end, I conducted two focus groups in each city using a semistructured instrument, as opposed to a probabilistic-based public opinion survey (Berg 2000; Merriam 1998). The methodology used here differs from the two usual methods applied to Latin America: "intensive case study" and "large numbers" (Large-N); the latter was used in chapter 3 in discussing the land-use survey findings. In this chapter, I use the "intensive case study method" (also called the "small numbers method," or small-N), analyzing the same topic in a limited number of settings while systematically contrasting the data. Historic districts proved to be an ideal geographical setting for this method.

For the field research in the study sites, I spent nine weeks in Havana (June–July 1998), four weeks in Cartagena (June 2000), and three weeks in Cuenca (June 1997). During previous field research visits in these neighborhoods, I had noticed an absence of public announcements inviting the community to join in discussions about neighborhood issues related to heritage tourism and its attendant problems (especially since planning departments told me that the local governments were implementing projects). While I believe it would be naive to assume that political enfranchisement leads directly to social justice (Calabrese and Burgelman 1999, 3), I anchor my intellectual and personal sympathies in a democratic model of local governance and urban planning. Accordingly, during these case study visits I combed newspapers and looked at public billboards for announcements. The only written notices about urban revitalization and historic preservation I found were in Habana Vieja and Cartagena. In the latter, the Office of the City Historian always labeled construction sites with information about the project name, the architect in charge, the construction firm, and related matters. However, I never saw any announcement of a public meeting called by the municipal government and its agencies. In Cartagena, I saw more planning department signs plastered on doors where building code violations were evident than in any other city in my study. Nevertheless, I never saw or read in the Cartagena newspapers any call for a public forum about planning, housing, or tourism matters.

I also combed local newspapers and examined newspaper archives for signs of investigative journalism. In Latin America, there is ample evidence that an active press can help redress social justice and community-planning issues (Scarpaci and Frazier 1993). In Western democracies, there is a rich history of investigative reporting and agenda building. In particular, investigative journalism can lead to what is called a mobilization model. In this sequence of events, a series of sustained published media investigations leads to changes in public opinion. In turn, these changes result in public policy reforms, remedying or setting a path to positive change (Protess et al. 1991, 12–13). Occasionally, I found op-ed pieces in Cartagena and Cuenca about the value of historic preservation. In Cuba, only laudatory articles about historic preservation appeared in the daily national newspaper *Granma*. Models linking journalism, investigative reporting, and public policy reforms were not germane in this study.

I was also struck by the absence of public announcements about a building, land-use, or public space conversion in any of the nine study sites during my eight months of field research over the past thirteen years. My conversations with public officials revealed a wide range of attitudes about community participation and local planning issues that ranged from disinterest at one end, to paternalism at the other. Therefore, the overall aim of this stage of my research was to understand specific dimensions of the revitalization process, with an investigation of the meanings of certain urban and residential dimensions. Put simply, what did the locals think about historic preservation and heritage tourism?

I conducted focus groups to gather information about how local residents of three historic districts interpreted the renovations taking place in their neighborhoods. I cast urban renovation as neutrally as possible: usually as neighborhood revitalization (*reanimar el barrio*) or neighborhood change (*cambios en el barrio*). To avoid a predetermined response from the informants, in no instance did I use terms such as displacement (*desplazamiento*) or gentrification (although Anglicized, the term *gentrificación* is recognized among professionals and academics but never among locals). I conducted each focus group either in the backroom of a

restaurant (for privacy), or in a private residence within the neighborhood. Group size ranged from nine to seventeen, with an average of thirteen informants. I drew on Hardoy's now classic piece about the demographic makeup of the inhabitants of Spanish American historical centers.
I selected a mixture of male and female; black, Indian, or white; households headed by a female versus those headed by two adults; retirees;
property owners; and tenants (Hardoy 1983, 156–160). Informants were
older than eighteen years of age and had lived in the neighborhood for at
least two years.

I led forty- to seventy-five-minute discussions by posing a half-dozen
semistructured questions aimed at assessing residents' perceptions about
neighborhood change. The key term here was *neighborhood change;* I did
not define it, but rather I allowed the respondents to interpret it individu-
ally or derive some collective agreement about its meaning. Informants
knew that I was a U.S. university professor writing a book on historic
neighborhoods in Latin America, which in itself helped specify in some
fashion the kind of "change" I was interested in hearing them discuss. I
paid no one for his or her participation but did arrange for day-care
services (at my expense) in two focus groups. Nonalcoholic beverages, a
locally fried food (frituras), and sweet cakes were served at the focus
groups. Everyone knew that the sessions were audiorecorded, and the
microphone was placed in the center of the room for all to see. Anonymity
was granted to all informants. Focus group sessions were transcribed into
Spanish but not English. I coded for both manifest and latent content
analysis, looking for simple and readily definable trends.

Findings reveal that in Havana and Cuenca, historic district residents
hold strong feelings about public authorities, investors, tourists/tourism,
and the future of their neighborhood (table 4.1). Generally, residents of all
three historic districts were not optimistic about the future, had negative
things to say about local authorities, and felt that tourism will bring more
harm than good.

Residents thought little of local authorities. They expressed frustration
with their attempts to get local officials to focus on what they (the residents) thought were important concerns. A typical sentiment about local
authorities, generally used to refer to the mayor, the mayor's office,
the city historian (in Havana), and the planning department, was aptly

Table 4.1   Selected categories of neighborhood change used in manifest and latent content analysis, based on focus groups in three historic districts, 1997–2000

Category	La Habana Vieja			Cartagena de las Indias			Cuenca		
	Pos.	Neutr.	Neg.	Pos.	Neutr.	Neg.	Pos.	Neutr.	Neg.
Public authorities (*auto-ridades públicas*)	7	0	42	2	0	36	6	0	28
Chi-square		27.78			37.06			15.44	
P		0.0001			0.0001			0.0001	
Investors (*inversionistas*)	3	0	12	6	2	4	1	1	18
Chi-square		5.78			Not significant			14.723	
P		0.0162						0.0001	
Tourists/tourism (*turistas, turismo*)	4	2	18	12	1	10	2	2	24
Chi-square		6.28			0.392			15.84	
P		0.01			0.531			0.0001	
Neighborhood future (*el futuro del barrio*)	13	0	11	8	2	16	0	0	9
Chi-square		0.17			1.39			Pearson: 9.0	
P		0.68			0.24			$P > 0.0027$	

Source: Author's field research, 1997–2000. See text for discussion.

expressed in Habana Vieja. An Afro-Cuban woman in her mid-forties, living two blocks from the Plaza Vieja, said:

> They [local authorities] go and spend millions of dollars in blowing up the [underground] parking garage. But for years, I've been asking [the local Committee for the Defense of the Revolution] for some plaster and mortar so I can repair the leak in my roof. And what have I gotten? Nothing.

An Indian man dressed in traditional garb who sells produce in the Cuenca market was equally skeptical of local authorities. His concern, however, was grounded in a long-standing dispute:

For four hundred years they [European Ecuadorians] did not care one bit about us, so why would rising rents matter to them now?

A single mother of three young girls who had inherited her father's home in Cartagena felt helpless in the face of planning authorities and the market:

> The local authorities are not interested in people like me. We have to put forward a large amount [of] capital to make changes. We cannot even afford the application fee for remodeling. We have to make changes on the interiors without the authorities knowing. Who in this room has the kind of money the French [Sofitel Corporation] do? Our neighborhood [San José] has its enchantment, and while we are pleased that tourists enjoy it too, we could be suffocated by the market if it runs wildly. My personal opinion is that as long as taxes remain low, we can hold on to our homes. But, the temptation to sell or to lease out the ground floor or the front room of our homes is great. This [grappling with this decision] is not easy.

Residents of Habana Vieja and Cuenca held strong negative views about tourists. They saw little advantage accruing to them because of the onslaught of tourists or tourism. *Cartageneros* (Cartagenans), though, held statistically significant negative views. Urban renewal and gentrification brought in by money laundering and real-estate schemes, as well as a strong demand by European jet-setters, had increased the demand for property between 1990 and 1995. An anti-money-laundering law passed in 1995, coupled with a recession, cut into demand in the late 1990s. One widow from a focus group remarked:

> I'm waiting for my European prince to arrive and offer me $500,000 [U.S. dollars] for my house so I can retire happily in the countryside with my kids!

The remark underscores the material rewards that heritage tourism brings to some property owners.

Cuencanos were ambivalent about the success that their family members have had overseas. Economic survival justified the transformation of old Cuenca, as the following statements show:

Of course our children have to go away and work; the economy is depressed here, as it has been for a long while. But, hey, we cannot hide the prosperity that the shipments [*envíos* or *giros,* both synonyms for money transfers] bring to Azuay [Province]. These improvements are happening. I doubt my grandchildren will be able to live here when they grow up, but Cuenca will always live, Cuenca is a part of us. . . . We will always have these tired buildings looking down on us, always. We don't have to live inside the historic shell [casco antiguo] to enjoy it, do we?

A young, male art-gallery owner who leases property from an absentee landlord residing in Quito also recognizes trade-offs in Cuenca's historic preservation process:

This is a double-edged sword. Without the commerce and tourism, the neighborhood will collapse. The municipality has only provided money for ceremonial structures: plazas, churches, and the like. My rents rise, but my landlady fixes up the building, the plumbing, the electrical wiring, and pays taxes. I couldn't run my business without her. So, yes . . . uh, I know this is complicated but the mayor has no money, and Quito doesn't know we exist.

A second set of tests was run on the content analysis findings. The null hypothesis was that the distribution of negative attitudes about these four dimensions of neighborhood change was equal in all cities. I rejected the null hypothesis and accepted the alternative that negative sentiments were uneven among the three study sites. This was determined by conducting a contingency analysis of each content-analysis category, across the three sites. The variable "neighborhood future" had a Pearson coefficient of 8.1 ($p = 0.02$) and shows that there are significant differences in how locals perceive the future of their cities and neighborhoods. Only cuencanos held exclusively negative views about the future of their neighborhoods, while the sentiment in both Havana and Cartagena was mixed (table 4.1). "Tourists and tourism" generated a Pearson coefficient of 11.13 ($p = 0.004$). While Havana and Cuenca expressed mostly negative comments about tourism, cartageneros held less critical sentiments.

Xavier, a twenty-three-year old father in Habana Vieja, had this to say:

The shipyards are not hiring, and I have to solve [*resolver*] my own problems for me and my family. To get by, I do what I have to do: cigars, [making referrals to] home restaurants [*paladares*], whatever. All this attention to the hotels and colonial mansions is fine, but it only helps me indirectly. My parents talk about the "old days" of the 1980s when the food-ration book [libreta] was enough [to get by], when there were things to buy in national currency [pesos]. Now, it is all dollars and more dollars. I can show you tenement houses [*cuarterías*] that the tourists don't see ever. So I guess you could say I'm a fighter, but many people, especially the older people, have no way [to cope].

A Colombian father of four who works as a busboy in a restaurant in the walled city assesses the relatively good situation of Cartagena compared to the rest of the nation.

My parents still live in Bucamaranga, and the stories they tell me about life there . . . the uncertainty, the violence [shaking his head]. The news-papers are full of problems elsewhere in Colombia. We are an island [he places his two hands together to form a circle], an island, a small one, and we are out of the main line of fire. Yes, here in Cartagena, we have Nelson Mandela [the shantytown outside Cartagena where many war-displaced victims from the highlands reside], but the tourism brings us hope and employment. This is all relative, then, you see? I say, "Mr. and Mrs. Tourist, come on down!"

Conclusion: Between Apathy and Empowerment in the Global Realm

Heritage tourism serves as a window to better understand the ambiguous process called globalization. This chapter has related the general experi-ence of how tourism and its attendant leisurescapes have changed three centros históricos: Cuenca, Havana, and Cartagena. As a variety of actors "discover" these places — UNESCO, international architects, art historians, urban planners, hotel operators, tourists, and travel agencies — we see how the neighborhoods operate and their residents' lives have been trans-formed. These changes, in turn, are part of a larger public-private debate about how national and local economies should respond to the unfettered forces of the world market.

At the macrolevel, I have shown how tourists, investors, and relatives living outside historic districts interact in complex ways. I have tried to sketch some of the patterns that the remittances play in Cuenca and Havana. Cuenca's transformation, for instance, derives in good measure from remittances sent by cuencanos laboring in the United States. Although remittances affect Cartagena less than Cuenca and Havana, Cartagena's real-estate market has been the target of money-laundering operations as well as second-home purchases by Europeans. Study of that Colombian seaport also shows how transnational hotel operations transform neighborhood land uses.

Focus group results show that local residents hold firm opinions about these changes, and they have strong sentiments about tourism, local authorities, and investors. Residents of Cuenca's and Cartagena's historic districts are not optimistic about the future of their neighborhoods, while those in Havana are more ambiguous about what tomorrow might bring. Generally, there is little contestation of how these districts are changing. A lack of class consciousness in Ecuador (where the disenfranchisement of indigenous groups has prevailed for centuries) and Colombia (where nearly half a century of civil war undermines confidence in public authority) suggests that conventional responses of community participation or electoral politics will produce little change. Although there is some disquiet about how redevelopment in Habana Vieja is unfolding, there is little formal outlet for protest or meaningful dialogue under the current system.

These research findings add to a growing literature that argues that community, political, and social mobilization among urban residents around the world may be highly romanticized and exaggerated. Andrew Calabrese (1999) refers to this as "ambivalence," which stifles the role of citizen activism because of distrust, a sense of hopelessness, and disillusionment. While he recognizes the historical importance of social movements and the role the citizenry can play in altering structural conditions of oppression and injustice, countervailing global forces hold firm. My focus group results suggest that global forces have derailed, or at least delayed, collective local action, by bringing a sense of hopelessness. "The disquieting condition of ambivalence about the prospects for democracy and democratic communication in a world governed by capitalist cartels should be accepted as steady-state. However, ambivalence is more satisfying than resignation, because the ambivalent view holds open the door to opportunity to benefit from new forms of democratic expression, whereas a resigned view may offer little more than eloquent epitaphs over the grave of democracy" (Calabrese 1999, 273).

The findings in my case studies of Habana Vieja, Cuenca, and Cartagena also corroborate those by Alejandro Portes, Carlos Dore-Cabral, and Patricia Landolt (1997), who demonstrate that popular participation in community organizations in Caribbean Latin America is now rather low. While Cuenca falls outside the Caribbean realm, the community perception is similar. In a classic Western model, a free and informed press, coupled with a literate public, might also serve as a venue for change. Mass communication and journalism scholars note the role of the media in setting agendas and modifying social policy. A common model linking the media to social policy change is the mobilization model, whereby journalists latch on to issues and manage to alter the salience of a matter that translates to policy change. The Cuban case study does not apply to that model because of state censorship and a lack of independent and private presses on the island. My review of Cuenca's and Cartagena's newspapers shows little focus on historic preservation, local planning, or social justice issues.

The three case studies offered here provide an empirical contribution to how locals confront globalization and heritage tourism. The social construction of public spaces in Habana Vieja, Cartagena, and Cuenca derives from locals' experiences in historic districts and their awareness of processes that originate beyond those barrios. Future research should continue to trace the nexus among the various scales of globalization so we can better understand contested and changing spaces in the Latin American historic district. The low level of community participation may stem from Mancur Olson's free-ridership dilemma: Why should residents participate in collective action when they perceive that their status remains the same regardless of whether they participate or not? (Olson 1965; Miller 2000). Discerning the experiences of those who live in these places will be a fruitful step in showing whether or how those spaces are questioned. It will also debunk the myth that there are common local responses to global processes, and that the downtrodden in Latin American cities speak in a single voice leading to collective action.

5 Heritage and Land Valuation in Cartagena de Indias

Planning and Paying for Cultural Patrimony

Cartagena de Indias (population 790,000), on Colombia's northwest coast, is unrivaled in architectural beauty and Spanish colonial charm (figure 5.1). Like many cities around the world, though, its inner city is characterized by "dilapidation, poor housing and economic deprivation" (Johnston, Gregory, and Smith 1994, 290). Among Cartagena's many maladies is an aging infrastructure requiring comprehensive modernization. Other predicaments include Colombia's role in the international narcotics industry, as well as lingering guerrilla warfare in the highlands and Amazon lowlands. Guerrilla strife consumes a large share of the national public budget. The city is geographically isolated from the highland war and is not part of the cocaine-producing or cocaine-processing zone (though marijuana is cultivated in the coastal plains around the city). Undeterred, displaced peasants arrive at this Caribbean port seeking refuge from war-torn areas. This migrant group has compounded the unemployment rate of 22 percent in 1999, and 21 percent in June 2000 (CCC 2000; personal communication, Herman Afiune, June 23, 2000, Cartagena Chamber of Commerce, Cartagena). Immigrant workers toil in such unskilled trade jobs as coffee vendors (*tinteros*), shoe shiners, and street vendors, especially in the city's old quarters.

Tourism and historic preservation in the Ciudad Amurallada, a 1982 UNESCO World Heritage Site, remain vital to the city's formal economy. Although architecture and colonial monuments are the main attraction, Cartagena suffers from the lack of a carefully devised tax policy for urban revitalization and economic development. Because of the regional and national economic slump, there are few policy stakeholders concerned about displacing local residents in the old city's historic barrios. This

Figure 5.1 Private residence, San Diego neighborhood, in Cartagena's historic district.

policy challenge cannot divorce itself from problems at the metropolitan, regional, national, and global levels.

This chapter reports on how Cartagena finances cultural patrimony. In other words, who pays for the upkeep of the city's UNESCO World Heritage Site designation? In answering this question, I analyze the tensions inherent in Cartagena's efforts to administer and implement tax, land-use, and zoning policies in its historic district. I begin with a review of some methodological pitfalls that are inherent in land valuation and housing market analyses, drawing on key literature on taxation in Latin American historic districts. Next, I explain planning and administration features of Cartagena's historic district that are central to this topic: land use, financing of heritage sites, and tax policies and revenues. The main section of the chapter turns to the implementation and regulatory challenges faced by authorities. I also present certain design and planning issues to show the common features that link heritage tourism, property taxes, and revitalization in important but not well-understood ways. A brief review of some conceptual parameters defining land and housing markets helps to situate this case study.

On Capturing Land Value

In their benchmark analysis of land-market and land-price analysis, Jones and Ward (1994) outlined research, design, and methodological issues in a single compendium. The case studies in that volume revealed how research and design can lead to different results, priorities, and policy prescriptions in capturing land values in the 1980s. Case studies show how the underlying assumptions of political economy versus Neoclassical paradigms shape outcomes and policy prescriptions.

Fueling the global economic upswing of the late 1980s and 1990s, The World Bank has aggressively promoted neoliberal orthodoxy that encourages the withdrawal of the state and the workings of unconstrained and free markets (see also chapter 4). It supports productivity, growth, and efficiency under the label of the New Urban Management Program (NUMP). However, Gareth Jones and Peter Ward caution that governments cannot divest themselves completely of all responsibilities for protecting vulnerable groups, and their case studies support that premise. For example, when industrialization in Mexico and Brazil "took off" during the 1950s and 1960s, there was no trickle-down benefit of more equitable wage labor. Therefore, why should the transfer of the entire housing market to private investors yield major improvements in the land-acquisition and housing position of Third World city dwellers? (Jones and Ward, 1994, 9). This questioning is particularly germane for residents of the historic district of Cartagena.

A more recent Inter-American Development Bank funded study by architect Eduardo Rojas (1999) explored the public-private partnerships in historic preservation as practiced in Cartagena; Recife, Brazil; and Quito. He found that Cartagena is unique because the private sector spearheads most of the initiatives in historic preservation, leaving the historic city susceptible to market fluctuations.

Historic Cartagena's Volatile Real-Estate Market

Three general features characterize Cartagena's housing market at the start of the new millennium. One aspect in the vicissitudes of the housing market is measured by construction permits requested for work in the old city. Requests for building permits rose markedly between 1992 and 1994 because of a housing market that "soared beyond the reach of most families interested in purchasing them" (Rojas 1999, 40). Later, efforts to remodel in the UNESCO site fell markedly in 1995, rose two years later, and then leveled out in the year 2000 (figure 5.2).

Conflating factors account for this seesaw trend. First, the Colombian national Congress passed Law Process 8,000 in October of 1995 as part of the anti-money-laundering platform of President Ernesto Samper (1994–98). It is unclear, however, whether the decline in construction is the result of this law (which aims to bring "transparency" to Colombia's financial institutions), or whether the law coincided with a downturn in the economy nationwide. Regardless, Law Process 8,000 ensures that no one invests, deposits, or makes transactions without documenting the source of the funds. This protocol might have dampened investments in historic properties, especially since Cartagena had become increasingly fashionable since the 1980s as a second-home resort for drug lords and their minions.

A second feature of Cartagena's housing market comes from the general downturn in the national economy evidenced by inflation and guerrilla warfare, both factors eroding investor confidence. The country confronts great political and economic uncertainty. Guerrilla forces continue to displace rural residents and drive them to the cities. Squatting in Colombia's urban centers is on the rise in ways the nation has not seen since the 1950s and 1960s when the infamous *violencia* period drove migrants from the countryside. Construction permits, mostly for renovation, rose sharply in Cartagena in 1997, but the financial bubble burst shortly thereafter. The Colombian government was forced to intervene in nine major banks and insurance companies in 1999, producing a tremendous credit crunch and "the greatest [financial] crisis of its history" (Guerrero 2000, 127). Scandals at the presidential level in the year 2000 dampened the political and economic future of President Andrés Pastrana. Meanwhile, back in

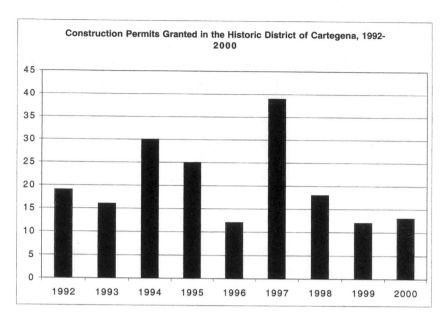

Figure 5.2   Construction permits issued in the historic district of Cartagena, 1992–2000. Data sources: Unpublished archival data collected by the author in *Control Urbano,* a publication of the Cartagena Planning Office, no. 1, July 1997 and June 2000; and *Control Urbano,* no. 2, June 2000, Municipality of Cartagena, Colombia. I also used unpublished archival records to compile the time-series data.

Cartagena, investors' interest in the historic district remained flat throughout 2000. The National Chamber of Building Construction (CAMACOL) even closed its branch office in Cartagena in 1999 because there was so little building construction.

To summarize, uncertainty looms heavily. By mid-2000, demand for historic district real estate had fallen off, and prices had decreased by roughly 25 percent since the mid-1990s (personal communication, Joaquín Pombo, general manager, Inmobiliario Gómez Pombo, June 27, 2000, Cartagena de Indias). The outlook in 2001 proved equally unpromising, and by 2003 U.S. military advisors had been killed in guerilla-controlled portions of the Colombian countryside.

A third feature of Cartagena's housing sector is the major changes in banking regulations. Although interest rates on residential and commercial mortgages stood only at 11.8 percent in July 2000, ambiguity in mortgage laws dampens investment in the built environment. Specifically, the Ley de Vivienda (Housing Law) regulates mortgage rates, but it has not clearly established how the banking industry will determine mortgages. In late 2001, the Unidad Valor Real (Real Value Unit) was to have been pegged to the rate of inflation. The legislature and court systems found the law illegal. Therefore, borrowers are reluctant to acquire mortgages without a promise that the rates will not balloon. Cartagena has had a glut of houses in the historic district for five years (1995–2000). Again, because of the uncertain mortgage and financial markets, buyers are reluctant to enter the housing market for refurbishing or buying existing properties. Figure 5.3 depicts the web of political and economic forces that shape Colombia's housing market.

Land Use and Taxes in Cartagena's Three Historic Neighborhoods

In 1982, UNESCO first listed the historic district of Cartagena as a World Heritage Site. It praises the district because "the monuments and architectural ensembles included in the list were located within the unique natural setting of the bay of Cartagena, the Committee also recommended that the bay be given the best protection possible" (UNESCO 1984). One out of twenty cartageneros lives in the ninety-seven-hectare site consisting of three neighborhoods of roughly equal area that together constitute the old city: Centro, San Diego, and Getsemaní (figure 5.4). Cartagena's elite neighborhoods outside the UNESCO district include Bocagrande, Laguito, and Castillogrande. Large single-family units and luxurious condominiums prevail in these neighborhoods. A modern strip of high-rise hotels in Bocagrande dating from the mid-1970s alleviates the imprint of tourism on the old city (Díaz and Paniagua 1993). This hotel district lies along a densely built peninsula to the south of the old city, and offers modern, full-service hotels.

The Centro Neighborhood

Centro, also called Catedral, is the original settlement of the old city and contains the largest collection of historic buildings, ramparts, museums,

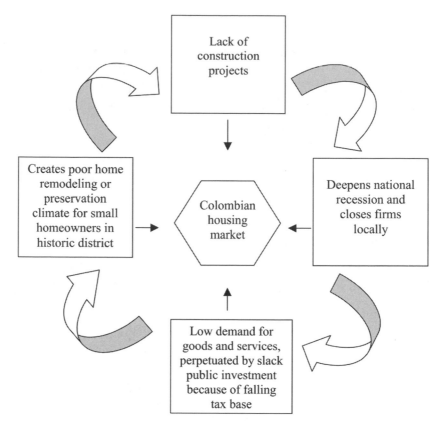

Figure 5.3 Schematic representation of Colombia's housing dilemma.

and civic and religious buildings within Ciudad Amurallada. Twelve of the city's site-specific heritage sites are located in Centro. The city's elite traditionally resides here, and there is a cluster of banks, government offices, real-estate firms, legal services, and corporate offices. A Colombian company redeveloped the former Santa Teresa Convent into a luxurious five-star hotel that anchors a plaza at the southern end of the neighborhood (figure 5.5, number 5). This property conversion from institutional use to a hotel has gentrified homes and encouraged upscale boutiques and antique markets to locate along adjacent streets. The streets between the Santa Teresa Hotel and Santo Domingo Plaza (figure 5.5,

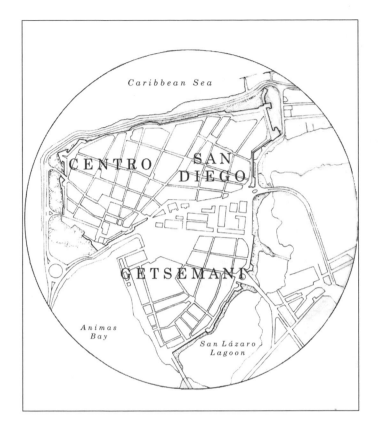

Caribbean Sea

CENTRO SAN DIEGO

GETSEMANI

Animas Bay

San Lázaro Lagoon

Figure 5.4 Cartagena's historic neighborhoods.

number 10) reflect these land-use changes, and it was here that President Clinton strolled during his September 2000 visit to Cartagena.

The San Diego Neighborhood

San Diego is a largely middle-income neighborhood that used to house many convents, schools, and businesses. In recent years, several buildings have been restored, and services connected to tourism have spread into San Diego (Díaz and Paniagua 1994a). Notable among these recent projects is the renovation of the former Santa Clara Convent (the twentieth-largest firm in Cartagena), which the Sofitel Corporation restored in 1994

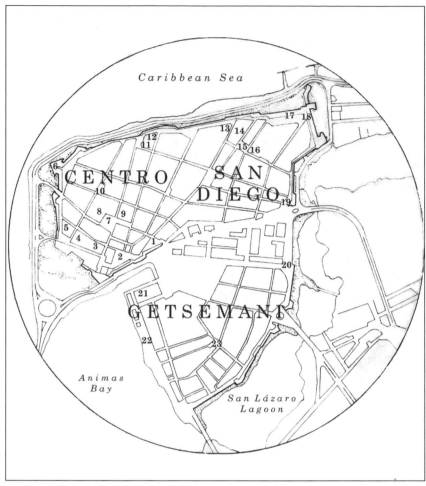

1. Plaza de los Coches
2. Plaza de la Aduana
3. San Pedro Claver Church
4. Naval Museum
5. Santa Teresa Convent (Hotel)
6. Santo Domingo Bastion
7. Bolívar Park
8. Inquisition Palace
9. Cartagena Cathedral
10. Santo Domingo Plaza
11. Heredia Theater
12. Jorge Tadeo University
13. García Márquez house
14. Santa Clara Convent (Sofitel Hotel)
15. San Diego Park
16. School of Fine Arts
17. Las Bóvedas (former barracks)
18. Santa Catalina Cisterns
19. San Pedro the Martyr Bastion
20. San Miguel Bastion
21. Cartagena Convention Center (former site of City Market)
22. El Arsenal (street/strip)
23. Trinidad Plaza

Figure 5.5   Location map of prominent features of Cartagena's historic neighborhoods.

into a five-star hotel (CCC 1999a, 9) (figures 5.6a–5.6e; see also number 14 on figure 5.5). The hotel pays only 5.5 percent property tax compared to 4.5 percent to 6.5 percent for residential properties; such discrepancies will be discussed later in the chapter. The San Diego neighborhood shows other land-use conflicts that gentrification and heritage tourism have brought to Cartagena.

Land-Use Conflict in San Diego Park. Until the mid-1990s, the park was the "living room" for the neighborhood.[1] Residents used it during most of the twentieth century as a place to celebrate formal and informal events. On December 29–30, the neighbors hosted a Festival de Boleros: evening dances of the slow rhythm bolero song style. Residents also held a New Year's Eve *fandango,* an event where a girl would dance to traditional Colombian songs. For Three Kings Day (Los Reyes Magos) on January 6, dancing in the park turned to "La Salsa de Ayer," a revival of salsa tunes from earlier years.

Land-use conflicts center on what merchants want to do with public space and what the local residents (often called the *comunidad raizal,* or "native community") wish. San Diego Park (El Parque San Diego, actually a town square) is one of two main plazas in the neighborhood. Traditionally, locals organized softball meetings in San Diego Park (figure 5.5, number 15). Neighborhood teams from outside the walled city came to the park to get tips on how to organize, find sponsorship, and schedule their games with the San Diego League (the field is just outside the wall, between the ocean and the old balustraded walls built in 1594). Senior citizens socialize in the square during the day, as do children, but less than in the past when there used to be a swing (removed in 1995 when the park was remodeled by Sofitel, a French hotel chain, and the Hotel Santa Clara). Students from the School of Art would also congregate there in the evening, but not anymore.

Although some of those activities still happen today, several features of the park's design and use have changed. First, the hotel removed a beautiful fountain with functional water pump that once graced the middle of the park during remodeling in 1995, and the hotel has not returned it. As noted above, a swing and slide set for children was removed. Second, local restaurateurs now dominate the space in the evenings by putting tables

a

b

c

into the center of the square. It is noteworthy that none of these entrepreneurs has permits to open restaurants around the square because it is within one hundred meters of a school at the northern end of the square (School of Arts: figure 5.5, number 16). Apparently, the restaurateurs have allies in city hall, which explains why the tables persist. The restaurateurs generate taxcs by selling food and beverages to tourists, though they violate planning codes.

Land use changed quickly when Sofitel revamped the convent in 1994. At lunchtime, ambulant food vendors, canteen trucks, and shaved ice ("snow cone") providers came to the park to sell meals and drinks. While

d   e

Figure 5.6a Figures 5.6a–5.6e show various perspectives on the remodeled Santa Clara Convent, Cartagena.
Figure 5.6b Facade bracing supports original exterior wall (right).
Figure 5.6c Vaulted ceiling along hallway.
Figure 5.6d Patio garden and fountain in hotel lobby draw on thick vegetation and coolness from shade to create a traditional setting.
Figure 5.6e Former convent courtyard used to hold gardens and fruit trees. Today, a swimming pool sits atop an underground parking garage.

many residents allege that the 180-room Santa Clara Hotel is beneficial to the neighborhood, it has generated externalities. For example, a discotheque opened in front of the hotel in 1998. The discotheque owner transformed her garage into this new facility. While the noise was not a problem, parking on the colonial streets was horrible. The police allowed discotheque patrons to park anywhere they could find space, and that meant blocking the entrances to the homes. Some residents even had to crawl over the hoods of cars to get into their houses. Police arrested one cigarette and chewing gum vendor outside the discotheque for selling cocaine that she hid underneath her basket of wares.

Authorities twice in 2000 arrested another merchant who operated a pizzeria facing the park for also operating a brothel, on the second floor, for affluent foreign tourists. Still, the merchant continued his business even though he — like other restaurateurs — has no legal right to operate a restaurant and serve alcohol, much less operate a brothel.

The conflicts surrounding San Diego Park have created unexpected alliances. Luis Daniel, the French Sofitel administrator/manager of Santa Clara Hotel, has given "unconditional" support to the San Diego association, for he too wants to see the restaurateurs disappear because they divert patrons from his hotel's three restaurants. The hotel pays for the park's lighting, but it is now reconsidering whether it should continue to subsidize its competitors' electric bills. The hotel chain also financed the redesign of the park in 1995.

A neighborhood newspaper describes the land-use debacle this way:

> The community of San Diego is dedicated more than ever to recuperating its park. The park is arbitrarily occupied by restaurateurs located on the streets adjacent to this public space. Among the many courses of action to be taken by the residents are some very clearly defined legal ones that entail questioning the legality of the restaurateurs' actions and the permissiveness of authorities. They have also elaborated a landscape architectural project so that the park will be pleasant and inviting as it always was. ("Así será el parque," 2000)

In the meantime, the Asociación de Sandieganos (Association of San Diegans), a neighborhood organization, continues to monitor the neighborhood for egregious violations of the law. It petitions city hall for a dismantling of the restaurants around the square.

The Getsemaní Neighborhood

Even though Getsemaní is a working-class neighborhood of the historic district, tourism is spreading to this corner of old Cartagena. The last of the three neighborhoods encased by the city walls in 1634, Getsemaní typically housed seamen, former slaves, and servants (Rojas 1999, 49). If it is the poorest district within the UNESCO site, El Arsenal Street and El Arsenal District fronting the bay are also undergoing rapid gentrification.

Restored buildings are opening for residential use, restaurants, coffee shops, nightclubs, and private and public offices (figure 5.5, number 22). One professional mother and her ten-year-old son had to move from her apartment because of the noise from a downstairs dance club.

> Friday and Saturday nights? Don't even talk about trying to get to sleep at that apartment. I just think it was a bad idea to allow a nightclub into a residential barrio. And if it was not the music thumping through the floors, then it was the large air conditioners outside the alley windows and in the back of the building, crying out all night long, forcing me to use my air conditioner just to cover up the noise. I had to pay the electricity bill for the air conditioner, which was a waste on nights when an open window or a fan would have sufficed. But my neighbor did not have an air conditioner, and she could not afford to move.

I asked about noise ordinances and whether the local authorities could have helped. "Noise ordinances?" she responded incredulously. "They have a license for the club, and that is all the local authorities care about."

Until 1979, the city market operated there on the waterfront, but in 1982 municipal authorities tore it down to make way for a modern convention center. The modern center, along with an extended parking lot, separates the neighborhood from the waterfront, where much fishing and marina activity happened. Since the mid-1980s, the largely Afro-Colombian community has restored its annual Carnaval parade held in November (figure 5.7). A cultural NGO (Getsemaní Cultural) promotes the revival of traditional arts, crafts, folklore, culture, and local history of the neighborhood (Díaz and Paniagua 1993).

Land Use

In 1992, I made my first visit to Cartagena, thanks to a series of lectures I delivered in Bogotá and Pereira as part of an Academic Specialist assignment arranged by the U.S. Information Agency. That assignment allowed me to travel to Cartagena when the lectures ended, where I surveyed the historic district. As discussed in chapter 2, I used the doorway as the unit of analysis. In all, 2,142 entrances, comprising all the doorways in the

Figure 5.7 Carnaval poster from Cartagena's Getsemaní neighborhood, 1999.

historic district, were assigned to one or more of seven variables, ranging from the most benign (residential) to the most noxious (abandoned or under construction) (figure 5.8).

The historic district balances residential and commercial land uses. Many cartageneros both work and live in the old quarters, unlike in some historic districts that turn into "ghost towns" at the end of the business day. One unique feature of Cartagena is the absence of large parking lots; many residents keep their cars within their courtyards or use restrictive street parking on specified roads in the old city.

Paying for Heritage

One approach in maintaining a healthy and just tax base is to use site-value taxation methods. Henry George, a nineteenth-century political economist, promoted a tax system that assessed the relative location of a property as the primary criterion in assessing taxes, versus the conventional method of assessing mainly the value of the building. William Doebele (1997) has argued that Henry George's ideas of appropriate land taxation are essential elements in creating prosperity. However, such land taxation has not been widely implemented in developing nations. "To the

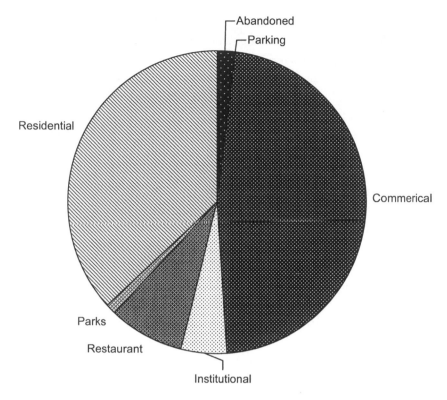

Figure 5.8 Historic Cartagena, land uses, 1992. Percentage breakdown: residential 37.02%, parks 0.70%, restaurant 8.03%, institutional 5.00%, commercial 47.01%, parking 0.23%, and abandoned 2.01%.

contrary, the active manipulation of land markets by both private and public interests — especially in urban areas — has been tolerated or even encouraged in many nations" (Doebele 1997, 57). Cartagena fits this characterization well.

The city's richest assets are its monuments and architectural treasures, but no public agency maintains the walls surrounding nearly 70 percent of the UNESCO site. During the twentieth century, several proposals even contemplated destroying parts of the walls and the fortress, Castillo San Felipe de Barajas (the largest Spanish colonial fortress in the Western Hemisphere). In the late nineteenth century, one politician wanted to dismantle San Felipe and use the rubble as landfill so the city could expand into the adjacent lagoons. In the 1930s, one mayor, allegedly with a drinking problem that impeded his judgment, opened an entrance to the city by tearing down 30 percent of the walls to make way for four lanes of traffic and a new bridge. One casualty was the large expanse of wall torn down between the San Pedro the Martyr and San Miguel Bastions (figure 5.5, numbers 19 and 20).

In 1924, a group of local elites organized to form the Society for Public Improvements of Cartagena (Sociedad de Mejoras Públicas de Cartagena). This private organization functions as a nonprofit entity that preserves and maintains parts of the city's historic sites and monuments. Until the 1970s, their meetings were infrequent and their projects site-specific: repair a bulwark here; excavate an underground passageway there. No comprehensive plan for restoration or preservation existed because there was no line-item budget from city hall. In the 1970s, the society began operating full time. Although national and international tourists come to Cartagena precisely because of its fortifications and colonial architecture, the city does not earmark funds for historic monuments and districts, although since 1988 a professionally trained anthropologist has directed the society. The only source of revenue for the maintenance of the fortress and the ramparts is the entrance fee of six thousand Colombian pesos (about US$3).

Just over half a million tourists visited Cartagena in 1998, one in five of them foreigners. That same year, 136 cruise ships called on the Port of Cartagena, carrying 123,000 passengers. Survey data show that fewer than 2 percent of all visitors to Cartagena visit the San Felipe fortress. The society contends that to enter the grounds, tourists should pay the entrance fee. However, one can easily stroll through the lower half of the complex before reaching a gate where a clerk requests a ticket. From there, visitors can walk up to higher levels and explore the inside of the fortress. Most tour buses coming from cruises stop at the bottom of the fortress, where the tour guide explains the history of the monument. Hardly any of the cruise ship passengers — almost all of them foreigners — pay the entrance fee. Colombian tour operators refuse to press the matter or include an admission fee in their land excursion fares. Most Colombian tourists, on the other hand, pay the equivalent of the US$3 entrance fee.

Hotels charge guests an additional US$1.25 daily to their tab when they stay in the old city or in the modern Boca Grande District. This small tax appears as a "Convention Center Fee" on their hotel bill. Although there is a Convention Center in the Getsemaní neighborhood of Cartagena, the fee goes to the Ministry of the Treasury in Bogotá, the nation's capital. Even the nearby Rosario Island National Park charges a US$1.50 park entrance fee for protecting the coral reefs of the park system. For Cartagena's bulwarks, ramparts, and castles, restoration funds must be approved by both chambers of the national Congress. With Colombia deeply entangled in a civil war with the FARC and several other guerrilla and paramilitary groups, as much as 30 percent of the national budget goes to the armed struggle. Moreover, tens of thousands of Colombians have been displaced from large expanses of the nation — perhaps half of the total territory — and many have resettled elsewhere (Weymouth 2000). For instance, one squatter settlement in Cartagena, Nelson Mandela, located in the mud lands and swamps of the city's back bay, has perhaps fifty thousand illegal residents, and this community of refugees is only five years old. Fiscal pressures to provide social services for groups such as these militate against preservationists' efforts to secure funds for Cartagena's cultural patrimony. In brief, no one who walks along the walls of the walled city pays for it directly, and the status of preservation funding remains tenuous. Historic preservation does not come cheaply. In 2000, the society was spending US$30,000 monthly for salaries, materials, utilities, and maintaining the fortress and ramparts (personal communications, María Pía Mogollón, director, and Franklin Howard, assistant director, Sociedad de Mejoras Públicas de Cartagena, June 24, 2000, Cartagena).

When new funding opportunities arise for improving self-financing, local and national authorities are slow to respond. For example, in 1995 excavations began in two large cisterns under the Santa Catarina Bastion (figure 5.5, number 18). These cisterns (*aljibes*) each occupy an area of approximately fifty thousand square feet within the walls (figure 5.5, number 18). During colonial times, Spanish soldiers stored vast amounts of rainwater in these chambers. With the advent of the Republican era (1830 onward), the cisterns were abandoned and used as garbage dumps. When the society decided to excavate the cisterns to determine how vast an area these historic vaulted rooms encompassed, little did they expect to find that 90 percent of the area within the Santa Catalina Bastion had been filled with waste and silt. No city, state, or national funding reached the excavation and restoration project. Consequently, the work was slow and financed solely by the entrance fees to the fortress.

In July 2000, the society formally dedicated and reopened the cisterns. The society is considering several revenue-generating uses of the reno-vated cisterns in order to broaden its financial base. These proposals in-clude renting them out for weddings, young girls' fifteenth birthday cele-brations (*quinceañeras*), poetry readings, musical recitals, an art gallery, a restaurant, or a museum. Again, the society must defer to the national Congress for final authorization over the use of the cisterns because the Santa Clara Bastion is a historic landmark. Naturally, the society admin-istration considers congressional oversight unjust and overly centralized. This decision making is also undemocratic because politicians who live hundreds of kilometers from Cartagena determine appropriations for Cartagena's UNESCO site, while local citizens and politicians have little say in the matter. Clearly, the society merits decentralized funding and decision-making ability because Colombia's 1991 Constitution strongly embraces the concept.[2] This funding and administrative dilemma is a microcosm of broader problems plaguing intergovernmental relations among local, regional, and national levels.

Tax Policies and Revenues

The Colombian government uses a series of "strata" to determine the level of property taxes. This variable is established for each lot in Cartagena and all cities throughout Colombia. The scale ranges from one, the least formidable quality and style of housing stock, to six, the most elaborate and priciest property. Appraisers determine these strata based only on a curbside assessment of facade quality and a rough estimation of the area of the structure on the lot. It is a controversial methodology because it does not consider precise measurements, number of residents, quality or type of infrastructure (plumbing, flushed commodes), or the Henry George notion that the relative location to commercial subcenters should determine property taxes (Brown 1997). Based on these strata, then, Cen-tro encompasses largely stratum five, San Diego three and four, and Get-

Table 5.1   Tax rates for urban properties according to residential strata and land use, 2002

Land Use	Rate (per million)
A. Housing	
Residential strata	
1 and 2	2.0
5	4.5
5	6.0
5	6.5
6	6.5
B. Commercial	9.5
C. Industrial	10.5
D. Hotel	5.5
E. Educational entities	7.5
F. Nonprofit organizations	7.5
G. Mixed commercial and residential	
Residential strata	
1 and 2	3.0
6	6.5
4, 5, and 6	8.0

Source: Alcaldía Mayor de Cartagena de Indias D.T. y C. Secretaría de Hacienda Distrital (2000), Article 74, pp. 26–27.

semaní three. Rent-generating land uses such as hotels and mixed (residential strata three and commercial) actually pay a lower tax than some private residential properties (table 5.1).

Tax incentives for restoring historic properties are tepid. Article 73 of Accord 44 passed in December 1999 provides a five-year 50 percent tax reduction as an incentive to restore historic properties. Article 71 declared that the planning inspection office (Control Urbano) would determine whether a property complies with historic preservation guidelines. In Cartagena, the "peak" years for renovation appear to have been when the national economy was awash in capital, before the 1994 construction boom.

The levels of property tax payments are also uneven (table 5.2). None of

Table 5.2 Property values and tax payments, Cartagena's historic neighborhoods, 1999

Neighborhood	Number of properties	Percentage of properties in historic district
Getsemaní	1,256	31%
San Diego	962	24%
El Centro	1,872	45%
Total	4,090	100%

Neighborhood	Property taxes filed	Value declared (pesos)	Average declaration	Average in U.S. dollars
Getsemaní	893	959,114,612.00	1,074,036.52	$537
San Diego	855	1,049,396,829.00	1,227,364.71	$614
El Centro	1,560	3,833,531,140.00	2,457,391.76	$1,229

Neighborhood	Actual properties paid	Total payments	Average payment	Average payment in U.S. dollars
Getsemaní	605	438,705,487.60	725,133.04	$363
San Diego	682	551,023,782.06	807,952.76	$404
El Centro	1,243	1,432,423,376.00	1,152,392.10	$576

Source: Unpublished data, Departamento de Hacienda, Impuesto Predial, June 2000.
Notes: Conversion rate at 2,000 Colombian pesos per dollar.
Rojas (1999, 47) states that there are 1,457 lots in the historic districts of Getsemaní, Centro, and San Diego. His data are taken from the planning office. However, the property tax office in the City Treasury Department shows 4,090. My own survey revealed 2,142 doorways leading to different or mixed land uses. These discrepancies point out the gap between coordinating property tax assessment and collection by the planning and the tax offices, as well as different methodologies. They also point out the dilemma facing researchers of land valuation, as noted by Jones and Ward (1994), that was discussed earlier.

the three principal neighborhoods in the historic district has paid more than half of their property taxes: Centro leads with about half of their property taxes paid, followed by Getsemaní at about one-third, and San Diego at a quarter. The payment pattern departs from a positive correlation with neighborhood income: Getsemaní is the poorest neighborhood yet it complied more than San Diego. Centro's average property value (US$1,229) is about 2.25 times that of Getsemaní ($537). Regardless of the uneven valuation and capturing mechanisms, the municipality of Cartagena does not fully benefit from the historic district's potential tax base. When I inquired at the municipal property tax office as to why so many properties were in arrears, all of the employees claimed that most cartageneros were awaiting some sort of "amnesty" to be given by the mayor or the municipal government. Alas, the welfare state powers of the executive branch serve as a tool for political favors.

Old Cartagena is not a ghost town; it has a desirable balance of commercial and residential land uses. As mentioned earlier, a good number of cartageneros work and live in the old quarters, and they give the district a local vibrancy. An updated survey would likely reveal a rise in commercial land uses and a concomitant drop in residential uses.

Design Issues

Paired Images of the Past

The passing of time is unkind to historic districts. Besides matters of urban heritage preservation, other cultural and socioeconomic factors are at play. Structures are reconverted from residential to commercial uses, and owners do not always inform planning authorities of conversions or remodeling in progress. Many property owners lack the funds to undertake quality restorations. Therefore, facades and interiors change subtly and without any consistent attention to architectural authenticity, which is an elusive goal in any preservation project. Inner-city tenements in Cartagena take root without any noticeable changes to the exterior of a home. By the time housing authorities realize that multiple tenants occupy a former single-family residence, the original design may have been transformed to accommodate the overcrowding.

Figure 5.9a   Calle de la Iglesia, Cartagena, 1900.

Yet, many streetscapes superficially, at least, suggest the charms of the past and a blend of colonial and Republican designs. Cartagena mines these images and promotes them in tourist literature. Strategically, the city is careful to project itself as part of the war-free sun-and-surf zone of the "Caribbean," as opposed to the war-ridden highlands. One can travel to many points in the old city and appreciate streetscapes that have changed little in the past century or so (figures 5.9a–5.9b, 5.10a–5.10b, and 5.11a–5.11d). These images of the past have powerful allure in promoting the historic images of Cartagena in the tourism industry.

Panzas (Bay Windows)

The habitat of a city reflects the richness of a place, not just some public spaces or ceremonial government and religious buildings. Everyday resi-

Figure 5.9b   Calle de la Iglesia, Cartagena, 2000.

dences leave a defining mark on historic districts. One vernacular design element that distinguishes Cartagena from other historic districts is a special bay window. Called *ventanas de panza* (literally "belly windows"), these extended "interior" spaces protrude slightly into the sidewalk and function as a place for socializing and "people watching." Increasingly, they also allow neighbors to keep an "eye" on the streets for crime watch purposes.

Cartagena's bay windows adorn the city at the street level, and they mark a transition between the public street and the private living room (figure 5.12). Found gently protruding into the sidewalks, they stem from design features found in Andalusia, Spain. Germán Téllez and Ernesto Moure (1982) trace these windows back to eighteenth-century Spain. Until recently, it was common for young women living in these homes to speak with male suitors through the panzas while remaining within earshot of family chaperones. Today, they serve mainly as resting places for sitting, reading, sewing, and chatting with neighbors, or as a decorative display of plants and vines that shade the interior of the home. Their rectilinear tops anchored by smooth plaster bottoms make them a local design feature in their own right (figure 5.13).

Figure 5.10a   Calle del Estero, Cartagena, photo circa 1900.

As the city's population grew and the crowding of sidewalks became a concern to many residents in the late nineteenth century, some of these decorative elements were removed. Vandals smashed some of the remaining ones in the twentieth century. These two events led to recessing the windows until they became flush with the facade of the house. By 1982, Téllez and Moure (1982) report, only thirty-two ventanas de panza remained in the city. In June 2000, I could find just two dozen of them.[3]

Some Residents Are More Equal than Others

One of the most notable changes in the gentrification of the walled city happened in the early 1970s, when well-known national figures started to

Figure 5.10b   Calle del Estero, Cartagena, photo 2000. The recent photo reveals height and balcony modifications, but the essence of the streetscape remains.

move into the district. Celebrities and political and artistic figures soon began acquiring second homes in Cartagena's historic quarters. By the 1980s, an international jet set had targeted Cartagena as a charming and safe second-home resort. Investors perceived the old city as a solid place to invest their money.

A celebrated house in the historic district is the residence of Nobel literature laureate Gabriel García Márquez. "Gabo" (as he is affectionately known to the locals) bought a property in San Diego, right next to a major bastion on the walls and across the street from the Santa Clara Convent (figure 5.5, numbers 13 and 14, respectively). Until 1993, the corner lot of his current residence was a warehouse. With the conversion of the convent into a hotel, the writer's architect argued that an extension to the height of the wall was needed to ensure privacy from the prying eyes

a

Figure 5.11a Figures 5.11a – 5.11d show Cartagena's Convento de Santa Clara, in 1900 (5.11a), 1992 (5.11b), 1997 (5.11c), and 2000 (5.11d). *The photograph from 1900 courtesy of the Fototeca de Cartagena; all others by the author.* 1900: The corner of what today are called Stuart and Calle del Torno Streets became in 1603 the home to the Clarisas Order of nuns, who were always cloistered and devoted to artisan endeavors. By 1650, the colonial core of the convent (shown in each of the time periods) had been built (Díaz and Paniagua 1994a). The elongated annex was appended in the nineteenth century and is the Republican wing of the convent. In 1900, the convent still functioned, though paved streets in the walled city did not arrive until the 1950s.

Figure 5.11b 1992: The convent is abandoned. After the nuns left the building in the early twentieth century, it functioned as a morgue, a medical school, and a hospital until the mid-1970s. A year after I took the picture, Sofitel started renovations on the five-star hotel.

Figure 5.11c 1997: Here the hotel comes into full operation. A fire escape has been added, and the hotel has directed and paid for the repaving and remodeling of the street and park (San Diego Park, to the left, not shown).

Figure 5.11d 2000: The fire escape has been removed, and the hotel has added two signs that denote reserved parking for taxis. Hotel administrators did not request a city permit (nor has one been granted) for the taxi stand, and the hotel's appropriation of these scarce parking spaces in San Diego is a point of contention with resident automobile owners who do not have courtyards

c

d

for parking their cars (see also the section "Land-Use Conflict in San Diego Park" in chapter 5). The corner building to the left of the hotel (with the two white balconies) houses a pizzeria on the ground floor. Twice, the owner was arrested for operating a second-floor brothel catering to foreign tourists.

of tourists (figures 5.14–5.14b, and 5.15a–5.15b). Although I found no record in the Permits Office that the city had granted permission, the wall is now one meter higher than surrounding walls. In addition, García Márquez's new home exceeds the two-story height of the original structure (even though keeping redeveloped properties in historic districts as close as possible to the original size, architectural design, and building materials are key precepts in historic rehabilitation) (figure 5.16). However, because García Márquez is a beloved figure who has set some of his novels and short stories in Cartagena, few would challenge these seemingly minor design violations. The design and planning exceptions such as these reinforce a Colombian value that those who have access to power are entitled to exercise it. As discussed below, that cultural value translates into withholding property tax payments as well.

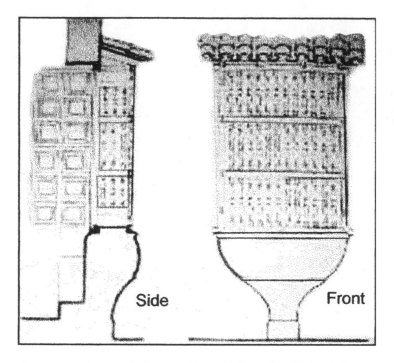

Figure 5.12 Panza design profile modified after Téllez, Moure, and Balen (1985, 94).

Implementation and Regulatory Challenges

Historic Cartagena has a sufficient number of property tax and planning laws on the books to support the role of a state government capable of nurturing urban heritage preservation. The proof reviewed here suggests that some structural conditions beyond the city's control will continue to impair efforts to enhance revitalization and to ensure community participation in resolving local conflicts.

In 2000, cities across Colombia began implementing new master plans as stipulated by the Constitution of 1991. These new master plans, in the singular, called POT (Plan de Ordenamiento Territorial), mandate community participation in framing local planning agendas. Many stakeholders with whom I spoke — planners, community leaders, local residents, and hotel operators — expressed cynicism about the future of the

Figure 5.13 Panza and street front, Cartagena, San Diego neighborhood, 1999.

POTs. On the one hand, local residents and even staff members of the City Planning Office conjecture that the elite and corporate interests will co-opt the planning process as they always have. On the other hand, public officials realize that the citizenry is skeptical of state-driven efforts in planning. Cynicism is rampant in Colombia, where for decades "might makes right" was evidenced by political violence and drug wars instigated by the Medellín and other drug cartels. In Cartagena, few citizens knew where and when meetings were being held by the planning office. Nevertheless, by October 31, 2000, Cartagena established a master plan that was, normatively at least, shaped by community input.

Efforts to promote the POTs cannot come too soon. Cartagena is not alone in this regard because the entire nation lags behind in the process. By June 2000, only 900 of 1,004 cities had completed their master plans. Therefore, an extension was granted until October 2000 (Miranda 2000). A recent Inter-American Development Bank study concluded that Cartagena would "benefit from a management plan for its historic city center to coordinate the activities of various levels of government, facilitate

Figure 5.14a García Márquez house, Calle del Curato, San Diego neighborhood, 1993.

Figure 5.14b García Márquez house, Calle del Curato, San Diego neighborhood, 2000.

private investment, and encourage diversification of services and real estate endeavors" (Rojas 1999, 29). The same report commented on the social effect of gentrification: "Because investments were not coordinated in Cartagena, the social impact issue was neither quantified nor addressed. Clearly, however, low-income households in what were decaying buildings were driven out by private investment in preservation and rehabilitation. The displaced families have joined others living in informal settlements in outlying areas of the city or moved to other slums in the city center" (39).

Figure 5.15a Former warehouse on the corner of the García Márquez lot, Calle del Curato Street, viewed from Santa Clara Convent, second floor, San Diego neighborhood, 1993.

Figure 5.15b Renovated warehouse structure as seen in 2000, complete with a pool, is now a home to Colombian author and Nobel laureate, Gabriel García Márquez. "Gabo," as he is known locally, visits his home a few times a year.

Figure 5.16 García Márquez house, Calle del Curato Street, viewed from the exterior walls of the old city, San Diego neighborhood.

A "culture of not paying" undermines the regulation and implementation of tax assessment and collection. Historic Cartagena is replete with buildings that may be functionally obsolete, but most are not physically obsolete. While financing is a challenge in all historic districts, Cartagena's good housing stock is markedly different from that of its Caribbean neighbor, Habana Vieja (see table 3.3). The condition of Cartagena's built environment bodes well for a reasonable-cost approach to rebuilding the old city, especially in the much-neglected Getsemaní neighborhood. Although there are reports of redlining (e.g., not lending money in certain neighborhoods whether applicants are creditworthy or not), that issue remains secondary given the nation's mired housing and mortgage markets. Once the housing market improves, the city's "urban curators" need to expedite the review process of building permits that has been criticized by builders and realtors for its lengthy delays.

What factors will shape the policy deliberations for perfecting or raising taxes to improve the historic district? Because of the economic downturn and complicated tax structure, it is unlikely that any reform in property taxation is imminent. For example, in a comprehensive study of tax policies in Colombia, the Cartagena Chamber of Commerce examined business taxes in Cartagena, Barranquilla (another port city), and Bogotá. The study identified sixteen different business taxes in Cartagena (excluding property taxes), whereas Bogotá and Barranquilla had only nine each. Cartagena also had the highest per capita property tax (us$18.62) compared to Barranquilla (us$8.54), Bucamaranga (us$4.97), and Manizales (us$15.02) (ccc 1999b). In short, no matter how flawed, unjust, and underreported Cartagena's property taxes may be, there is a perception that the city is already heavily taxed in absolute and relative terms. Because the previous mayor of Cartagena was arrested and imprisoned in 1999 for embezzlement, many property owners were hopeful that the president-appointed mayor would grant them a "property tax amnesty" in 2000 as a sign of political good-will. That amnesty was never awarded.

It is also important to recognize that Colombia faces external pressure to comply with International Monetary Fund mandates. Fulfilling these objectives will situate the nation more favorably with international lending and aid agencies. Such goals demand decreases in social spending and augmentation of reserves to bolster the national currency, balance of payments, and international reserves. For example, as of March 31, 2000, Colombia had surpassed its goal of safeguarding us$8.15 billion in net international reserves and fulfilled a reserve level of us$8.254 billion (Jaramillo 2000, 21). Austerity measures continue to call for more available capital such as that which an enhanced taxation program might supply. Thus, globalization and neoliberal reform unsettle Cartagena in various ways.

Conclusions: On Accommodating Multiple Investors and Users

Historic preservation and defining heritage in Cartagena are largely beyond the control of a beleaguered national government embroiled in civil war. A weakened state and regional government can, in the dire prognosis of Guenther Roth (1968) and Robin Theobold (1990), lead to a "re-privatization" of the state. In other words, "in an overall context of economic scarcity and political instability a growing proportion of people withdraw or are forced to withdraw into black marketeering, smuggling, drug-dealing, banditry and the economy of violence which such conditions tend to nurture" (Theobold 1990, 167). While Colombia creeps toward that sinister fate, such a scenario is not yet absolute.

Cartagena is unique in Latin America because of the powerful role of its private sector, and the limited role of public subsidy and policy in shaping its heritage preservation. This UNESCO site remains vital because the commercial core of the city still functions in the Centro neighborhood. Geography has graced urban historic preservation by allowing Laguito and Bocagrande to siphon off the Miami Beach–like and Cancún-like modern tourist complexes found elsewhere in the Caribbean basin—supporting Carrión's (1992) contention that the Latin American CBD and centro histórico are discrete places with unique features. Tourism contributes 5 percent of the total value generated by Cartagena's one hundred largest firms (CCC 1999a, 7).

Heritage tourism in Cartagena is off to a difficult start in the new millennium. Public services funded by property taxes will be enhanced greatly if both the method of land valuation and the tax payment system are modernized. The current convoluted formula for assessing land valuation is rife with methodological and operational problems. However, this does not suggest that a NUMP is appropriate.

This chapter has shown that urban revitalization in Cartagena's Ciudad Amurallada is ridden with conflict, and the San Diego neighborhood conflict highlights those grassroots issues. The debate surrounding the use of public spaces in San Diego Park reflects a city government timid about enforcing the law. Beyond these local conflicts is a broader ethos in Colombia of not paying taxes. This social value depletes the quality of public services and defers to powerful actors in the real-estate market. Clearly, it is unrealistic to divorce Cartagena's urban heritage preservation efforts from structural problems at the national and global levels (Díaz and Paniagua 1994b). In that spirit, it seems that major reforms of the national army, judicial system, police, and banking need to continue if heritage tourism and historic preservation are to be firmly restored. Pasuk Phongpaichit, Sungsidh Piriyarangsan, and Nualnoi Treerat's (1998, 264–65) harrowing study, *Guns, Girls, Gambling, Ganja*, about Thailand's illegal economy offers useful lessons for Colombia's path to reform: "There are no easy answers, no quick solutions. Thailand's illegal economy is firmly established. It is also well integrated with the power structure of police, politicians, and local influential people. Any attempts to control or limit the illegal economy must begin from popular pressure."

In Gabriel García Márquez's classical account of the mystical city of Macondo, he describes a village of twenty houses made of clay and wattle along the banks of a crystal-clear river. The river stones shine like enormous prehistoric dinosaur eggs, though the world seems fresh and new. Some Colombians might fantasize about a coastal Caribbean town much like Cartagena, but that was centuries ago. Today, Cartagena lacks even a primary water-treatment system, as evidenced by the poor-quality water in Animas Bay, the Caribbean Sea, and San Lázaro Lagoon. Still, the walled city holds a special allure. One can walk through its streets and go back in time without using a futuristic machine and appreciate that this built heritage is close to authentic, and not yet "Disneyfied." Cartagena de Indias allows visitors to see history with their own eyes. Its future will depend on the city's fiscal abilities and the extent to which it incorporates citizens and businesses into the land valuation and planning processes.

6 Heritage Tourism in Habana Vieja: Restructuring in a Post-Soviet Age

Reassessing "lo urbano"

Cuba's antiurbanism policies served the Revolutionary leadership well for the first three decades of its tenure. A "minimum of urbanism and a maximum of ruralism" helped to forge a socialist program that benefited communities outside Havana, a capital city of one million residents at the time of the Revolution. For example, in 1959, the government classified only 12 percent of rural housing in "good condition," a figure that had risen to 49 percent by 1999 (IPS 1999). Urban and regional planning also entailed the *debourgeoisement* of Cuban cities, which meant expanding health services and schooling (Eckstein 1977; Segre and Baroni 1998). Although the state did not entirely ignore the capital city, literacy, education, health care, and military preparedness consumed large portions of the national budget.

If the socialist leadership perceived Havana as a parasite leeching resources from the national body for centuries, then state resources would supplement economic development in small towns and provincial capitals. Havana embodied the worst of capitalist development: corruption, avarice, vice, prostitution, and a glaring disparity between social classes. To be sure, not all residents (*habaneros*) had prospered during the Republican era (1898–1958). Recall from the historical overview in chapter 2 that nearly one in twenty habaneros lived in shantytowns or tenement houses at the time of the Triumph of the Revolution, January 1, 1959. Under the aegis of the INAV (National Housing Institute), the state built one hundred thousand units between 1959 and 1961, six thousand of them in Havana. If city living conditions were dire, they paled compared to life in the countryside.

After the first few months of the Revolutionary victory, the state ended evictions and decreased rents by 30 – 50 percent. The Vacant Lot Law helped potential homeowners build and also helped end land speculation (Hamberg 1998, 3). Within the first two years of the Triumph of the Revolution, the government passed Laws 26, 135, 691, and 892 (among others), broadening the government's social justice program. In the housing sector, prefabricated units modeled after Soviet and European designs became a high priority. Socialist modernization efforts drew heavily on concrete because of its flexibility, endurance, and low cost (Violetta and Scarpaci 1999). Other building construction projects included technical schools, workers' centers, student dormitories, and research centers. New residential areas of Havana opened when northbound emigrants vacated houses and businesses. The state awarded houses to government officials, while many former servants (called *tías*) often remained in the houses of their former employers, only to bring their extended families from the impoverished countryside (Scarpaci, Segre, and Coyula 2002, chap. 3). Although these interventions were significant, little attention was paid to maintaining Havana's extant housing stock. Instead, housing resources addressed the needs of neglected and destitute areas of the countryside and provincial towns. Not surprisingly, safeguarding Havana's historic treasures was not a priority: that built environment symbolized a bourgeois and exploitative past.

At the start of the new millennium, Habana Vieja especially reflects this neglect. Decades of abandonment, a lack of basic building maintenance, the scars of overcrowding and amateur reconversion are visible at every corner. When UNESCO declared the 128-hectare expanse of Habana Vieja a World Heritage Site in 1982, few could fully appreciate its implications for international tourism. After all, designs and plans of the colonial (1519–1898 under Spanish directive) and Republican (1899–1958, under direct or indirect U.S. influence) eras symbolize the very intervention and hegemony that the Revolution sought to redress (Scarpaci 2001).

The present-day socialist leadership seeks to remedy the tattered fabric of Havana's built environment by drawing on a comparative advantage: tourism. Since 1959, tourism had not been a leading economic factor. Fidel Castro often vowed that Cuba would not become an island of bartenders and chambermaids as had other Caribbean nations. Accordingly, in 1975, just twenty-five thousand nonmilitary foreigners visited Cuba. Following the UNESCO recognition, few planners, architects, and politicians imagined that in just six years, the USSR would collapse, and Cuba's economy would enter a tailspin. The Revolutionary leadership, in typically uncanny fashion, saw opportunity in a time of crisis (Codrescu 1999), and it began to pin its hopes on economic development in Habana Vieja, the city's original gateway to the world. By 2002, the tourism figure had risen to just under two million.

This chapter examines three defining features of heritage tourism in Habana Vieja: historic preservation, revitalization, and restructuring. A state company headed by the city historian, Habaguanex has overseen all aspects of public works, historic preservation, and refurbishing of older buildings since the early 1990s. Its budget comes from hard-currency operations in tourism. Indirectly, historic preservation unleashed gentrification in Habana Vieja. In U.S., Canadian, and Western European cities, the "gentry class" tends to be better educated and more affluent than local residents but are usually of the same nationality. Gentrifiers in Cuba are a transient group made up of foreign tourists or businesspeople from Canada, Spain, Italy, other Western European nations, and Latin America.[1] *Revitalization* refers to the general physical and socioeconomic enhancement of a designated built environment. In the United States and Canada, it often entails public-private partnerships. In Habana Vieja, the process depends mainly on joint-venture deals or direct intervention by Habaguanex, S.A. (S.A. stands for Sociedad Anónima or "incorporated"). I use the term *restructuring* to identify how global capital transforms nations and cities. This chapter ends with five examples of how restructuring, an outgrowth of the internationalization of capital, is reshaping Habana Vieja.

We begin with a brief discussion of the global political economy that made the socialist leadership rethink the centro histórico.

The Special Period and the Rise of Opportunity

The Habana Vieja municipality was immune from the scheduled and unscheduled blackouts that afflicted Cuba in the first half of the 1990s. Such was not the case in adjacent municipalities, such as Centro Habana, Marianao, Miramar, Víbora, and other suburban municipalities in Havana City Province (figure 6.1).[2] The real virtue of Habana Vieja, though, was

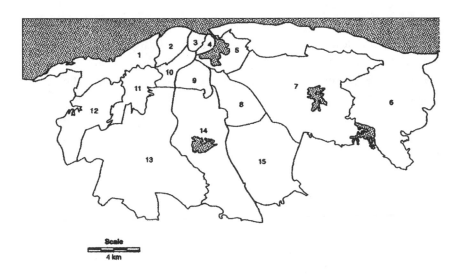

1. Playa
2. Plaza de la Revolución
3. Centro Habana
4. Habana Vieja
5. Regla

6. Habana del Este
7. Guanabacoa
8. San Miguel
9. Diez de Octubre
10. Cerro

11. Marianao
12. La Lisa
13. Boyeros
14. Arroyo Naranjo
15. Cotorro

Figure 6.1   Havana City municipalities.

not its privileged public lighting status but its architectural heritage and tourism potential. Opportunity came knocking unexpectedly, but none too soon.

Calamity created Habaguanex. In June 1993, an architect from the National Center for Conservation, Restoration, and Museum Science (CENCRM) was escorting a journalist from the British newspaper the *Independent*, through Habana Vieja. At one stop along the walking tour, the Cuban architect pointed out buildings around Old Square (Plaza Vieja), a district full of grand old *casas-almacenes* that served as nineteenth-century houses and warehouses (Segre 1995). As the journalist paused to photograph a turn-of-the-century structure that was undergoing renovation, the building fell down. Recent rains had saturated the crushed-rock materials (mampostería). Apparently, a load-bearing column had collapsed.

After the collapse, the British media reveled in the striking photographs and in the physical decay of Habana Vieja. Syndication and wire reports spread the story. "No one died in the collapse of Plaza Vieja. . . . Neither, remarkably, was anyone killed later that evening when a second building imploded on the Malecón [the seaside promenade]." One Cuban architect aptly described the relationship between environment and colonial architecture: "In this weather (86 degrees, 100 percent humidity and frequent storms) . . . we can expect there to be several more collapses" (Glancey 1993).

Coincidentally, perhaps, the Council of State approved Law Decree 143-93 shortly thereafter, creating Habaguanex. The company is part of the Office of the City Historian, headed by the historian Eusebio Leal Spengler. Habaguanex assumed the legal right to operate restaurants, museums, gift shops, and hotels that other state agencies (CIMEX, Gran Caribe, Horizontes, Havanatur, and Rumbos) had managed previously. As part builder-developer and part tourism promoter, Habaguanex claims (in English) on its Web site that there is an "intense and happy nightlife [in Habana Vieja] that creates in cafeterias and restaurants, open 24 hours, a festive and bohemian ambience of quality and pleasure" (Habaguanex, S.A., 2000.[3]

The Office of the City Historian designs and implements the Master Plan for Old Havana's revitalization. It also manages land-use and investment priorities for the 214-hectare and 242 blocks of the Habana Vieja municipality. The area includes some four thousand buildings, of which just under a quarter (nine hundred) have heritage value (figure 6.2). Development projects concentrate heavily in the northeast corner of Habana Vieja, around the Plaza de Armas, Plaza de San Francisco, the cruise ship terminal, and Plaza Vieja. If *sustainability* is a term debated widely around the world (Dyck 1998), in Habana Vieja it has surely come to mean self-financing (Grogg 1999; Scarpaci, Segre, and Coyula 2002).

Habaguanex is a unique public entity. It is one of the few Cuban companies in post-1959 Cuba to manage dollar-operated facilities without having to remit profits to the main legislative body, the National Assem-

Figure 6.2 Master Plan for Old Havana's revitalization. Modified slightly by the author. Data source: Habaguanex (2000).

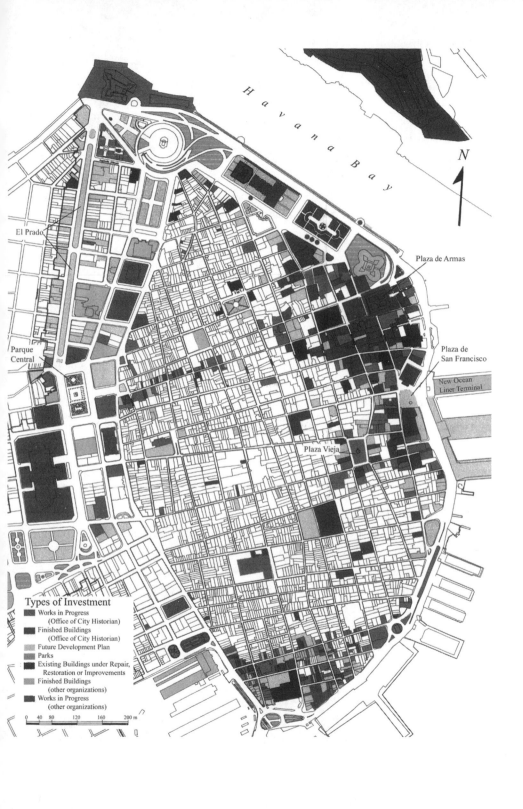

H a v a n a   B a y

N

El Prado

Plaza de Armas

Parque
Central

Plaza de
San Francisco

New Ocean
Liner Terminal

Plaza Vieja

Types of Investment

- ■ Works in Progress
  (Office of City Historian)
- ■ Finished Buildings
  (Office of City Historian)
- Future Development Plan
- Parks
- Existing Buildings under Repair,
  Restoration or Improvements
- Finished Buildings
  (other organizations)
- Works in Progress
  (other organizations)

0   40   80   120   160   200 m

bly. Nor must it arrange joint venture deals for historic preservation through the Ministry of Foreign Investments (MINVEC) as do all other public entities. Instead, it negotiates historic preservation and new construction projects directly with foreign capitalists. Its fiscal autonomy and decentralized decision-making ability are unique in socialist Cuba. From a design and planning perspective, its principal duties allow the firm to use profits to refurbish the UNESCO district. Elsewhere in Cuba, the general tenets of the Foreign Investment Act of 1995 stipulate the conditions under which joint ventures must operate.[4] Habaguanex, though, has considerable autonomy.

This legal framework spells good news for historic preservationists and more than a few European and Canadian tourists. However, much discussion about historic preservation and restoration tends to overlook the residents of Habana Vieja. Throughout this book, I have argued that authenticity in historic preservation projects is an elusive goal because social classes have different allegiances to the built environment. The tensions between architectural authenticity and social actors — politicians, tourists, investors, and local residents — fashion the collective memory of places. Habana Vieja, like other historic centers, begs the question: Whose history and collective memory will be forged under Habaguanex's charge?

Habaguanex's main responsibility is to generate dollars. In 1995, it generated US$5 million in gross revenues. Its 1997 figures were estimated to be greater than $10 million. According to journalist Chandler Burr, in early 1999, the figure stood close to $40 million and by the year 2002, Habaguanex was expected to reach $200 million (Burr 1999, 73). Unfortunately, no public documents such as balance sheets or income statements are printed and distributed. Habaguanex CEO Eusebio Leal stated in 1999 that investment in Habana Vieja exceeded the previous four years combined (Leal 1999). Although it hires three thousand construction workers — many of whom reside in Habana Vieja — the economic multiplier effect for local residents is limited. The construction workers end up with pesos, which have restricted spending potential and are not spendable in dollar stores. Dollars are obtained through tips, black marketeering, or remittances. Because it is a commercial enterprise,[5] it has a different legal relationship with the residents of Habana Vieja than, say, the Ministry of Housing does; the latter cannot generate its own revenue

Figure 6.3   Sierra Maestra cruise ship terminal, Habana Vieja.

through retailing, and its focus is on a national scale and not a single barrio. Through its Cuban building partner, Fénix (Phoenix), and its real-estate agency, Aurea, the company engages in the most ambitious construction projects in the old city since American businesses set up banks and corporations there between 1902 (the formal end of U.S. military occupation) and 1920 (the year of the "dance of the millions," an eminently successful sugar-harvest year when sugar reached thirteen cents a pound, and then plummeted to three) (Weiss 1950; Llanes 1993).

Several Habaguanex interventions are noteworthy. These include the restoration of buildings on the Plaza de Armas, Plaza de la Catedral, and Ambos Mundos Hotel (where Ernest Hemingway resided). Another major project is the renovation of Havana's former stock market (Lonja de Comercio) on San Francisco Square, facing the new Italian-financed renovation of the ocean terminal at Sierra Maestra docks (figure 6.3). The Lonja de Comercio project relied on Spanish investment capital of about US$12 million. Intervention in the building's interior entailed moving the front stairway to the back of the building, installing two pairs of elevators,

Figure 6.4a   Benetton boutique, Habana Vieja.
Figure 6.4b   Plaza de San Francisco, Habana Vieja.

updating office space for new technology (FAX and Ethernet connections), building a café and post office on the ground floor, and constructing a dark-glass encased floor on the roof.[6] Adjacent buildings surrounding San Francisco Square (figure 6.4b) include another post office, a money exchange house, an upscale teashop and restaurant, and the Italian clothing chain Benetton (figure 6.4a). To many local residents it is a great irony that an $85 pair of jeans, equivalent to a half year's earnings for an average Cuban worker, is sold in a socialist city where many basic needs are unsatisfied.

The Habaguanex strategy is not unlike the planning and design strategies of the Republican era that aimed to forge a good impression on visitors who gazed out from the rails of steamers coming into Havana Harbor (Schwartz 1997). Officials want to make sure that San Francisco Square "impresses" cruise ship passengers as they spill into streets of Habana Vieja. What waterfront visitors do not count on, however, is the foul stench of Havana Bay. It is one of the most heavily contaminated bodies of water in the Caribbean, receiving several tons of organic material and oil products daily (Díaz-Briquets and Pérez-López 2000, 245–47).

Historic preservation in the old city also creates tension between foreign joint-venture investors (who tend to favor turnkey hotel and construction operations and architects from their countries) and Cuban professionals. One case in point is the Dutch-operated (Tulip) Parque Central located on the park of that same name. Cuban architects submitted many designs for Parque Central Hotel at the west-central edge of Habana Vieja (figure 6.2). In the end, a feasibility and design project submitted by a Spanish outfit, allegedly for tens of thousands of dollars, won the design competition. One Cuban architect remarked, "With that type of money, dozens of local architects could have received a stipend for two months of work while they were completing their Parque Central submissions. It would have given them money to buy drafting materials too. And I bet we could have come up with a project just as good as the Spanish one, if not better" (personal communication, E. Cárdenas [professor of Architecture, Instituto Superior Politécnica José Antonio Echeverría], Hotel Parque Central, Havana, October 15, 1999). Such foreign investment control over the use of design professionals smacks of an earlier, pre-Revolutionary era when local talent and projects were crowded out by foreign influences (Rigau 1994).

Urban Revitalization and Globalization

The previous discussion of heritage tourism and restructuring in Habana Vieja resembles transformations common in the market economies of Vancouver and Toronto (Ley 1996), New York (Holcomb and Beauregard 1982; N. Smith 1979, 1987), Paris (Noin and White 1997), Montevideo (Benton 1985), Quito (Jones and Varley 1994, 1999a), and Worcester, England (Vilagrasa and Larkham 1995). One notable distinction is that preserving Cuban architecture of the colonial (pre-1898) or the Republican eras (1899–1958) shows the relationship between capital and colonialism, and therefore serves as a political message about the globalization of socialist culture and capitalist exploitation (King 1990). There are also no "young urban professionals" residing in Habana Vieja.[7] This feature attests to the Revolutionary view of the socialist city as defined by an absence of "young Cuban Americans."[8] Most residents of Habana Vieja who are displaced by historic preservation move to Habana del Este, across the bay on the eastern side of the city. This is the site of some of the first public housing projects in the 1960s. Many habaneros consider it unattractive because of its poor sites and services, public transportation problems, and badly maintained grounds (Hamberg 1994). Although no official figures have been released, I estimate that at least two hundred residents were displaced between 1998 and 2000.

How can the government justify the displacement of local residents in socialist Cuba? At a presentation before the World Economic Forum in Davos, Switzerland, on January 27, 1995, Carlos Lage Dávila, then secretary of the Cuban Council of Ministers, described the seeming contradiction of foreign investment juxtaposed against austere conditions among Cubans this way:

> The disappearance of the socialist bloc and the USSR, along with the strengthening of the U.S. economic blockade . . . abruptly threw Cuba into the most complex moment in its [socialist] history. . . . The steps that we have been taking for the sake of the country's economic recovery are part of an integral concept and not the result of isolated measures. . . . We're not trying to fool anyone. We are not offering our foreign partners a transition to capitalism. Cuba is and will continue to be a socialist country. (Conas 1995, 7–9)

Like many political assessments of a nation's current situation, Lage's theorization of Cuba can only be assessed within the logic of his arguments. Few Cubans, or foreigners for that matter, doubt the Cuban leadership's resolve to ride out the Special Period.[9] Yet Habaguanex is a reflection of how the state views its new role in the global economy; a shift to the market will inevitably create uneven development.

Meanwhile, common citizens wait for improvements in their residences as this uneven development manifests itself at different geographic scales of analysis. Nationwide, the government has downsized nearly half a million workers from state jobs since 1990. Those who have not retired seek employment among the new self-employed, *cuentapropistas*, who amount to about 150,000 workers in a nation of eleven million. On average, they earn as much as 3.5 times more than state workers. Many self-employed work in the old quarters of Havana (Peters and Scarpaci 1998). Since 1993, the decriminalization of the dollar has created a dual economy, one of pesos and the other of hard currency. More than a few residents of Habana hold animosity toward hustlers (jineteros) who work in the black market or with tourists (see Elinson 1999). Havana now rivals Bangkok as a primary destination for sexual tourism. Full accounts on how to "negotiate" the Cuban commercial sex industry are readily available on the World Wide Web. Cuba is closer geographically and culturally to Western Europe, and Spanish and Italian men find it easier to speak Spanish in Cuba than to cope with Thai or broken English in Bangkok. Much of this commercial sexual trade takes place in Habana Vieja, where couples can disappear easily into the most densely settled neighborhood on the island (Cornebise 2003).

To crystallize this discussion about how political economy influences daily life, I briefly review how residents perceive historic preservation in Habana Vieja.

The View on the Streets

UNESCO's World Heritage Site label afforded the old quarters an international badge of distinction. However, few UNESCO funds have come from the Geneva headquarters to renovate Habana Vieja. Instead, refurbishing the old city depends on for-profit European joint ventures (usually Italian or Spanish), as well as nonprofit organizations such as professional architectural organizations from Andalusia or Catalunya (Catalonia) in Spain. Habaguanex works jointly with both types of financiers. Because of the large stock of colonial buildings, restoration efforts have largely tackled those Spanish-colonial style structures that create tourist-friendly spaces. In the process, however, the issue arises about the extent to which residential housing needs are met. It is noteworthy that nearly 54 percent of Habana Vieja's housing stock dates from before 1920, leaving a balance of twentieth-century structures (Nickel 1990, 79).

Planners insist that only half of the roughly eighty-five thousand residents occupying Habana Vieja should reside there. Crowding exacerbates inner-city slums and tenements: cuarterías, *solares*, and *accesorias*. In addition, poor structural conditions have worsened because of humidity in walls, leaks in roofs, low levels of ventilation and lighting, and waste removal problems. Of the 60 percent of the nation's poor or very poor housing stock found in Havana, Habana Vieja contains a disproportionate percentage of that amount. Although revitalization efforts have long-term goals about generating hard currency, short-term outcomes are just as germane to the quality of life.

Plaza Vieja

One restoration project that raised concern among local residents is the Plaza Vieja (Old Square) site. In the 1950s, the automobile defined both Havana and the nation itself. President Batista (1952–59) supported public works projects, especially highway construction. Abdicating public transportation to the automobile and bus lobby led to removing the electric streetcar system (figure 6.5) that radiated out of the old city's train stations and plazas to the outer suburbs (Schwartz 1997). Automobile dominance made Havana's urban design more of a North American city than a Latin American one, though its original design is European in conception. In Habana Vieja, not even the switch to one-way streets could resolve the dilemma of automobile traffic and pedestrian safety. For example, cars encroached on sidewalks for parking space, and parked cars often illegally blocked entrances to residential courtyards (patios).

One solution to the parking problem was the construction of an underground parking garage to hold the bulky American cars. Plaza Vieja's surface rose about one meter above the street to accommodate the roof for the subterranean parking. Forty years later, though, the design and function had become anachronistic. Gasoline prices are costly (about US$1.00 per liter) compared to U.S. prices. Both price and fuel rationing have greatly curtailed private automobile travel. Tourist rentals and state-owned cars dominate the roads. As a result, bicycle ownership has increased twelvefold in Havana from about seventy thousand in 1990 to over one million by the middle of the decade (Scarpaci and Hall 1995).

In 1996, demolition crews imploded the underground parking garage at Plaza Vieja (figures 6.6a–6.6b). The intervention provoked concern among local residents. Habaguanex, unlike the County Planning Department, was not required to comply with other state agency regulations. To the author's knowledge, no community meetings, public hearings, or town planning sessions were held. Habaguanex set out to renovate the third most important square in the old city (after Arms and Cathedral

Figure 6.5   A streetcar stop in Habana Vieja, at Plaza de Armas square, c. 1950, about two years before streetcar service was discontinued throughout the entire city. *Photographer unknown.*

Squares). Residents, though, expressed reservations. One resident of a cuartería near Plaza Vieja remarked in 1998: "The back half of the roof in my kitchen has been off since the last hurricane blew through here. I've brought this to the attention of the municipality, the local CDR [Revolution Defense Committee], and even the City Historian's Office. But nothing. And now they use dynamite and all that cement to blow up the parking garage and level it. It's great for the tourists, but what about me?"

Interviews with other area residents during five months of field research between 1995 and 2000 revealed similar concerns.[10]

In a recent study, Arnold August (1999) also notes the tensions surrounding Havana's revitalization and the response of local governance. One case study he reports happened in nearby Vedado, Plaza Municipality, in the city of Havana, and the influence of the city historian is evident. In the following passage, Arnold (1999, 401) relates the experiences of an elected official (delegate) who attempted to resolve a problem

Figure 6.6a Plaza Vieja under renovation after imploding the underground garage (1997).

Figure 6.6b View of Plaza Vieja from adjacent building. The fenced-off fountain made of Italian marble is at the right center of the image (1999).

for a group of constituents. The residents requested that a state construction company (Cubalse) that renovated a park and a theater clean up leftover building materials at the site.

> The delegate acted because of grievances by the citizens in the accountability meetings. He wrote letters to the Ciudad de La Habana historian [Eusebio Leal] which did not bring any results, seeing that the city historian understandably insisted that the construction company remove the construction material before anything could be done. [The delegate] then met with Carlos Lage, one of the National Assembly deputies for the constituency, to arrange a meeting with the representatives of the construction company doing the restoration of the theater. Since then, the construction material has been removed from the park and the park's restoration has been taking place.

Figure 6.7a   Building on northeast corner of Plaza Vieja, 1991. Occupied by local residents. Plaza in the foreground is the top of underground parking garage built in 1952.

Figure 6.7b   Plaza Vieja, renovated and nearly completed building to be occupied by foreign business community, 1999. The underground parking garage has been removed, and the plaza is recessed to street level.

The passage underscores the occasional need for national-level leaders to resolve problems that are decidedly local in scope and origin.

As stated earlier, the state built new housing in the early 1960s for those displaced from eradicated settlements because one in twenty Havana households lived in squatter settlements. Habana Vieja absorbed a sizable share of relocated squatters. One building specifically represents what has happened elsewhere in the old city (figure 6.7a). On the northeastern corner of the Old Square rests a stately apartment complex built in 1904. Much of the ornate plasterwork and some of the balconies had fallen off the six-story apartment building over the years. By the late 1960s, the former single-family apartments had become homes to several families each. Crowding compounded the deterioration. In 1996, an Italian-Cuban joint-venture project began renovating the structure into condominiums (figure 6.7b). Future occupants will be foreign businesspeople working in Cuba, not residents of Habana Vieja. Foreigners will rent the apartments from Habaguanex and will pay in dollars, not pesos. The adjacent Plaza Vieja has been restored with an ornate Italian-marble fountain in the center of the plaza, while metal spheres to prevent vehicular traffic frame the perimeter of the plaza.

Officials at Habaguanex justify such building renovation, civic beautification, and limited residential displacement.[11] In the end, the preservation of a collective, socialist order will be ensured, since social property remains the sine qua non of the Cuban Revolution. Habaguanex and the socialist leadership are, in the words of one company official, "in [the preservation business] for the long haul."[12] However, as table 6.1 shows, Habaguanex has financed some social works (*obras sociales*) in the old city.

Officials argue that local residents will eventually see tangible signs of how this guarded Habaguanex operation has benefited the quality of life as well as the built environment. However, the housing crisis in the old quarters remains severe. "Forty-three percent of the 22,516 housing units there have structural problems with their roofs. A quarter show signs of gradual sinking, while more than half suffer from water leaks in the roofs, and a third showing leaks in the walls" (Grogg 1999; Leal 1996).

Conclusions: Marketing Heritage in Socialist Cuba

In many parts of the world, revitalization, historic preservation, and restructuring are complex and tension-ridden phenomena. The contested spaces of Latin American historic districts that are undergoing restoration benefit some citizens more than others. Habana Vieja is not immune from these unevenly distributed geographic and social benefits, and historic preservation efforts are "walking along the thin line between paralysis and disaster" (Coyula 2002, 69).

Not since the U.S. investment of the early twentieth century has the pace of revitalization in Havana been so quick. Outcomes include some gentrification, residential displacement, and restructuring. In the short term, residents of the old city will not benefit greatly from Habaguanex's new

Table 6.1 Social projects funded and organized by Habaguanex in Habana Vieja, 2003

Project
Earmarking a large Canadian donation exclusively for residential housing, not tourism.
Construction of three hundred apartments across the bay in the eastern township of Alamar, Habana del Este Municipality. These units will house those who are displaced from renovation projects.
A detailed revitalization plan of the UNESCO district that focuses on the subdistricts of San Isidro, Belén, and Catedral. In particular, residential housing for locals will be prioritized.
Free daily breakfasts at one primary school in Habana Vieja.
Refurbishing a cloister of the Belén Convent as a musical conservatory, to be used especially by talented youth and artists in Habana Vieja.
An elderly day-care facility in Belén Convent.
A maternal-infant care facility, on the corner of Lamparilla and Mercaderes Streets.
The San Isidro residential redevelopment project, targeted to the neighborhood of the same name, in the southern end of Habana Vieja.

Source: Author's field research 1999–2003, and Leal (1999).
Note: I would be remiss if I did not mention that the city historian referred to one of my earlier publications about heritage tourism in which I mentioned that there were "winners and losers" in the old city's heritage tourism. In the city historian's plenary address to an international architecture conference, he stated emphatically: "Ladies and gentlemen, [in Habana Vieja] there are no losers, only winners" (Leal 2002).

investment strategies. The improvements, rather, are anticipated to be long term. Curiously, this is not unlike Walt Rostow's trickle-down notion of development that underpins modernization theory (Rostow 1961). Habana Vieja's public spaces have become, in Jones and Varley's terms, "contested spaces" (1994, 1999b), and they underscore different urban agendas among residents in Latin American historic districts and in the local state, as well as underscoring different outcomes of commodifying the built environment (Ward 1993).

Following Michael Smith and Joseph Feagin (1987, 13), we can identify at least five ways that heritage tourism in Habana Vieja manifests itself in what Marx might have labeled the new international division of labor. First, economic restructuring and tourism drive development as Cuba opens to the travel and leisure industries. This chapter has argued that community input has not been a central premise of heritage tourism in Habana Vieja. One study by a team of Cuban social scientists who examined the effect of Habaguanex in one part of Habana Vieja — San Isidro — concluded that "there is a need to create spaces for debate that include informative aspects [of community development] . . . [and] it is necessary to recognize different actors that are involved in this community work and to specify the roles they will have" (Collado, Mauri, and Coipel 1996, 117). Another Cuban urban and regional planning team assessing Havana's problems in the next millennium found a need to "increase neighborhood participation in proposing and implementing solutions to community problems" (Oñate, Brito, and Oliveras 1996, 112). These community roles have not been a regular feature of community development in Habana Vieja, yet they would help to mitigate the strains of global economic restructuring.

Second, state restructuring is evident on every corner. Habaguanex searches out capital for urban revitalization in multiple venues. As Smith and Feagin (1987, 27) argue, restructuring urban space in cities entails "the interplay of global capitalism, the state, and activities of urban residents. . . . Major economic investment and location decisions shape the built environment of [capitalist] cities." Capital has been urbanized, and *plusvalía* (appreciation) in the old quarters of Havana is not unlike real-estate investments in market economies (Harvey 1985).

Third, households in Habana Vieja are not immune to economic restructuring. Laid-off public workers and new self-employed workers now ply their trades (legal and otherwise) throughout the old city. New employment appears as legal self-employed workers (cuentapropistas) and hustlers (jineteros). Downsizing has made bartending, hotel work, and tourism in general a new choice in socialist Cuba. Foreign investment exacerbates income differentials. As Gillian Gunn observed (1995, 15):

Present conditions in Cuba suggest that while rising foreign investment is undermining Castro's power in several important ways, this subversive effect is balanced by other sociological results of foreign investment that actually consolidate the system. . . . That balance could easily change, however. If investment rises faster and spreads further from the tourism enclaves . . . then the class of privileged workers will grow, and the contrast with the hardships of their neighbors hired in state enterprises will become more evident.

A decade or so after her observation, such contrasts are even more striking, especially in Habana Vieja. Income disparity and the contrast of housing stock between tourist facilities and locals call attention to a long-standing debate in socialist planning about moral versus material incentives (Zhao 1995; Rohter 1995; Szlenyi 1982).

Fourth, community restructuring symbolizes the way in which Habana Vieja has become commodified. Not unlike Orlando, Florida, and the "Disneyfication" of its landscape, Habana Vieja revives the semiotics of its colonial and exploited past and is marketing its cityscape so that it will provide a unique "tourist gaze" for visitors (Urry 2002). From the old haunts, restaurants, and bars of Ernest Hemingway, to the fortresses that once held precious minerals stolen through the Spanish conquests of Incas and Aztecs, Habana Vieja is slowly becoming a "living museum." Foreigners can experience this urban heritage for a price. Caribbean folklore that reflects buccaneers and pirates is now part of the tourist trinkets sold in Habana Vieja, just as symbols of Caribbean heritage have been marketed for years in Ocho Rios, Jamaica, or Georgetown, Gran Cayman Islands. In the end, Habaguanex will mold a collective memory of land use, urban design, and architectural style in its own image. Comparable efforts in Great Britain and the United States show us how the symbolism and beneficiaries of historic preservation reflect the dominant interests of certain social groups who successfully lay their imprint on the urban fabric (Barthel 1996, 152–54). Habana Vieja is not immune from those dominant interests.

Fifth, the new international division of labor entails geographic restructuring. Habana Vieja's streets have never been more demarcated between dollars and tourist venues, at one level, and pesos and Cuban residents, at another. A deepening segregation exists between habaneros and dollar-laden tourists.

Habaguanex will continue to serve as the redevelopment engine of Habana Vieja, and this chapter has questioned that development. As geographer Michael Edwards, former civil society specialist of the World Bank, argues, the past fifty years have been characterized by corporate and state meddling in the lives of the poor. The next fifty years, he contends, should see cooperation as the dominant discourse in development circles. "The changing global context makes co-operation both more necessary and more possible. There has never been a better time to pursue the vision of a more co-operative world" (Edwards 1999, 23).

Civil society in Cuba faces significant legal reforms. In May 2002, after a constitutionally sanctioned petition drive among human rights groups gathered more than ten thousand signatures to call for a constitutional referendum, President Jimmy Carter spread the word to millions of Cubans in a nationally televised speech. During his visit to Havana, the former president often spoke about the project by name (Project Varela, named after a nineteenth-century Cuban priest). The following month, though, the Cuban government initiated a referendum of its own: to make socialism eternal. More than 80 percent of eligible voters signed the petition, quashing any challenges to the socialist establishment. A number Cubans with whom I spoke in June 2002, and again in January, February, March, and April 2003, said that Committee for the Defense of the Revolution members visited households where individuals had not signed. Fears of recrimination, persecution, and lost jobs and of other threats led to an unknown number of Cubans signing the referendum. These national-level machinations reflect local-level planning that creates a kind of Orwellian single-speak.

While few Cubans can go on record to talk about coercion or censorship, there is a local saying about civil society's role in speaking out against the regime: "En Cuba, no hay una cultura de crítica" (There is no culture of criticism in Cuba). Political propaganda billboards throughout the countryside pronounce: "Dentro de la Revolución, todo. Afuera, nada." (Within the Revolution, everything. Outside of it, nothing). To cast a basic civil liberty (freedom of speech, freedom of assembly) as a cultural element "packages" and "sugarcoats" a basic truth: you are either for us, or against us. In March 2003, more than seventy dissidents in Cuba were given stiff prison terms for collaborating with the U.S. government. That same month also witnessed new U.S. Treasury Department plans to not renew licensed travel for civic and cultural groups to the island, a significant and high-end component of Havana's tourist revenues. In April 2003, three young men were executed for trying to hijack a ferry to the United States. In response, the administration of President George W. Bush is threatening to both eliminate the number of Cuban Americans who visit the island (that would amount to about 70 percent of total U.S. visitors [personal communication, U.S. Interests Section 2002]), and to suspend the legal transfer of remittances to the island. If implemented, the tourist industry would surely suffer, and residential-housing needs would take a backseat to a larger national economic crisis.

Restructuring in Habana Vieja unfolds without consulting local residents; neither tourism nor revitalization is developed at the grass roots. In this instance, we would do well to recall one of Chris Rojek and John Urry's (1997) arguments about global tourism: perfecting the built environment into a homogenous and ubiquitous landscape can carry a price. If planners continue striving to erect a uniform, Spanish-colonial setting, Habana Vieja's uniqueness could be homogenized and lost. Socialist planning in the old city has gone from an antiurban bias, rejecting a capitalist past, to one seemingly unable to commodify the colonial city quickly enough. In so doing, it runs the risk of becoming another Caribbean port such as Old San Juan (Puerto Rico), Santo Domingo (Dominican Republic), Veracruz (Mexico), or Cartagena (Colombia). Only Habaguanex can bring Habana Vieja into the new millennium and avoid the kinds of economic and social exclusion that urban revitalization and restructuring create in historic districts well studied outside the island. Faithful adherence to a socialist project and the geography of heritage depend on it.

7 Tourism Planning and Heritage Preservation in Trinidad, Cuba

Trinidad (pop. forty-two thousand) is a colonial gem on the south-central coast of Cuba (figure 7.1). Chapter 2 highlighted its geographic isolation, tucked away at the foot of the scenic Escambray Mountains. The chapter also noted that this historic villa was the fourth of seven initial settlements forged in 1514 by Velázquez, indicating that its quincentennial anniversary approaches, making Trinidad the oldest case study location in the book. Trinidad's economic history took it from a remote secondary port, to a major sugar-producing center, to decline, and, recently, to revival.

In this chapter, I wish to show the way that broader processes at foot in international tourism are tethered to local outcomes — in this case Trinidad — but filtered through the present leadership in Cuba. In the 1990s, seventy cents on every investment dollar in Cuban tourism went to hotel construction. By 1999, Cuban and foreign investment had added sixty hotels to the island's stock, elevating it to the second-largest hotel capacity in the Caribbean (Gutiérrez and Gancedo 2002, 78). But the demand brought by international heritage tourism does not simply fill economic vacuums left by an eroded state or by collapsed Soviet aid, as the Cuban leadership contends. Rather, it is important to situate how the Cuban government interacts with provincial and municipal liaisons in the pursuit of economic growth, with varying degrees of success. Michael Radu (1998, 700) describes the behavior of Cuban government agencies this way:

> Because the party leadership directly controls all institutions, all-important decisions, from management to personnel to planning and production targets, are dependent upon the central policymaking apparatus, the Politburo. Hence, the ability to respond promptly to any challenge or unexpected development is severely hindered, and individual responsibility by institutional leaders is inhibited. Attempts at

Figure 7.1   Trinidad's Main Town Square. The Sánchez Iznaga house to the left is currently the Architecture Museum. The Ortiz house in the middle, whose original owners became wealthy from the slave trade, functions as an art gallery. At the horizon, the Caribbean Sea.

institutional reform — whether "workers self management . . . or decentralization of planning . . . failed because they did not (and, by the logic of communist system, could not) escape from the party's ultimate control."

Over the past decade, new wealth has come to Trinidad in the form of tourism. The Ministry of Tourism has been promoting Trinidad as a "tourist pole" along with Santiago (east), the keys and archipelagoes (north-central), and Havana-Varadero (northwest) (Gutiérrez and Gancedo 2002). Specifically, they seek investors to develop the Ancón Peninsula just nine kilometers south of Trinidad. However, the ministry's five-year plan is at odds with the goals of the City Restoration Office. My research question is whether a cultural heritage site could possibly be compromised given its international reputation, its UNESCO World Heritage status, and articulate and passionate leadership by architects at the local level.

This dilemma encapsulates the tensions inherent in "glocal" studies: Who jeopardizes Trinidad's colonial charm in the name of hard currency? On one hand, the Cuban leadership needs hard currency to sustain its social provision. On the other, local officials in Trinidad believe an unfettered international tourism market bound for its town and beaches could spoil an international heritage site. I argue that while intergovernmental collaboration among various local, regional, and national agencies is always rife with conflict, the Trinidad case study strikingly shows a top-down approach to economic development and planning.

This brief chapter provides a close-up on tourism and heritage planning in Trinidad and the adjacent Sugar Mill Valley (Valle de los Ingenios). The case study highlights the dilemma of intragovernmental collaboration and the challenges that small centros históricos face in Latin America.

Ancón Beach and Trinidad's Centro Histórico

Forty years ago, CIA director Richard Bissell argued that Playa Ancón should be the site of the ill-fated Bay of Pigs Invasion, and not Girón Beach located to the east. Unlike the Bay of Pigs (surrounded by thick mangroves and layers of coral reefs), Ancón Beach is flat and very accessible. Today, a new invasion is expected. In late 1999, the Tourism Ministry sought investors to build four thousand hotel rooms in the only part of the greater Trinidad area that can handle such growth: the Ancón Peninsula. Since the announcement in 2000, only one facility, with three hundred beds, has been built (Trinidad al Mar), and it was financed by Cubanacán, a Cuban company. Just two other hotels (Hotel Ancón, 279 rooms; Hotel Costa Sur, 131 rooms) occupy the peninsula. By early 2003, the ministry had lowered its desired number of new units to three thousand (personal communication, architect Nancy Benítez, April 19, 2003). Although the actual level of construction, then, is different from the original four thousand units the ministry desired, challenges between ministry and local expectations linger.

The main conventional tourist attraction outside the historic center of Trinidad is the four-kilometer beach with sugary white sand, Playa Ancón, on the Caribbean Sea (figure 7.2). Architecturally, however, the peninsula's largest hotel is unattractive. Hotel Ancón is typical of the thousands

Figure 7.2   Aerial photograph of Ancón Peninsula with Ancón Beach and the Caribbean Sea to the left (west), looking north with the Escambray Mountains in the background, 1999.

of prefabricated buildings that were erected during the first two decades of the Revolution. Schools, factories, office buildings, and hotels adopted a series of premanufactured models that were used in France, Yugoslavia, Scandinavia, and Canada (Machado 1976). Prefabrication in Cuba was economical and symbolic because the structures "became reference points for the Revolution's modernization efforts . . . [and] spread to the most unlikely and remote corners. . . . The enduring nature of Soviet power had been reaffirmed by victory over barbarian Nazi forces. Soviet planning sought to show new features and rights of the unfolding socialist society" (Scarpaci, Segre, and Coyula 2002, 198). To some degree, this philosophy is evident in Cuba's use of prefabrication as well. Although prefabrication exists on the beach and in the postcolonial quarters of the city, there is none in the historic district.

Historic Trinidad (figure 7.3) has an unusual tourist infrastructure. No hotel exists within the 1988 UNESCO-declared World Heritage District. A two-star hotel, Las Cuevas, built a few years before the Revolution and

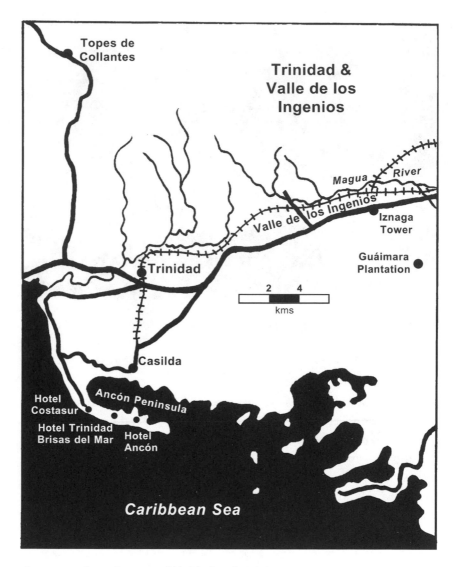

Figure 7.3 Location map, Trinidad and vicinity.

Figure 7.4 Entrance to the nonmotorized zone in the historic center of Trinidad.

operated by the Cuban company Horizontes, sits on the side of a hill just north of the old city. However, there are scores of mostly illegal, privately operated bed-and-breakfast establishments in the old city charging about $20–$30 daily. Although very limited private enterprise has been permitted since 1993 (see chapter 6), engineering authorities are concerned with this type of lodging because it will increase water consumption, lower water pressure, and create more raw sewage. Completing even half of the three thousand desired units may jeopardize historic preservation and will certainly place economic development interests on a collision course with architectural historians. The current water and sewage capacities in the old city have already been reached. Although standard thirty-passenger buses as well as all other motorized traffic cannot enter the colonial core of Trinidad because of gated streets (figure 7.4), city planners and conservators are concerned about the impact of dozens of additional buses that might bring tourists from the peninsula to the town. The Cuban- and Italian-trained director of the City Restoration Office, architect Nancy Benítez, remarked, "Imagine dozens of larger buses parked outside the historic center, with their air-conditioning units running. The vibrations will shake the streets and buildings, while thousands of tourists flood the historic center. They're going to need restaurants and bathrooms. The pressure on the old city will be incredible" (personal communication, April 19, 2003). The vibration problem is not unlike the problems faced in Quito's heavily trafficked historic district described in chapter 2 (see Figure 2.17a).

Attracting Investors

Three major allures may encourage tourism, which, in turn, will attract investment. Foremost is the colonial charm of old Trinidad. The design of elite homes reflects a blend of Spanish and French styles, especially evident in the traditional ceramic roof tiles. The French came when sugarcane planters fled the 1791 slave revolt in nearby Haiti. With the Louisiana Purchase in 1803, more French growers resettled in this corner of the West Indies. Economic prowess grew into what historian Moreno Fraginals (1976) calls Cuba's "sugar aristocracy" or "sugar-ocracy." The result is a rich blend of Spanish, French, and Creole architecture, graced by cobbled streets made from ship ballast or rocks from nearby streams and quarries.

The City Restoration Office is the primary entity handling historic preservation in Trinidad. Formed in 1988, the office has restored dozens of mansions that have been turned into museums and cultural centers. Since 1997, the office has been renovating a large residential quarter in the eastern part of the city called Tres Cruces (Three Crosses) (figure 7.5).

Second, Trinidad is one of the few beach areas (in a region that geologically speaking has a "submerged coastline") on Cuba's south coast, reflecting the tourist preference for the aquamarine waters and beaches that abound off the north coast. With a paved airport runway that dates back to the 1950s, the town airport receives small commercial flights several times daily from Havana, Varadero, Camagüey, and Santiago de Cuba.

Third, Trinidad offers tourists an attractive relative location. It serves as

Figure 7.5   Only the lower half of a residential exterior door is being restored in the Tres Cruces neighborhood of Trinidad. Imported cedar from Belize is costly, about US$500 a cubic meter.

a departure point to explore the Escambray Mountains and the Topes de Collantes health-resort complex that sits at an elevation of about 830 meters, just one hour away. The town is also adjacent to the Sugar Valle de los Ingenios, which once held dozens of mills from the late eighteenth and early nineteenth centuries (figure 7.6). The valley is the only natural landscape (not a town or city) designated a UNESCO World Heritage Site in Cuba (Old Havana, and, of course, Trinidad, are the other two heritage sites).

Funding Small-Scale Heritage Projects

Architects, planners, geographers, and engineers make up the twenty-four professionals of the Trinidad Restoration Office. In a short time, they have established an organization to attend to archival, technical, economic, construction, and training endeavors (figure 7.7). They direct the renovation of several sugar plantations in the valley and hope to open a sugar

Figure 7.6 Iznaga Tower on the former Manaca Sugar Plantation located thirteen kilometers east of Trinidad, in Valle de los Ingenios. Built between 1835 and 1845 for the overseer (*mayordomo*) to watch over slaves in the field atop the forty-three-meter, seven-level structure, its staircase was in disrepair for most of the twentieth century. One of the first restorations undertaken by Trinidad's Restoration Office in 1988 was to reconstruct the stairwell. Hand-sewn tablecloths and other embroidery by local women hang on clotheslines to entice tourists.

museum in one of the former homes (figure 7.8). Old slave quarters and toolsheds will be restored or converted into bathrooms and small restaurants. Restorationists seek investors for reconverting specific properties in the valley both to relieve some of the tourism pressures in Trinidad and to revive old buildings that still contain frescoes painted by Italian and French painters in the 1830s.

All companies that charge in dollars within Trinidad (including the historic district, the larger city, and the county of the same name) must now remit a 2 percent tax of their gross revenues to the City Restoration Office. Companies that conduct business with the Cuban peso are taxed 1 percent of their gross revenues. Architect Benítez notes that since 1998—the first year of revenue sharing—the budget has gone from a few thousand dollars to about $450,000 in 2001. The Office proposes a more modest

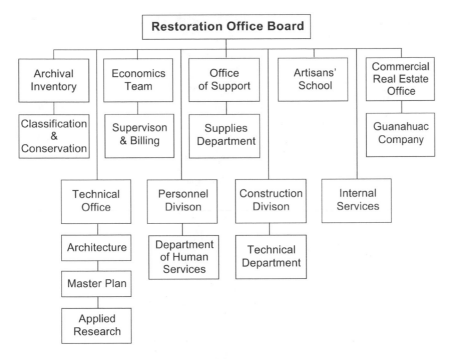

Figure 7.7   Trinidad Restoration Office, organizational chart.

investment strategy that would encourage investors to build small hotels in restored colonial buildings. For example, a nineteenth-century home (figure 7.9) sits abandoned just two blocks south of the Plaza Mayor, and the Restoration Office has been looking for an investor for several years. "It would be the perfect five-star, small hotel," remarked the late Office Director and Trinidad native, Roberto "Macholo" López.[1] To date, though, no one has come forward. "In general, hotel investors do not want to spend money on restoration," adds Benítez. "They prefer a new, clear site, where they can start fresh" (personal communication April 19, 2003).

While Cuba's financing scheme for heritage preservation is both innovative and serves as a window to Cuba's new political economy, a few obstacles remain. Many companies that operate in either national currency (pesos) or hard currency (dollars) do not always pay. Some firms are so far in arrears with the Restoration Office that the small group of architects has had to take the "debtors" to court and sue them for payment.

Figure 7.8   Side view of the landlord's house at the former Guaímaro Plantation twenty-one kilometers southeast of Trinidad. The original structure at the right was built in the 1830s and is covered by French-style "locking" roof tiles (versus the more common Spanish "curved" tiles). Bountiful sugar harvests in the 1840s allowed the landlord to add a colonnaded arcade to serve as a porch-gallery at the house entrance (left). The anteroom contains frescoes and murals painted by Italian masters 160 years ago. The City Restoration Office seeks investors to convert the mansion into the Museum of the Sugar Mill Valley (El Museo del Valle de los Ingenios), where artifacts from the slave-driven sugar economy will be displayed. Mechanization, especially stream engines and boilers, launched the Trinidad region into decline around 1860.

Litigation cuts into the limited resources of the Restoration Office. Thus, like in market economies, where cooperation is not always forthcoming, intragovernmental coordination is not always easy, even in the centrally planned economy of Cuba.

The Cuban cities of Trinidad, Habana Vieja, Camagüey, and Santiago de Cuba serve as models for historic preservation, heritage tourism, and sustainable development in several important ways. First, they target specific revenues from a larger pool of funds for upgrading the built environment of their neighborhoods. A cash-strapped state does not have to

Figure 7.9   An abandoned nineteenth-century home, two blocks south of the Plaza Mayor, Trinidad. It is zoned to become a small, upscale hotel in the historic district.

divert funds from health, education, or related public welfare sectors for this purpose. Instead, funds come from state entities that generate their own revenues. Thus, for example, in Trinidad the cost sharing is minimum (2 percent) and widely distributed throughout the businesses that operate in the city of forty-two thousand.

Second, dollar-paying facilities earn their revenues from tourists, not Cubans. In that sense, one can make the argument that tourists should be (indirectly) responsible for maintaining heritage sites, not the Cuban people who have seen deterioration in their standard of living.

Finally, the financing scheme is sustainable in that the revenues are proportionately commensurate with the volume of tourists passing through. In some way, then, the Restoration Office budget will "rise and fall" with the ebb and flow of tourism. Holding constant for the moment the possible consequences of the four thousand beds on the beach, the 2 percent tax will allow for the constant and steady upgrading of the UNESCO site so that costly intervention is not necessary later this century.

Conclusion: Prioritizing Residential Housing in Trinidad

The post-Soviet era sent shock waves throughout Eastern European nations and Cuba (Horowitz and Suchlicki 2003). Forced to compete without preferential prices, Cuba entered the global market like never before. Since the early 1990s, it has drawn on tourism, a traditional comparative advantage, as a source of hard currency. In particular, it promotes heritage tourism as a venue to complement the traditional sun-and-surf outlets inherent in Caribbean tourism. This chapter has shown how local heritage tourism setting is immersed in the broader patterns of globalization, but with the socialist government as the intermediary force.

In contemporary Cuba, economic development decisions made at the national level override local planning goals. In Trinidad, the City Restoration Office was notified of the goal of four thousand beds after the Tourism Ministry made its decision. The differences of opinion between local and national decision-makers underscore the locals' concern with authentic heritage preservation and the latter's search for hard currency. A final determination on hotel construction was to be made by late 2000, but by mid-2004, there was still no word on the project. Post–September 11, 2001, downturns in international tourism may have scared off investors, at least for the short term.

In the 1970s, E. F. Schumacher's celebrated work, *Small Is Beautiful,* echoed a passionate plea for development projects that were locally defined, bottom-up, and small in scale. Schumacher railed against the mammoth development projects of the day: the Alliance for Progress in Latin America as well as a spate of World Bank–funded works in Africa, Asia, and Latin America. Tourism planning and heritage preservation in Trinidad, Cuba, embody a number of those tenets. Nevertheless, this chapter has shown that firms operating in centrally planned economies are not necessarily more altruistic and cooperative than their counterparts in market economies. Also, opportunity comes knocking at local heritage tourism offices in ways that are serendipitous, if not tragic. Trinidad's Restoration Office currently benefits from a budget that exists in good measure because of the demise of the former USSR, and the dissolution of Cuba's traditional trading partners in Eastern Europe. No one could have anticipated the global ramifications for Trinidad after the events in 1989. Perhaps the real mettle of this new financing scheme will be demonstrated when the intragovernmental differences about beachfront development are resolved, and the residential quarters of Tres Cruces neighborhood are fully restored without mandates from the national government.

8 Globalization's Pressures in the New Millennium

This book has identified various transformations of those old neighborhoods known in Spanish America as centros históricos, cascos históricos, cascos antiguos, or ciudades viejas. Heritage tourism is increasingly the venue by which outsiders come to know these places, and the Latin American centro histórico enables visitors to see history with their own eyes. However, these "living museums" are teeming with locals who maintain long-standing traditions and labor at tasks not always connected to tourism. Locals socially construct the attributes, challenges, and meanings of their own everyday experiences. These experiences, in turn, increasingly coexist with the forces of globalization.

The nine case studies in this book reflect considerable geographic variety: agricultural versus mining and manufacturing centers, ports versus inland locations, and large versus small cities. I have tried to show how the histories of these plazas and barrios are layered with meanings, symbolism, and occasionally conflicts that belie their benign colonial exteriors. Economic development, modernity, and globalization have unevenly left their marks in the built environments of these places. The economic histories show that recessions in the colonial era were cyclical and that the Bourbon reforms of the late eighteenth century changed local and international commerce, often for the better. British capital financed waterworks, sewers, and port facilities in Montevideo and Buenos Aires; U.S. capital prevailed in Cuba. Some of the cities (Havana, Buenos Aires, Puebla, Montevideo, and Quito) became national transportation and economic hubs in the nineteenth or twentieth centuries. Others remained untouched by modernization until the latter half of the twentieth century. During the twentieth century, some government and private agencies modernized the larger metropolitan areas by building factories at the city edge, while the historic quarters were spared major disruptions. In the new millennium, centros históricos play host to "smokeless industries," posing opportunities and challenges for the future.

In this final chapter, I arrange some of the principal findings thematically. They include

— land use
— taxation, finances, and remittances
— heritage preservation and local planning
— community participation and gentrification
— urban design and the automobile
— urban and regional theory

I end with a discussion on what globalization and heritage tourism portend for the centro histórico.

Land Use

Despite sharing some common historical legacies in the fifteenth and sixteenth centuries, today these districts exhibit different land uses. To my knowledge, no research to date has described the empirical and aesthetic dimensions of these architecturally rich neighborhoods. Chapter 3 presented the findings of the most comprehensive and systematic land-use study of the Latin American centro histórico. My research question was whether one could build an aggregate assessment of how land uses in one Latin American centro histórico differ from those in another. I used a curbside approach involving an analysis of nearly thirty thousand doorways in establishing a land-use profile for each centro histórico in nine historic districts. Each location sampled included the recognized historic district of each city, shown by either the national or the international (UNESCO) landmarks agency. For comparative purposes, I used statistical means to show general trends in these corners of the Latin American city.

Cuban cities showed the highest proportion of residential land uses as well as the poorest condition of the built environment. The most meaningful finding concerns commercial activity, vital to all neighborhoods, especially in historic districts around the world. General retailing ("twenty-four–seven") keeps the historic district from being dominated by tourists. Commercial activity consumed one-third of street-level land uses in this study (34.6 percent). Historic Quito topped the list with its vast low-end general retailing. Puebla's historic district is also a major regional retailing and wholesaling center in central Mexico. Cartagena's historic district (Ciudad Amurallada) has kept its low-end, traditional mom-and-pop retailing while building modern shopping complexes beyond the walled city. In Cartagena, retailers ply their trades at the street level and often live above their businesses, or else they rent out these upper-floor apartments. The presence of mom-and-pop retailing corroborates much of the literature that heralds owner-occupancy and mixed land uses (versus single zoning) in Spanish American, North American, and Western European cities. The land-use survey also showed that Montevideo and Buenos Aires have the highest levels of abandonment: over 5 percent of all units were abandoned compared to a survey average of half that level. Ciudad Vieja and San Telmo, neighborhoods in two of the most "modern" nations included in the study, reflect more of the low-income "ghetto" aspect described by the Chicago urban ecologists in their portrayal of downtown U.S. cities.

Building quality varied widely across the study sites. Generally, historic districts in Cuba and the Southern Cone cities had the lowest-quality building facades. At the other end, the Ecuadorian and Mexican cities had the best-quality buildings. These findings underscore the benefits of governments (Mexican and Ecuadorian) that maintain steady involvement over decades in heritage preservation as opposed to the sudden, disjointed intervention seen in the Cuban and Southern Cone cities.

Not surprisingly, the pace of modernity has moved irregularly and has created a range of building heights and skylines in these centros históricos. Buenos Aires topped the list (2.9 floors) followed by Montevideo (2.7), and Havana (2.4) at the upper limits. Bogotá (1.9), Puebla (1.94), Cartagena (1.8), and Trinidad (1.04) featured the lowest skylines. Skyscrapers and modern buildings around most Spanish American CBDs cluster beyond the centro histórico, supporting Carrión's (1992) argument that there is a "sorting-out" process of building type and urban scale, either by design, default, or change. For instance, the districts of Vedado and Centro Habana developed higher skylines than Habana Vieja's. In Montevideo, Carrasco and districts near Montevideo's airport absorbed buildings that would have transformed Ciudad Vieja, while Palermo and the

Costanera are home to Buenos Aires' towering buildings. This sorting-out process does not mean that modernity has violated the colonial imprint of these cities or that urban morphology evolves according to some natural, "organic" laws. Whether by design or default, though, the skylines of Latin American historic districts testify to the economic and architectural landscapes of the past. Modernity and urbanization may ensure high-quality building stock, but they also produce great extremes in the "look" of the Latin American city. Part of that look stems from the capital available to transform these districts.

Taxation, Finances and Remittances

The case studies represent a variety of financing mechanisms for enhancing the look of the historic district. Bogotá, like Quito, enlists a public-private corporation. Both entities address matters of historic preservation, particularly in public spaces (plazas, sidewalks). The Bogotá entity is also charged with promoting small businesses, while Quito's administrative agency is coping with an abundance of retailing. The Cuban study sites are markedly different. Habaguanex in Habana Vieja enjoys a fiscal autonomy otherwise unheard of in this socialist country. However, lack of financial transparency means that no one can assess the veracity of their claims about historic preservation and hotel renovation on the one hand, nor the benefits of social projects in the local community on the other. Across the island, in Trinidad, the Restoration Office funds only social projects (e.g., private residences). A 1 or 2 percent tax imposed on businesses funds restoration projects in Trinidad in a fashion that embraces the much touted but rarely operationalized concept of "sustainability" (cf. Dyck 1998). The Restoration Office proposes a more modest investment method for historic preservation, even though it may conflict with the powerful Ministry of Tourism. The Trinidad case study reveals that dedicated local administrators — empowered with a financing mechanism linked to the ebb and flow of heritage tourism — can produce substantive historic preservation that integrates the locals' need for shelter. However, even centralized planning in socialist Cuba cannot minimize litigation that taxes the limited resources of the Restoration Office as it seeks payment from Cuban companies.

Remittances are also important sources of capital in shaping urban change. Citizens of Havana and Cuenca receive considerable funds sent by relatives from the United States. In Cuenca, a small banking district tucked away inside the historic district has grown appreciably. Although new banks adopt neocolonial facades, they cannot disguise the displacement of the Indian population because of rising rents. More field research will show the connections between remittances and heritage preservation.

This research has shown that taxes are not major sources of capital for historic preservation. An ethos of not paying local taxes confounds Cartagena's efforts to administer and implement taxes, land-use regulation, and zoning regulation. Levels of property tax payment in Cartagena are also uneven, often favoring business owners over residents, though Cartagena's sixteen different business taxes create a perception that the city is overtaxed. Uneven valuation and capturing mechanisms deprive Cartagena of the full potential of its tax base. While tourists come to Cartagena because of its colonial architecture, the city does not target specific funds for historic monuments and districts. As in many other historic districts, those who visit Cartagena do not pay for it directly. Therefore, preservation funding is tenuous. As demonstrated in the other study sites, historic preservation in Cartagena is not inexpensive, and funding comes from a hodgepodge of capital sources. Even if the municipal government had the political will to support residential-housing improvements and historic preservation, it does not have the money to restore private residences. Nonetheless, cartageneros, accustomed to a beleaguered and unegalitarian state mired in civil strife, do not expect such social programs. A weak national government in Bogotá does not allocate money for heritage purposes, ostensibly because of war, but there is little proof it did so before the strife. In the other eight study sites, urban heritage preservation efforts suffer from structural problems at the national and global levels. These conundrums pose special challenges for heritage preservation and local planning agencies.

Heritage Preservation and Local Planning

Early in the book, I noted that the 1967 Carta de Quito and UNESCO's designation of World Heritage Sites have cast international attention on historic preservation. Still, cultivating and defining authenticity, heritage, and historic periods are challenging tasks. While the UNESCO "badges of honor" are good publicity for the centro histórico, they do not carry large financial aid packages.

During the 1990s, neoliberal policies took hold in Latin America. In some places, the global capital markets undermined a state that international socialism had abandoned (e.g., post-Soviet Cuba). In others, civil war (Colombia's Revolutionary Armed Forces, narcotics traders, right-wing militias) or national fiscal and political crises (Argentina) wreaked havoc. The effect was to make the funding of heritage projects a lower priority than it was in the 1980s and before.

Planning officials in centros históricos face a special challenge distinct from the challenges of delivering "standard" public services such as water, waste removal, and police and fire protection. Heritage preservation presents both "low" and "high" cultural capital matters to planners. This book has argued that how those matters are prioritized, funded, and implemented varies widely in the region. The domain of "low" cultural capital in the Latin American urban core includes the vernacular architecture and public spaces beyond the main plazas. Urban poverty in the Latin American inner city is more "disguised" than in its North American counterparts and compounds the tasks of local planners. In addition, inconsistent regulations governing what kinds of retailing planning the departments allow must compete with the needs of tourists and locals (Scantelbury 2003). As the example of the "señora de la chalupa" symbolizes (figure 1.6), street vendors' rights to work in the historic centers may be perceived as colliding with "high" cultural capital and may be discouraged or outlawed. The specific changes in Puebla highlighted in table 2.1 underscore this conflict.

The case study of San Diego Park in Cartagena discussed in chapter 5 shows how local communities can bring salience to a planning issue. In the example given, local residents had little "voice" in coping with the redesign of their plaza, with parking dilemmas, with drug dealing, and with prostitution—all the indirect results of heritage tourism near the San Diego Plaza and the conversion of Santa Clara Convent into a five-star hotel. Because heritage tourism and the Sofitel Corporation are so powerful, municipal authorities have failed to heed their call for reform. In addition, the example of Nobel laureate Gabriel García Márquez indicates that some cartageneros are "more equal than others" and that planning variances are either granted or ignored in a seemingly random fashion. Both Cartagena and Havana showed that historic preservation in the old city also creates tension between foreign investors (who tend to favor simple, turnkey solutions and nonlocal architects) and local residents and professionals.

Chapter 7 examined heritage planning in Trinidad, which reflects the struggles of weak local planning agencies as they face powerful national ministries. That chapter described how the Tourism Ministry wants to add four thousand hotel rooms to the only part of the greater Trinidad area that can handle such growth, the Ancón Peninsula. While investors have not come forth, the case study illustrates that even socialist planning can seek profits with little consideration for the local aesthetic and sensitive heritage tourism. The Cuban study sites indicate plainly the gap between a theoretical commitment to social justice and the short-term quest for hard currency.

Community Participation and Gentrification

Chapters 5 (Cartagena) and 6 (Havana) made clear that heritage tourism and historic preservation could create problems that include residential displacement, gentrification, and other social ills. Local communities face a local-global dilemma in resolving neighborhood problems. While residents may understand the cause of local planning issues, they are often powerless to resolve those same problems. This finding challenges the romantic notion that urban organizations and social movements are resoundingly successful in Latin America. Rather, I concur with Portes and Irigoshin (1994) that such characterizations have been exaggerated (cf. Escobar and Alvarez 1992).

To address more fully how the residents of centros históricos feel about these and analogous problems, I conducted focus groups with residents of the historic neighborhoods of Havana, Cartagena, and Cuenca (see chapter 4). This qualitative method sought to remedy logical positivist approaches espoused by the spatial organization school that has long dominated urban geography. I presented urban renovation to them as neutrally as possible, using such expressions as reanimar el barrio (neighborhood redevelopment) and cambios en el barrio (neighborhood changes). My findings show that in the other two cities, but not Cartagena, historic district residents hold strong feelings about public authorities, investors, tourism, and the future of their neighborhood. Residents do not expect local authorities to resolve their problems. Surprisingly, community input is not a central premise of Habana Vieja's transformation, despite the socialist program of the national government. In Habana Vieja, downsizing makes bartending, hotel work, and tourism in general new sources of new hope in socialist Cuba. Moreover, foreign investment in Cuba widens income differentials. Habana Vieja has become just as commodified as the market economies of the historic districts of Cartagena and Cuenca. In each city where I held focus groups, heritage tourism unfolds with little citizen input. If one of the tenets of globalization is that forces beyond national boundaries erode the ability of the nation-state to remedy its own problems (Waters 2000), then local governments are apparently no better equipped.

In chapter 5, I tried to understand one part of the complex relationships among tourists, investors, and relatives who live outside historic districts. Although Cartagena is less affected by remittances than Cuenca and Havana, money laundering influences its real-estate market, as does second-home purchasing by Europeans. At this stage, it is ambiguous whether the 1995 law (Process 8,000) can retard money laundering in Cartagena's real-estate market. Still, the focus group results in all three cities indicate that residents are not optimistic about the futures of their neighborhoods. I could identify few policy stakeholders concerned about the displacement of local residents. Moreover, there is little formal outcry about gentrification, again challenging the notion of class solidarity or even the existence of a unified voice in articulating local needs (cf. Radcliffe 2000). Subsequent research should continue to use carefully drawn case studies to clarify the relationships among the various scales of globalization and how heritage preservation unfolds in the centro histórico.

Urban Design and the Automobile

Spanish American centros históricos mine the images of cobblestone streets, colonial facades, and vernacular architecture in their tourist

Figure 8.1 Puebla shopping arcade, adjacent to the Main Town Square. The late nineteenth-century structure is endowed with high ceilings for cooling and natural light (owing to stained-glass panels), and it provides a variety of low- and high-end products and services.

literature, regardless of whether locals appreciate these amenities. The opening vignette in chapter 1 and the remarks of Lázaro Valdivieso underscore this lack of appreciation. The first two chapters identified the historic role of the grid, colonial laws, and symbolism in leaving these barrios with uniform urban design. The cultural ascription of urban meanings in most Latin American cities was established on "green sites." However, these preautomobile streets have responded to new forms of transportation in restoring and preserving the charm that the automobile attacks. Retailing from the preautomobile era will continue to prove captivating to locals and tourists when the built environment is alluring and balanced (figure 8.1).

The Modern Movement and the tenets of CIAM left urban planning in Latin American cities with few ways to fit the automobile into existing neighborhoods. The ideas of Le Corbusier and others helped make the suburbanization and commuting of the workforce a common practice among the middle classes. Today, though, there is a growing appreciation for clearing out automobile congestion. Quito has turned back to electric trams in an attempt to abridge the use of combustion engines (buses, trucks, and cars) in its historic districts. Habana Vieja has witnessed a dramatic rise in bicycling because of the higher cost of oil since Soviet subsidies ended in 1989. Rudimentary barriers such as concrete posts engender a "pedestrianization" of the historic district. Trinidad, Cartagena, and Barrio La Candelaria have fenced off streets and sidewalks to restrict cars from parking and moving through parts of the city.

Other efforts to restrict the automobile, however, have been more drastic. To illustrate this relationship, I focused on the special bay windows, called the ventanas de panza, in Cartagena. These bay windows adorn the urban design of the city at the street level, and they represent a midpoint between public and private spaces. Unfortunately, they have been hacked off over the years to make room for the automobile, or smashed by cars and trucks squeezing through the colonial streets or by vehicles parking on sidewalks. Conceptualizing how modernity and tradition confront each other in cases like this is a challenge for urban and regional theory.

Urban design and planning in the Spanish American historic quarters can be enhanced through a variety of "best practices" outlined in these case studies (table 8.1). These include myriad approaches to preserving the built forms of these places as well as creative social and cultural policies that emphasize local concerns over exclusively tourist-induced demands. No broad top-down management or policy template can be ascribed to all these places. However, a proper balance of international (UNESCO), national (heritage landmark designation), and local (practices and customs) can produce effective results. These outcomes range from the simplest of measures (figure 8.2) to creative and sustainable funding sources (Serageldin, Shluger, and Martin-Brown 2001, xii–xix).

Urban and Regional Theory

This review of the Spanish American city has shown that the centro histórico and the Central Business District (CBD) remain discrete entities. The

Figure 8.2 Cuenca authorities use concrete to fill in corners where load-bearing columns and buttresses protrude into sidewalks. They paint crosses on these places to discourage men from urinating there.

history of each case study revealed how colonial life evolved around different town squares, each with unique functions. In Habana Vieja, for example, the economic and social life of the district evolved around four major plazas. Today, those plazas are cornerstones of the revitalization process. The relationship between an urban historical geography of the past and the present promises to afford scholars an opportunity for understanding the role of urban morphology and its transformation over time. It also shows how abstract theory must be grounded in geographic space to illuminate the link between social theory and material life.

The Cuban cases reflect how the socialist leadership aims to mend the tattered fabric of Old Havana by using a standard market remedy: comparative advantages. That tourism was once considered bourgeois and anathema to the Revolution, but is now deemed to be in vogue, should be

Table 8.1   Selected "best practices" in Spanish American historic district urban design and planning

Spanish American centro histórico	Best practices
Bogotá (Barrio La Candelaria)	Sidewalk bumpers to reduce automobile parking. Mixed retailing to support university and institutional activities.
Buenos Aires (San Telmo)	Public and private promotion of theater, restaurants, clubs, and tango. Mixture of retirees, artists, cafés, tango shows, discos, antique and flea-market vendors, and tourists.
Cartagena (Ciudad Amurallada)	Private support for heritage preservation of sites and monuments. Functioning of vibrant retailing within walled quarters (*intramuros*).
Cuenca	Adherence to neocolonial design in expanding financial district. Simple deterrents to urinating in public.
Habana Vieja	Massive hotel construction and building recycling. New state-run urban development corporation (Habaguanex).
Montevideo (Ciudad Vieja)	Promotion of Afro-Uruguayan culture and music (*candomblé*).
Puebla	Long-standing heritage and conservation programs.
Quito	Pioneering heritage and conservation programs.
Trinidad	Use of 1 to 2 percent taxes on businesses earmarked just for residential housing improvements. Attention to revitalizing Tres Cruces neighborhood.

Source: Author's field research, 1992–2004.

instructive in encouraging planners, urban geographers, urban sociologists, and political scientists to move beyond the simple labels of "market economy," "neoliberalism," and "socialism." Explaining how the funding mechanisms work under these broader political economies can help us move from simple generalizations, to concrete examples about the role of the state and local communities. Habaguanex is committed to "trickle-down" economics, though it surely will not use that label to explain its operations. Indirectly, historic preservation unleashed gentrification because most redevelopment goes to dollar-generating properties. Significantly, there is no foreign speculation in Habana Vieja without careful state guidelines, and young Cuban Americans do not live there. The many dilemmas of contrived cultural spaces, from the tacky, tourist-trap facets of Old Havana through images of Ernest Hemingway, Caribbean pirates, and the music of the 1950s are all concerns because they enhance the tourists' gaze and not necessarily the locals' interests. Accepting Habaguanex's claim that there is a comprehensive social agenda behind their restoration efforts is to uncritically accept broad labels. Fieldwork in Trinidad, Cuba, however, showed that the small town is indeed committed to both quality public housing and heritage tourism. Human agency can be a powerful force in overcoming global, structural forces (figure 8.3). Planners and geographers need to continue to test broad suppositions through carefully grounded field research.

Globalization and Heritage Tourism

I began this book with two vignettes in different times and places: one in nineteenth-century Paris and the other in late twentieth-century Cuenca. Both tales showed how modernity (the rise of industrial capitalism and mass advertising, and a postindustrial information economy) has transformed older neighborhoods. The protagonists, de Amici in Paris and Valdivieso in Cuenca, responded differently to these changes: one was outraged while the other was complacent; one was affronted personally and aesthetically while the other was happy to profit from the changes. Each venue showed the ways that globalization and heritage tourism manifested themselves and how the powers of human agency reacted accordingly.

Figure 8.3   A husband and wife sift through rubble at a demolition site on Calle Obispo in Habana Vieja (1998). Various sieves will allow them to use the rubble to mix up their own concrete after various additives are purchased on the black market.

The transformation of the Latin American centro histórico is a useful way to understand recent theorization about globalization and neoliberalism. To review some of the early arguments laid out in chapter 1, a few suppositions are summarized here. First, globalization has made communications and immigration more fluid (figure 8.4). Certainly, the migration patterns from Cuenca demonstrate this.

Second, cultural and media influences are widely disseminated. As multinational hotel chains appear, national symbols (tango dancing; Afro-Latino music in Montevideo, Cartagena, Trinidad, and Havana; buccaneer motifs) become more evident in centros históricos. Amidst these national motifs, however, are generic features that homogenize these spaces. Just like in Italo Calvino's dreamlike story telling about the twilight of an empire in *Invisible Cities* (1974), where each fantastic place he describes to Kublai Khan and the young Marco Polo is really the same place, the marketing of centros históricos highlights similar generic

Figure 8.4 Plaza Santo Domingo, Ciudad Amurallada, Cartagena, July 2000. Several cybercafés like these bring international travelers—mostly young people—to check their e-mail and book reservations for their next stop in Colombia. Centros históricos afford travelers a postmodern mix of antiquity and modernity because of these and related amenities.

features of the colonial landscape. However, the empirical observations reveal significant differences.

Third, the community of nations is "shrinking" because of advances in transportation and telecommunications (O'Brien 1992). International travel makes centros históricos more accessible to North Americans and Europeans, as do local economic development Web sites, government Internet postings, and the home pages of multinational hotel chains. Such information allows tourists to choose among a wide array of destinations that eschew the sun-and-surf and ecotourism venues. Last, market niches produce segmentation of heritage experiences despite the widespread move toward a single global economy (figure 8.5).

Globalization has brought an ensemble of rich attributes of the Spanish American historic districts—castles, cathedrals, cobblestone streets, artisans, and colonial lore—into the world's "leisurescapes" or "pleasure

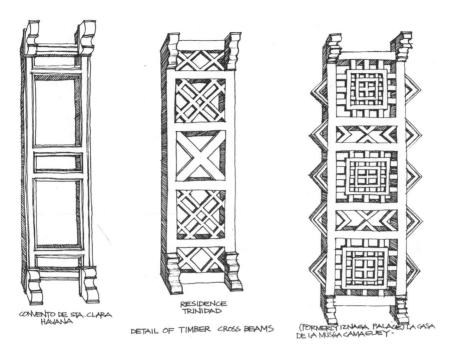

CONVENTO DE STA. CLARA
HAVANA

RESIDENCE
TRINIDAD

DETAIL OF TIMBER CROSS BEAMS

(FORMERLY IZNAGA PALACE) LA CASA
DE LA MUSICA CAMAGUEY-

Figure 8.5 A simple selection of cross-timbers in three Cuban cities reveals the variety in design and serves as a window to broader issues of building purpose, the economy at the time of construction, and local conditions such as the builder, the region, and the client. Heritage tourism draws on these niches to promote their unique markets. *Courtesy Marisa Magasanky.*

periphery." Heritage, I have argued, is etched into Spanish American historic districts and can be conceptualized as a duality that is anchored by economic factors at one end and cultural capital at the other. Spanish American historic districts display a remarkable and adaptive reuse of their built forms and a new appreciation of the sense of place. Central to the debate about place identity is the question: Whose heritage is represented?

Heritage tourism in Spanish America's centros históricos will thrive because it affords unique landscapes for domestic and international tourists. Simultaneously, globalization homogenizes these landscapes and chips away at the uniqueness of these places. As tourists come to expect certain levels of comfort and standardized services and facilities, foreign chain-hotel operations such as Sofitel and Golden Tulip will move in to satisfy those demands. Seen from the vantage point of the "logic of the market," these multinational firms perform a function. Yet, these case studies have shown that their power exceeds the specific hotel facilities. Sofitel has changed the daily operation and look of San Diego Park (plaza) in Cartagena. Externalities such as noisy discotheques and nightclubs, prostitution, drug dealing, and restrictive parking for locals now afflict Cartagena residents. Golden Tulip's hotel in Havana participates in a dual-wage system that — not unlike apartheid in South Africa — pays Cubans in pesos and the government in dollars. Moreover, the architectural design of Parque Central was outsourced to foreign (e.g., non-Cuban) architects and its aesthetic is controversial. In both cities, local citizens have had little input into transforming their neighborhoods. Heritage tourism imposes these prices on civil society in a globalized era.

Because of these globalizing forces, one might expect the recent antiglobalism forces to rally to the aid of residents in centros históricos. The Group of Eight summit in Genoa and the violent clashes between police and protesters, in July 2001 and earlier meetings in Seattle and Montreal focused world attention on environmental calamity, Third World debt relief, sweatshop and labor conditions, and related matters. I posit that heritage tourism will not secure a prominent place on the agenda of antiglobalization activists, because the centro histórico is geographically small, and the forces of globalization change these neighborhoods slowly. Intangible and jeopardized lifestyles are more difficult for the world to picture than, say, endangered species. If heritage tourism is factored into the antiglobalization agenda, it will likely be classified as a cultural globalization dilemma. In that category, it will have to compete with linguistic concerns (the spread of English), ethnic and religious minority rights, and the spread of a global consumer culture that downplays local culture and authenticity while celebrating foreign models of consumption. If local residents are to have a say in directing planning and economic development, they must rely on endogenous resources. Residents of Latin American historic districts may well appreciate Starbucks, Benetton, Gap, McDonalds, Coca-Cola, and other global chains because they bring employment and captivate tourists. How these firms and travelers are accommodated will determine the economies, lifestyles, and landscapes of the centros históricos of tomorrow.

Notes

Unless otherwise noted, all translations of Spanish quotations are my own.

Chapter 1

1. The historic core of Spanish American cities carries a variety of local names: *casco antiguo, casco histórico, centro histórico, ciudad vieja,* and *barrio histórico* are often used in local parlance. However, none of the labels has any bearing on whether the neighborhoods are officially recognized as historic landmarks.

2. Cuba's centrally planned economy minimizes private-sector activity and is treated separately in chapters 6 (Habana Vieja) and 7 (Trinidad).

Chapter 2

1. Full reference, Pablo Babini (1967, 8).

2. Reducciones were Jesuit-built Indian reservations in Paraguay that served as military outposts and defensive lines against the Portuguese.

3. Throughout the book, Bogotá and Santa Fé de Bogotá are used interchangeably, as the official name has been changed over time.

4. A ration book that allows Cubans to purchase subsidized food in pesos and is allocated to all Cuban households.

5. I follow George Pendle (1978), who notes that by 1825 or 1830, all Spanish colonies except Cuba and Puerto Rico had embarked on their Republican agendas.

Chapter 4

1. I do not suggest that the idea of scale is unproblematic and pregiven. Scales that differ between locales can be examined to understand how political and economic processes function. See Bryon Miller (2000, 17–20).

2. Nancy Churchill Conner (2001a, 8, n. 8) defines the trade this way: "The *coyote* or *pollero* is the agent who arranges the trip across the border, shepherding his charges safely to the other side in return for payment that must be received before he frees them on the other side of the border."

Chapter 5

1. Sources for this subsection: author's field notes, June 30, 2000; personal communication, Carlos Jiménez, vice president, Asociación de Sandieganos, June 30, 2000, and other San Diego residents.

2. There is considerable variation in financing arrangements among Caribbean World Heritage Sites. Havana and Cartagena, the two Latin American cities with the largest collection of fortresses, ramparts, and castles, are good examples. The Morro-Cabaña complex in Havana, Cuba, charges US$1 to enter the grounds and another US$3 to enter each castle. The Society for Public Improvements of Cartagena administration refuses to impose one fee for Colombians (cartageneros or otherwise) and another one for foreigners. Cubans, however, charge nationals one-twentieth the fee that foreigners pay to explore the UNESCO World Heritage Site fortresses around Old Havana. The difficulty in true decentralization is not unique to Cuba or Colombia. See Ignacio Irarrázaval and Scarpaci (1994) and Dick Netzer (1997).

3. Other smaller bay windows that are similar to the ventanas de panza include the *ventanas de caja, ventanas de repisa, ventanas de copa,* and *ventanas de reja.* Regional variations can be found in other parts of northern South America and southern Spain. See Javier Covo (1996).

Chapter 6

I am indebted to Roberto Segre, Nathalie Neaves, Phil Peters, Matthew Hill, and Orestes del Castillo Jr. for helpful comments. All errors and omissions remain mine alone. A version of this chapter originally appeared in *Urban Geography* 21:724–44 (Scarpaci 2000b).

1. Although there may be a very small gentry class of artisans and "hustlers" living in Old Havana, they lack the kind of purchasing power required to enter the dollar-driven foreign-housing market. Even if they had enough money, they could not legally purchase new construction under current law.

2. Although there are "suburbs" in Havana in the sense that residents once commuted from there to work in Vedado, Centro Habana, or Habana Vieja, they are actually small satellite cities. This is especially true for Marianao and Víbora, while Miramar reflects more of the "garden suburb" variety that sprang out of the City Beautiful movement that emerged in the late nineteenth and early twentieth centuries in the United States and Western Europe.

3. According to Chandler Burr (1999), the company was launched in 1994 with just $20,000 in state financing. Today it runs 4 hotels (including the four-star Santa Isabel), the Ambos Mundos (Hemingway's old haunt), 13 restaurants, 13 cafeterias, 10 open-air bars, 22 shops, a bakery, 9 markets, and a pastry shop. By 2004, the company should have 25 hotels either under construction or completely operational.

4. On September 5, 1995, the National Assembly of People's Power of the Republic

of Cuba passed Law No. 77/95 of Foreign Investment, which annuls Decree Law No. 50, passed in 1982. The latter had broadened the legal framework for economic associations between foreign entities and Cuban counterparts. For an English-language discussion of the act and related commentaries, see the publication of a consulting firm, Conas (1995).

5. The U.S.-based real-estate company and franchise RE/MAX tried to operate in Cuba. In May 1999, its Web site's home page had registered more than one hundred thousand hits. Enticingly, the opening lines state: "The purchase of Real Estate in Cuba is now a reality! Condos, Homes, Office Space and more. Probably the most anxiously awaited real estate opportunity in the Americas. Hundreds of units have already been sold to astute buyers." These units, however, are mostly in Miramar and the Monte Barreto complex in the western suburbs. See http://www.realestatecuba.com/ (accessed December 2003).

6. A black-glass wall envelopes the roof (*azotea*) of the original structure. It is a modern design that stands out several blocks away, and it contrasts with the sober turn-of-the-century facade. A radio station and communication operations are located behind the black glass. Unaccompanied foreigners cannot enter this area. Located at the eastern edge of Havana Bay, the view is exceptional.

7. Although Yuppies are not present, there is concern among urban planners and architects about a "what if" scenario should Cuban Americans in Miami suddenly appear in Old Havana. In that case, the YUCAS (Young Urban Cuban Americans) would likely find much real estate to their liking. Other concerns about a potential onslaught of Florida influences include "Miamification" (high-rise waterfront construction), creation of contrived cultural spaces, and "McDonaldization" (onslaught of chain retailing) in Havana. These points of reflection exceed the scope of this book. For a consideration of them, see the home page and related links of Cuban American architect Andrés Duany and his partner and wife, Elizabeth Plater-Zyberk at http://www.dpz.com. It is noteworthy that despite the highly polemical debate about the desires of Cuban Americans to transform Havana, there is strong agreement that it should not become another Miami (e.g., turning its back to the sea, becoming a highly automobile-reliant metropolis, and other maladies of late twentieth-century suburban sprawl). See Kunstler (1996) for a succinct review.

8. For a hypothetical discussion of how Havana might have looked had the Triumph of the Revolution not occurred in 1959, see Scarpaci, Segre, and Coyula (2002, chap. 10).

9. The Special Period (short for the Special Period in a Time of Peace [El período especial en un tiempo de paz] was dubbed by the Cuban leadership as the post-Soviet and post–Soviet bloc period that wrought economic hardship on the island from the early 1990s until the present.

10. Statistically representative sampling and in-depth focus groups are difficult for foreigners in Cuba without a research visa from the Foreign Ministry, cosponsorship by a research or teaching facility, and often approval by local government (Poder Popular).

Cuban scholars engaged in qualitative ethnographic research contend that even their own findings cannot "give definite conclusions"; nor can they "assume that points of views should be interpreted as the only valid and acceptable ones" (Dávalos and Vázquez 1996, iv). For one sample of state-approved research, see Arnold August (1999). The description on the back of that book says that August is "the first non-Cuban who has directly attended virtually all the steps of the contemporary Cuban electoral process in order to write a book on the subject. He has based the contents [of the book] on many months of painstaking research, personal observation, and interviews in Cuba." The book was published by a Cuban publishing house, and, accordingly, it praises community participation at the local level.

11. Leal Spengler has requested payments to Habaguanex for his interviews, approximately US$1,000 per conversation. Generally, only prominent journalists or politicians can speak with him. This information comes from personal communication with journalists from the *Dallas Morning News, New Orleans Times-Picayune, Ft. Lauderdale Sun-Sentinel, Condé Nast Travel,* and *U.S. News and World Report.*

12. I had these interviews with two administrators of Habaguanex on March 6, 9, and 10, 1998.

Chapter 7

1. Roberto López Bastida, know as "Macholo," died suddenly at forty-five in June 2003. Trained at the University of Havana, he served as an informal "cultural ambassador" to hundreds of architects, planners, geographers, and tourists who came to visit his hometown. As of this writing (July 2004), his successor had not been named.

References

Afshar, F., and K. Pezzoli. 2001. Globalization and planning: Guest Editors' Introduction. Integrating globalization and planning. *Journal of Planning Education and Research* 20:277–90.

Aguilar, L. 1993. Cuba, c. 1860–c. 1930. In *Cuba: A Short History*, ed. L. Bethel. New York: Cambridge University Press, pp. 21–57.

Albrow, M. 2000. Travelling beyond cultures. In *The Globalization Reader*, ed. F. J. Lechner and J. Boli. New York: Blackwell, pp. 118–25.

Alcaldía Mayor de Cartagena de Indias, Secretaría de Hacienda Distrital. 2000. Estatuto Tributario Distrital (Acuerdo 44 de 1999). Cartagena: Alcaldía Mayor de Cartagena de Indias D.T. y C. Secretaría de Hacienda Distrital. Mimeo.

Alvarez Tabío, E. 1994. La Habana hablada a tres. *3ZU* 3 (ETSAB [Escola Tècnica Superior d'Arquitectura de Barcelona], Barcelona): 16–21.

Amaral, A. 1994. Editor. *Arquitectura neocolonial: América Latina, Caribe, Estados Unidos*. Mexico City: Fondo de Cultura Económica.

Análisis Internacional. 2002. Temas relevantes: ¿Dolarización en América Latina? (http://www.analisisinternacional.com/analisis/dolar.html) (July 7). 4 pp.

Angelópolis: Programa de Desarrollo Regional Angelópolis 1997. VHS. Puebla: Puebla Municipios Conurbanos, Programa General. Produced by Rebattu Video Studio, Río Conchos 5510, Colonia San Miguel, Puebla, Mexico.

Appadurai, A. 1986. *The Social Life of Things*. New York and Oxford: Cambridge University Press.

Arana, M., and A. Mazzini. 1990. Montevideo. In *Centros históricos: América Latina*, ed. G. Carbonell. Bogotá: Junta de Andalucía, Universidad de los Andes, pp. 272–81.

Arreola, D. 1980. Landscapes of nineteenth century of Veracruz. *Landscape* 24:27–31.

———. 1982. Nineteenth-century townscapes of eastern Mexico. *Geographical Review* 72:3–19.

Artucio, L. 1971. *Montevideo y la arquitectura moderna*. Montevideo: Nuestra Tierra. Fascicle 5.

Ashworth, G. J. 2003. Globalisation or localization: Towards convergence in the European city. Paper presented at meeting of the Association of American Geographers, New Orleans, March.

Así será el parque. 2000. *La Plaza: Cultura Urbana* (Cartagena) 1, no. 4 (May): 16 (back cover).

August, A. 1999. *Democracy in Cuba and the 1997–98 Elections.* Havana: Editorial José Martí.

Babbie, E. 1999. *Social Science Research Methods.* Monterey, Calif.: Wadsworth.

Babini, P. 1967. *Buenos Aires con ganas.* Buenos Aires: Editorial Sudamericana.

Barberia, L. G. 2002. The Caribbean: Tourism as development or development for tourism? *ReVista: Harvard Review of Latin America* (Winter): 72–75.

Barthel, D. 1996. *Historic Preservation: Collective Memory and Historic Identity.* New Brunswick, N.J.: Rutgers University Press.

Benton L. 1985. Reshaping the urban core: The politics of housing in authoritarian Uruguay. *Latin American Research Review* 21 (2): 33–52.

Berg, B. L., 2000. *Qualitative Research Methods for the Social Sciences.* 4th ed. Boston: Allyn and Bacon.

Bethel, L. 1993. *Cuba: A Short History.* New York: Cambridge University Press.

Blakewell, P. 1997. *A History of Latin America.* Malden, Mass.: Blackwell.

Bogetic, Z. 2000. Economías ya dolarizadas. *Perfiles del Siglo XXI* (Mexico), no. 81 (April): 34–35.

Borges, J. L. 1969. *El fervor de Buenos Aires.* Buenos Aires: Editorial Emecé.

———. 1998. *Collected Fictions.* Trans. Andrew Hurley. New York: Viking.

Borrero, A. L. 1992. Las migraciones y recursos humanos: Situación reciente y tendencias. In *Cuenca y su futuro.* Cuenca: Corporación de Estudios para el Desarrollo, pp. 93–172.

Bradford, W. 1952. *Of Plymouth Plantation 1620–1647.* New York: Knopf.

Brading, D. A. 1980. The city in Bourbon Spanish America: Elite and masses. *Comparative Urban Research* 8:71–85.

Brett, D. 1996. *The Construction of Heritage.* Cork: Cork University Press.

Broadway, T. 1999. "Shrines near NATO targets vulnerable." *Roanoke Times,* May 29, B-5. (reprinted in *Washington Post*).

Bromley, R. D. F., and G. A. Jones. 1995. Conservation in Quito: Policies and progress in the historic center. *Third World Planning Review* 17:41–60.

———. 1996a. The conservation cycle in the cities of the developing world: Implications for authenticity and policy. *Urban Geography* 17:650–69.

———. 1996b. Identifying the inner city in Latin America. *Geographical Journal* 162:179–90.

Brown, H. J. 1997. *Land Use & Taxation.* Cambridge, Mass.: Lincoln Institute of Land Policy.

Buenos Aires por los caminos de Borges. 2002. Zubieta, Martín (http://www.leedor .com/literatura/buenosairesporborges.shtmlve a la ciudad) (accessed July 2002).

Buisseret, D. 1980. *Historic Architecture of the Caribbean.* London: Heinemann.

Burr, C. 1999. Capitalism: Cuban Style. *Fortune* (international edition), March 1, pp. 72–74.

Burtner, J. 2002. Boycotting pleasure and violence in the land of eternal springtime. *ReVista: Harvard Review of Latin America* (Winter): 52–55.

Bussey, J. 2000. Ecuador embraces U.S. dollar as its national currency. *Miami Herald*, March 10, p. 12-A.

Cabrera Infante. G. 1971. *Three Trapped Tigers*. Translated from the Cuban novel *Tres tristes tigers* by D. Gardner and S. J. Levine in collaboration with the author. New York: Harper and Row.

Calabrese, A. 1999. The welfare state, the information society, and the ambivalence of social movements. In *Communication, Citizenship and Social Policy: Rethinking the Limits of the Welfare State,* ed. A. Calabrese and J. C. Burgelman. Lanham, Md.: Rowman and Littlefield, pp. 259–77.

Calabrese, A., and J. C. Burgelman. 1999. Introduction. In *Communication, Citizenship and Social Policy: Rethinking the Limits of the Welfare State,* ed. A. Calabrese and J. C. Burgelman. Lanham, Md.: Rowman and Littlefield, pp. 1–16.

Calhoun, P. 1996. Social theory and the public sphere. In *The Blackwell Companion to Social Theory,* ed. B. S. Turner. Oxford and Cambridge: Blackwell, pp. 429–70.

Calvino, I. 1974. *Invisible Cities*. New York: Harvest Books.

Caplow, T. 1949. The social ecology of Guatemala City. *Social Forces* 28:113–35.

Caprio, J. 1979. *Cuenca: Su geografía urbana.* Cuenca: López Monsalve Editores.

Carbonell, G. 1990. Centros históricos de América Latina. In *Centros Históricos: América Latina,* ed. G. Carbonell. Bogotá: Colección SomoSur, pp. 10–11.

Carpentier, A. 1977. Prologue. In *Ecue Yamba O*. Havana: Arte y Literatura Editions, p. 11.

Carrión, F. M. 1992. Quito: Una política urbana alternativa. *Medio ambiente y urbanización.* 9, no. 38 (Buenos Aires, Instituto Internacional de Medio Ambiente y Desarrollo [ILLED], América Latina) (March): 55–70.

Carta internacional sobre la conservación y la restauración de monumentos y sitios. 1964. Issued by the Congreso Internacional de Arquitectura y Técnicos de Monumentos Históricos, held in Venice in 1964. Published in *Summa*, no. 77 (Buenos Aires): separate appendix.

Castellanos, A. 1971. Historia del desarrollo edilicio y urbanístico de Montevideo. Montevideo: Biblioteca Artigas.

CCC (Cámara de Comercio de Cartagena). 1999a. Las cien empresas más grandes de Cartagena. Cartagena: Cámara de Comercio de Cartagena. Mimeo.

———. 1999b. Ultimo Estudio Económico: Política de fomento empresarial y estrategias de generación de empleo en Cartagena de Indias. PowerPoint file. Cartagena: Cámara de Comercio de Cartagena. Mimeo.

———. 2000. *Estadísticas básicas de Cartagena, 1998–1999.* Cartagena: Cámara de Comercio de Cartagena.

CED (Centro de Estudios del Desarrollo) 1990. *Santiago: Dos Ciudades. Análisis de la estructura socio-económica-espacial del Gran Santiago.* Santiago: CED.

Clairmonte, F., and J. J. Cavanaugh. 1981. *The World in Their Web: Dynamics of Textile Multinationals.* London: Zed Press.

Clark, D. 1996. *Urban World/Global City.* London: Routledge.

Codrescu, A. 1999. *Ay, Cuba! A Socio-erotic Journey.* New York: St. Martin's Press.

Collado, R., S. Mauri, and M. Coipel. 1996. Revitalización urbana, desarrollo social y participación: La experiencia en el barrio San Isidro. In *Participación social: Desarrollo urbano y comunitario,* ed. R. Dávalos and A. Vázquez. Havana: Universidad de La Habana, pp. 106–18.

Conas. 1995. *Foreign Investment Act of Cuba.* Havana: Conas.

Conner, N. C. 1999. El Paseo del Río de San Francisco: Urban development and social justice in Puebla, Mexico. *Social Justice* 26:156–73.

———. 2000. Espacio e historia hegemónica del Puebla de los Angeles. *Bajo el Volcán: Revista Semestral de Ciencias Sociales* 2:45–66.

———. 2001a. Entre el aseo y la máquina: Ganando la vida en un mundo de transición. Paper presented at meeting of the Latin American Studies Association, Washington, D.C., September 6–8, 2001.

———. 2001b. Hacer cultura, hacer lugar: La lucha para el espacio social en el barrio de Analco, Puebla. In *Ciudad, Patrimonio y Gestión,* ed. M. Viladevalli I. Guasch. Puebla: Benemérita Universidad Autónoma de Puebla, Dirección de Fomento Editorial, Gobierno del Estado, Secretaría de Cultura, pp. 179–93.

Control Urbano. 2000. Unpublished archival data gathered by author. Cartagena Planning Office.

Cornebise, M. W. 2003. The Social Construction of Tourism in Cuba: A Geographic Analysis on the Representations of Gender and Race during the Special Period. PhD Diss., presented for the Doctor of Philosophy Degree, Department of Geography, University of Tennessee, Knoxville, April 2003. Preliminary draft.

Corporación Barrio La Candelaria. 1989. *Barrio La Candelaria.* Bogotá: Corporación Barrio La Candelaria.

Cosgrove, D. 1985. *Social Formation and Symbolic Landscape.* London: Croom Helm.

———. 1987. New directions in cultural geography. *Area* 19:95–101.

Covo, J. 1996. *La casa colonial cartagenera.* Bogotá: El Ancora Editores.

Cox, K. 1997. *Spaces of Globalization.* New York: Guilford.

Coyula, M. 2002. City, tourism, and preservation: The Old Havana way. *ReVista: Harvard Review of Latin America* (Winter): 66–69.

Crain, J. 1994. *Historic Architecture in the Caribbean Islands.* Gainesville: University Press of Florida.

Daniels, S., and D. Cosgrove. 1988. Introduction: Iconography and landscape. In *The Iconography of Landscape,* ed. D. Cosgrove and S. Daniels. Cambridge: Cambridge University Press, pp. 1–10.

Dávalos, R., and A. Vázquez, eds. 1996. *Participación social: Desarrollo urbano y comunitario.* Havana: Universidad de La Habana.

Díaz, R., and R. Paniagua. 1993. *Getsemaní: Historia, patrimonio y bienestar social en Cartagena*. Cartagena: COREDUCAR (Educational Development and Training Corporation), Colección Barrio Ciudad no. 1.

——. 1994a. *San Diego: Historia, patrimonio y gentrificación en Cartagena*. Cartagena: COREDUCAR (Educational Development and Training Corporation), Colección Barrio Ciudad no. 2.

——. 1994b. *Cartagena popular: Aproximación al análisis socio-cultural*. Cartagena: COREDUCAR (Educational Development and Training Corporation), Colección Barrio Ciudad no. 3.

Díaz-Briquets, S., and J. Pérez-López. 2000. *Conquering Nature: The Environmental Legacy of Socialism in Cuba*. Pittsburgh: University of Pittsburgh Press.

Dicken, P. 2003. *Global Shift*. 4th ed. New York: Guilford.

Doebele, W. A. 1997. Land use and taxation issues in developing countries. In *Land Use and Taxation*, ed. H. J. Brown. Cambridge, Mass.: Lincoln Institute of Land Policy, pp. 57–70.

Donald, J., and A. Rattansi, eds. 1992. *"Race," Culture, and Difference*. London: Sage/Open University.

Douglas, M., and B. Isherwood. 1979. *The World of Goods*. New York: Basic Books.

Duany, A., E. Plater-Zyberk, and J. Speck. 2000. *Suburban Nation: The Rise of Sprawl and the Decline of the American Dream*. New York: North Point Press.

Dyck, R. 1998. Integrated planning and sustainability theory for local benefit. *Local Environments* 3:27–41.

Early, J. 1994. *The Colonial Architecture of Mexico*. Albuquerque: University of New Mexico Press.

ECH (Empresa del Centro Histórico). 1998. Empresa del Centro Histórico. Quito: ECH, photocopy.

Echeverría, M. 2003. La fuga imprevisible de Macholo. *Escambray: Organo Oficial del Comité Provincial del Partido* (ISSN 9664-1277) (provincial, weekly newspaper). Sancti Spiritus, Cuba, June 14, p. 7.

Eckstein, S. 1977. The debourgeoisement of Cuban cities. In *Cuban Communism*, ed. I. L. Horowitz. New Brunswick, N.J.: Transaction Books, pp. 443–74.

Ecuador's switch to the U.S. dollar is in full swing. Associated Press, April 27, 2000 (http://www.rose-hulman.edu/~Edelacova/ecuador/dollar-swing.htm) (accessed December 2003).

Edwards, M. 1999. *Future Positive: International Co-operation in the Twenty-first Century*. London: Earthscan Publications.

El Salvador will bank on dollars 1/1/01. Associated Press, December 30, 2000.

Elinson, H. 1999. Cuba's Jineteros: Youth culture and revolutionary ideology. *Cuba Briefing Papers Series* no. 20. Washington, D.C.: Center for Latin American Studies, Georgetown University.

Escobar, A., and S. Alvarez. 1992. Theoretical and political horizons of change and contemporary Latin American social movements. In *The Making of Social Movements in Latin America*. Boulder, Colo.: Westview, pp. 316–29.

Ewen, S. 1988. *All Consuming Images: the Politics of Style in Contemporary Culture.* New York: Basic Books.

Fernández, M. A. 1994. Ecuador. In *Latin American Urbanization: Historical Profiles of Major Cities,* ed. G. M. Greenfield. Greenfield, Conn.: Greenwood Press, pp. 125–251.

Finch, M. 1981. *The Political Economy of Uruguay Sine 1870.* London: Macmillan.

FLACSO (Facultad Latinoamericana de Ciencias Sociales). 2001. Special issue "La nueva segregación urbana." *Perfiles Latinoamericanos* (Mexico City: FLACSO Sede Mexico) 10 (19).

Ford, L., and E. Griffin. 1980. A model of Latin American city structure. *Geographical Review* 37:397–422.

Foster, D. W. 1993. Popular culture: The roots of literary tradition. In *Imagination, Emblems, and Expressions: Essays on Latin American, Caribbean, and Continental Culture and Identity,* ed. H. Ryan-Ranson. Bowling Green, Ohio: Bowling Green State University Popular Press, pp. 3–28.

———. 1998. *Buenos Aires: Perspectives on the City and Cultural Production.* Gainesville: University Press of Florida.

Franco, J. 1999. *Critical Passions: Selected Essays.* Durham, N.C.: Duke University Press.

Frangialli, F. 2002. Understanding tourism: Development and beyond. *ReVista: Harvard Review of Latin America* (Winter): 2.

Fraser, V. 1990. *The Architecture of Conquest.* New York: Cambridge University Press.

———. 2000. *Building the New World: Studies in the Modern Architecture of Latin America, 1930–1965.* New York and London: Verso.

Gade, D. 1974. The Latin American central plaza as functional space. *Proceedings of the Conference of Latinamericanist Geographers* 5:16–23.

Gall, C. 2003. Tackling a tall order: The Bamiyan Buddha. *New York Times,* April 23, p. 13 (a special section: Museums).

Garson, B. 2001. *Money Makes the World Go Around: One Investor Tracks Her Cash through the Global Economy, from Brooklyn to Bangkok and Back.* New York: Viking.

Gilbert, A. 1994. *In Search of a Home: Rental and Shared Housing in Latin America.* Tucson and London: University of Arizona Press.

Girourard, M. 1985. *Cities and People: A Social and Architectural History.* London and New Haven, Conn.: Yale University Press.

Glancey, J. 1993. Architecture Page: Walls came tumbling down. *Independent* (London), October 20.

González, J. 1995. Análisis de un sector de los barrios de Analco, La Luz y El Alto de la ciudad de Puebla. In *Patrimonio Cultural: Estudios y Documento.* Puebla: Benemérita Universidad Autónoma de Puebla, Instituto de Ciencias Sociales y Humanidades, pp. 40–42.

Goodheart, A. 2003. In Richmond, a museum for the big leagues. *New York Times,* April 23, p. 8 (a special section: Museums).

Graham, B., G. J. Ashworth, and J. E. Turnbridge. 2000. *A Geography of Heritage: Power Culture and Economy.* London: Arnold.

Greenfield, G. M. 1994. Colombia. In *Latin American Urbanization: Historical Profiles of Major Cities,* ed. G. M. Greenfield. Greenfield, Conn.: Greenwood Press, pp. 134–58.

Grogg, P. 1999. Ciudades de America Latina: Habana Vieja, una ciudad para vivir mejor. August 2, InterPress Service, Third World News Agency, Montevideo, Uruguay.

Guerrero, G. 2000. La crisis del sistema financiero colombiano. In *Síntesis 2000: Anuario Social, Político y Económico de Colombia.* Bogotá: TM Editores, pp. 127–36.

Guillén, G. 2001. Ecuador busca apoyo contra el Plan Colombia. *El Nuevo Herald,* February 24.

Guillén Martínez, F. 1958. *The Tower and the Town Square: An Essay on Interpreting America.* Madrid: Ediciones Cultura Hispánica.

Gunn, G. 1995. Cuba's NGOs: Government puppets or seeds of a civil society? *Cuba Briefing Papers Series* no. 7. Washington, D.C.: Center for Latin American Studies, Georgetown University.

Gutiérrez, A. n.d. *Trinidad* (ISBN 959-7064-02-2). Trinidad, pamphlet.

Gutiérrez, O., and N. Gancedo. 2002. Tourism development: Locomotive for the Cuban economy. *ReVista: Harvard Review of Latin America* (Winter): 76–78.

Gutiérrez, R., ed. 1990. *Centros Históricos: América Latina.* Bogotá: Colección SomoSur.

Gutman, M. 1992. Presentación. *Medio ambiente y urbanización* 38 (March): 1–2.

Gwynne, R. 1986. *Urbanisation and Industrialisation in Latin America.* Baltimore and London: Johns Hopkins University Press.

Habaguanex, S.A. 2000. (Sociedad Anónima) (http://habaguanex.com), April (accessed December 2003).

Haddock, N. 2002. The legacy of human rights: Touring Chile's past. *ReVista: Harvard Review of Latin America* (Winter): 58–59.

Hall, S. 1995. New cultures for old. In *A Place in the World? Place, Cultures and Globalization,* ed. D. Massey and P. Jess. Oxford: Open University/Oxford University Press, pp. 175–214.

——. 1997. The work of representation. In *Representation: Cultural Representations and Signifying Practices,* ed. S. Hall. London: Sage, pp. 13–74.

Hamberg J., 1994. The dynamics of Cuban housing policy. PhD diss., Columbia University.

——. 1998. Revolutionary Cuba's spatial policies: Successes and challenges. Paper presented at the meeting of the Latin American Studies Association, Chicago, Palmer House Hilton Hotel, September 24–26, 1998.

Hannum, A. B. 2002. Tricks of the trade: Sex tourism in Latin America. *ReVista: Harvard Review of Latin America* (Winter): 60–61.

Hansen, A. T. 1934. The ecology of a Latin American city. In *Race and Culture Contacts,* ed. E. B. Reuter. New York: McGraw Hill, pp. 124–42.

Hardoy, J. E. 1983. The inhabitants of historical centres. *Habitat International* 7:151–62.

———. 1992. Theory and practice of urban planning in Europe, 1850–1930. In *Rethinking the Latin American City,* ed. R. Morse and J. E. Hardoy. Baltimore and London: Johns Hopkins University Press, pp. 20–49.

Hardoy, J. E., and M. Gutman. 1992. *Impacto de la urbanización de Iberoamérica: Tendencias y perspectivas.* Madrid: Mapfre.

Harris, M. 2001. How one woman followed the money. *Business Week,* March 5, p. 22.

Hartshorne, R. 1939. *The Nature of Geography.* Lancaster, Penn.: Association of American Geographers.

Harvey, D. 1985. *The Urbanization of Capital.* Baltimore and London: Johns Hopkins University Press.

———. 1996. *Justice, Nature, and the Geography of Difference.* London: Blackwell.

Herzog, L. A. 1999. *From Aztec to High Tech: Architecture and Landscape across the Mexico–United States Border.* Baltimore: Johns Hopkins University Press.

Hewison, R. 1987. *The Heritage Industry: Britain in a Climate of Decline.* London: Methuen.

Hitchcock, H. R. 1955. *Latin American Architecture since 1945.* New York: Museum of Modern Art.

Hobsbawm, E. J. 1990. *Nations and Nationalism since 1789: Programme, Myth, Reality.* Cambridge: Cambridge University Press.

Holcomb, H. B., and R. Beauregard. 1982. *Urban Revitalization.* Washington, D.C.: Association of American Geographers.

Horowitz, I. L., and J. Suchlicki. 2003. *Cuban Communism: 1959–2003.* New Brunswick, N.J.: Transaction.

IPS (InterPress Third World News Agency). 1999. Cuba: Disminuirá construcción de viviendas. Report (http://www.ips.org) (accessed February 23).

Irarrázaval, I., and J. L. Scarpaci. 1994. Decentralizing a centralized state: Local government finances in Chile within the Latin American context. *Public Budgeting and Finance* 14 (4): 120–36.

Irragori, R. V. 1980. *Análisis del ambulantismo y sus posibles soluciones.* Puebla: Ayuntamiento de Puebla.

Iyer, P. 2000. Bali: On Prospero's Isle/The Philippines/Born in the USA. In *The Globalization Reader,* ed. F. Lechner and J. Boli. London: Blackwell, pp. 111–17.

Jackson, J. B. 1984. *Discovering the Vernacular Landscape.* New Haven, Conn.: Yale University Press.

Jafari, J. 2002. Retracing and mapping: Tourism's landscape of knowledge. *ReVista: Harvard Review of Latin America* (Winter): 12–15.

Jaramillo, C. F. 2000. ¿Para dónde va la economía colombiana? Presentation delivered by the Technical Vice Minister of Treasury and Public Credit, Cartagena, June 14, 2000. Mimeo of PowerPoint presentation.

Johnston, R., D. Gregory, and D. M. Smith. 1994. *The Dictionary of Human Geography.* 3rd ed. Oxford: Blackwell.

Johnston, R., P. Taylor, and M. Watts, eds. 1995. *Geographies of Global Change: Remapping the World in the late Twentieth Century.* Boston: Blackwell.

Jones, G. A. 1994. The Latin American city as contested space. *Bulletin of Latin American Research* 13:1–12.

———. 2001. Under De-construction: Contesting modernity and identity in the Historic centres of Latin America. Paper presented at the Latin American Studies Association meeting, September 4, Washington, D.C.

Jones, G. A., and R. D. F. Bromley. 1999. Investing in conservation: The historic center in Latin America. *Built Environment* 25:196–210.

Jones, G. A., and A. Varley. 1994. The contest for the city centre: Street traders versus buildings. *Bulletin of Latin American Research* 13:27–44.

———. 1999a. Conservation and gentrification in the developing world: Recapturing the city center. *Environment and Planning A* 31:1547–66.

———. 1999b. The reconquest of the historic centre: Urban conservation and gentrification in Puebla, Mexico. *Environment and Planning A* 31:1547–1566.

Jones, G. A., and P. M. Ward, eds. 1994. *Methodology for Land and Housing Market Analysis.* London: University College London Press.

Jrade, C. L. 1998. *Modernismo, Modernity, and the Development of Spanish American Literature.* Austin: University of Texas Press.

King, A. 1990. Architecture, capital, and the globalization of culture. *Theory, Culture, and Society* 7:397–411.

Kirn, W. 2001. *Up in the Air.* New York: Doubleday.

Klak, T. 1998. *Globalization and Neoliberalism: The Caribbean context.* Lanham, Md.: Rowman and Littlefield.

Klosterman, R. E. 1990. *Community Analysis and Planning Technology.* Savage, Md.: Rowman and Littlefield.

Kobayashi, A. 1989. A critique of dialectical landscape. In *Remaking Human Geography,* ed. A. Kobayashi and S. Mackenzie. Boston: Unwin and Hyman, pp. 164–83.

Korten, D. C. 1995. *When Corporations Rule the World.* West Hartford, Conn.: Kumarian Press/Berret-Koehler.

Kostof, S. 1991. *The City Shaped.* Boston: Little, Brown and Company.

Kunstler, J. H. 1996. *Home from Nowhere.* New York: Simon and Schuster/Touchstone Books.

Lash, S., and J. Urry. 1994. *Economies of Signs and Space.* London: Sage.

Lavoie, D., and H. O'Neill. 1999. Family stumbled along path of blind faith. Life in Ecuador was poor, simple, and hard. But the streets of Bridgeport, CT proved harder. Associated Press. *Roanoke Times,* Sunday, May 30, p. A-14.

Leal, E. 1996. *Viaje en la memoria.* Havana: Oficina del Historiador de la Ciudad.

———. 1999. Opening remarks, plenary session, Fourth International Conference on Cultural Heritage and Historic Preservation, Ministry of Culture, National Center for Restoration, Conservation, and Museum Science (CENCRM), October 12. Spanish language presentation on audiocassette and transcribed by and available from the author.

———. 2002. Plenary address delivered to the international meeting of the Association of Collegiate Schools of Architecture, Habana Vieja, Convento de San Francisco, Salón Blanco, June 23.

Le Corbusier. 1925. *Buenos Aires*. Buenos Aires: Hachette.

Lemaitre, E. 1994. *A Brief History of Cartagena*. Medellín: Editorial Colina.

Lerner, F. J., and J. Boli. 2004. *The Globalization Reader*. Malden, Mass.: Blackwell Publishing.

Ley, D. 1996. *The New Middle Class and the Remaking of the Central City*. Oxford and New York: Oxford University Press.

Lezama, L. 1974. *Paradiso*. Trans. G. Rabassa. New York: Farrar, Strass, and Giroux.

Lindstrom, N. 1998. *The Social Conscience of Latin American Writing*. Austin: University of Texas Press.

Llanes L. 1993. 1898–1921. *Apuntes para una historia sobre los constructores cubanos*. Havana: Editorial Letras Cubanas.

———. 2001. *The Houses of Old Cuba*. New York: Thames and Hudson.

London, B. 1982. The social ecology of Latin American cities: Recent evidence. In *Urban Patterns: Studies in Human Ecology*, ed. G. Theoderson, rev. ed. University Park: Pennsylvania State University Press, pp. 374–78.

Loomis, J. A. 1999. *Revolution of Forms: Cuba's Forgotten Art Schools*. New York: Princeton Architectural Press.

Losch, A. 1954. *The Economics of Location*. New Haven, Conn.: Yale University Press.

Low, S. M. 2000. *On the Plaza: The Politics of Public Space and Culture*. Austin: University of Texas Press.

Lowell, B. L., and R. O. de la Garza. 2000. *The Developmental Role of Remittances in U.S. Latino Communities and in Latin American Countries: A Final Report*. Washington, D.C.: Inter-American Dialogue and Tomás Rivera Policy Institute.

Lowenthal, D. 1985. *The Past Is a Foreign Country*. Cambridge: Cambridge University Press.

Lynch, M. 2003. Latin officials' conference told of Bogotá turnaround. *Miami Herald,* June 26, p. 5-B.

Machado, O. 1976. La Habana: DESA [Desarrollo Económico y Social]. La industrialización de la construcción de la vivienda: El sistema IMS [Institute for Material Testing] en Cuba. Mimeo.

Mahieux, V. 2002. Rio de Janeiro's favela tourism. *ReVista: Harvard Review of Latin America* (Winter): 44–45.

Mander, J., and E. Goldsmith. 1996. *The Case against the Global Economy: And for a Turn toward the Local*. San Francisco: Sierra Club Books.

Marín, F. 1945. *Historia de Trinidad*. Havana: Jesús Montero.

Marín, V. 2002. Cuba: The preservation of architecture as seen as saving a legacy for humanity. In *Havana: Patrimony, Patience, and Progress: Architecture, Urban Planning, and Historic Preservation in Havana, Cuba*. New York: New School University, Vera List Center for Art and Politics at the New School and Heritage Trails Worldwide, pp. 27–34.

Marrero, L. 1983. *Cuba: Economía y sociedad.* Vol. 9. Madrid: Editorial Playor.

McGirk, T. 2002. Does Buddha sleep here? *Time,* August 5, p. 18.

Merriam, S. B. 1998. *Qualitative Research and Case Study Applications in Education.* San Francisco: Jossey-Bass.

Millán, G. M. 1995. *La modernización sistémica: La desconcentración comercial de la Ciudad de Puebla.* Puebla: Facultad de Arquitectura, Unidad de Investigación y Estudios de Posgrado, Dirección General de Fomento Editorial, Benemérita Universidad Autónoma de Puebla.

Miller, B. A. 2000. *Geography and Social Movements: Comparing Antinuclear Activism in the Boston Area.* Minneapolis: University of Minnesota Press.

Miller, T. 2001. *The Panama Hat Trail.* 2nd ed. Washington, D.C.: National Geographic.

Miranda, F. 2000. Urbanismo: Escollos para el Plan de Ordenamiento Territorial. Ciudades del 2010. *Lecturas Dominicales,* June 25, 2000 (Cartagena).

Mishra, 2000. Globalization and the Welfare State. City: Cheltenham, England: Edward Elgar.

Mitchell, W. J. T. 1994. Imperial landscape. In *Landscape and Power,* ed. W. J. T. Mitchell. Chicago: University of Chicago Press, pp. 5–34.

Moreno Fraginals, M. 1976. *The Sugar Mill: The Socio-economic Complex of Sugar in Cuba, 1760–1860.* New York and London: Monthly Review Press.

Morse, R. 1992. Cities as people. In *Rethinking the Latin American City,* ed. R. Morse and J. E. Hardoy. Washington, D.C.: Woodrow Wilson Center, pp. 3–19.

Morton, W. B. 1992. Forging new values in uncommon times. In *Past Meets Future,* ed. A. J. Lee. Washington, D.C.: Preservation Press, pp. 40–41.

Moya, J. 1998. *Cousins and Strangers: Spanish Immigrants in Buenos Aires, 1850–1930.* Berkeley and London: University of California Press.

Muir, R. 1999. *Approaches to Landscape.* London: Macmillan.

Netzer, D. 1997. The centralization and decentralization of government and taxation. In *Land Use and Taxation,* ed. H. James Brown. Cambridge, Mass.: Lincoln Institute of Land Policy, pp. 43–56.

Nickel, A. 1990. El casco histórico de La Habana: La situación de vivienda y los conceptos de renovación urbana en La Habana. *Revista Geográfica* 112:75–90.

Noin, D., and P. White. 1997. *Paris.* London and New York: John Wiley and Sons.

Núñez Jiménez, A., Zerquera, and F. de Lara. 1986. *Trinidad de Cuba: Monumento nacional.* Havana: Instituto Nacional de Turismo.

O'Brien, R. 1992. *Global Financial Integration: The End of Geography.* London: Royal Institute of International Affairs.

Olson, M. 1965. *The Logic of Collective Action.* Cambridge, Mass.: Harvard University Press.

Oñate, N., B. Brito, and R. Oliveras. 1996. Habana hace el 2000: Un enfoque metodológico para la obtención de la estrategia de desarrollo urbano. *Cuba: Investigación Económica* 4 (October–December): 104–26.

Open for business: While Marc Rich was fugitive, firm dealt with pariah nations. *Wall Street Journal,* February 23, 2001, pp. A-1, A-6.

Palabras del presidente Ernesto Zedillo, durante la ceremonia en la que inauguró el Centro de Convenciones Puebla "William O. Jenkins" (http://zedillo.presidencia.gob .mx/pages/disc/ene99/06ene99-2.html) (accessed December 2003).

Palomeque, S. 1990. *Cuenca en el Siglo XIX.* Quito: Abya-Yala.

Park, R., D. McKenzie, and R. Burgess. 1967. *The City.* Chicago: University of Chicago Press.

Pendle, G. 1950. *Uruguay.* London: Oxford University Press.

———. 1978. *A History of Latin America.* New York: Penguin.

Pérez, L. 2001. *Winds of Change: Hurricanes and the Transformation of Nineteenth-Century Cuba.* Chapel Hill: University of North Carolina Press.

Pérez-López, J. 1995. *Cuba's Second Economy.* New Brunswick, N.J.: Transaction Books.

Perry, R. D. 1997. *Blue Lakes and Silver Cities: The Colonial Arts and Architecture of West Mexico.* Santa Barbara: Espadaña Press.

Peters, P., and J. L. Scarpaci. 1998. *Five Years of Small-Scale Capitalism in Cuba.* Arlington, Va.: Alexis de Tocqueville Institute.

Phongpaichit, P., S. Piriyarangsan, and N. Treerat. 1998. *Guns, Girls, Gambling, Ganja: Thailand's Illegal Economy and Public Policy.* Chiang Mai, Thailand: Silkworm Books.

PNUD (Programa de las Naciones Unidas para el Desarrollo)/UNESCO. 1977. Documento final del "Coloquio de Quito." Quito: PNUD/UNESCO, Proyecto Regional de Patrimonio Cultural. Mimeo.

Portes, A., C. Dore-Cabral, and P. Landolt, eds. 1997. *The Urban Caribbean: Transition to the New Global Economy.* Baltimore and London: Johns Hopkins University Press.

Portes, A., and J. Irigoshin. 1994. The party of the grassroots: A comparative analysis of urban political participation in the Caribbean basin. *International Journal of Urban and Regional Research* 18:491–509.

Protess, D. L., F. L. Cook, J. C. Doppelt, J. S. Ettema, M. T. Gordon, D. R. Leff, and P. Miller. 1991. *The Journalism of Outrage: Investigative Reporting and Agenda Building in America.* New York: Guilford Press.

Quantrill, M. 2000. *Latin American Architecture: Six Voices.* College Station: Texas A&M University Press, Center for the Advancement for the Studies in Architecture (CASA).

Radcliffe, S. A. 2000. Civil society, social difference, and politics: Issues of identity and representation. In *Latin America Transformed: Globalization and Modernity,* ed. R. Gwynne and C. Kay. Cambridge: Cambridge University Press, pp. 203–24.

Radu, M. 1998. Cuba's transition: Institutional lessons from Eastern Europe. In *Cuban Communism,* ed. I. L. Horowitz and J. Suchlicki. 9th ed. New Brunswick and London: Transaction Publishers, pp. 697–718.

Rial Roade, J., and J. Klaczko. 1981. *Uruguay: El país urbano*. Montevideo: Ediciones de la Banda Oriental.

Rigau J. 1994. No longer islands: Dissemination of architecture ideas in the Hispanic Caribbean, 1890–1930. *Journal of Decorative and Propaganda Arts* 20:237–25.

Robinson, M., N. Evans, P. Long, R. Sharpley, and J. Swarbrooke 2000. *Tourism and Heritage Relationships: Global, National, and Local Perspectives*. Sunderland, England: Teleport, Doxford International.

Rodó, J. 1988 [1900]. *Ariél*. Trans. M. S. Peden. Foreword by J. W. Sumington. Prologue by C. Fuentes. Austin: University of Texas Press.

Rodríguez, E. L. 2000. *The Havana Guide: Modern Architecture 1925–1965*. New York: Princeton Architectural Press.

Rohter R., 1995. In Cuba, Army takes on party jobs, and may be only thing that works. *New York Times*, June 8, p. A-12.

Rojas, E. 1999. *Old Cities, New Assets*. Washington, D.C.: Inter-American Development Bank.

Rojek, C., and J. Urry, eds. 1997. *Touring Cultures*. London: Routledge.

Rose, G. 1992. Geography as a science of observation: The landscape, the gaze, and masculinity. In *Nature and Science: Essays in the History of Geographical Knowledge*. ed. F. Driver and G. Rose. Edinburgh: Institute of British Geographers Historical Geography Research Series no. 28, pp. 8–18.

———. 2001. *Visual Methodologies*. London: Sage.

Rostow, W. 1961. *The Stages of Modernization*. Cambridge, Mass.: Harvard University Press.

Roth, G. 1968. Personal rulership, patrimonialism, and empire-building in the New States. *World Politics* 20:194–206.

Rottin, L. 1949. *Buenos Aires: Ciudad, Patria, Mundo*. Buenos Aires: Talleres Artes Gráficas Miguel Briuolo.

Sánchez, R. 1991. *Puebla: Antología de una ciudad: Crónica y cartografía, 1531–1992*. Puebla: Ayuntamiento de Municipio de Puebla.

Sanz de Santamaría, C. 1989. Reminiscencias del Barrio La Candelaria. In *Corporación Barrio La Candelaria*. Bogotá: Corporación Barrio La Candelaria, pp. 3–11.

Sargent, C. 1994. Uruguay. In *Latin American Urbanization: Historical Profiles of Major Cities*, ed. G. M. Greenfield. Greenfield, Conn.: Greenwood Press, pp. 468–85.

Sassen, S. 1999. The state and the new geography of power. In *Communication, Citizenship, and Social Policy: Rethinking the Limits of the Welfare State*, ed. G. M. Greenfield. Lanham, Md.: Rowman and Littlefield, pp. 17–32.

Sassen, S, and P. Marcotullio. Forthcoming. In UNESCO *Encyclopedia of Life Support Systems: Human Settlements and Sustainability*. New York and London: United Nations Press.

Scantelbury, M. G. 2003. Review of "Tourism and Heritage Relationships." *Annals of Tourism Research* 30:268–69.

Scarpaci, J. L. 1990. Medical care, welfare state, and deindustrialization in the Southern Cone. *Environment and Planning D: Society and Space* 8:191–209.

———. 1991. Primary care decentralization in the Southern Cone: Shantytown health care as urban social movement. *Annals of the Association of American Geographers* 81:103–26.

———. 1993 On the Validity of language: Speaking, knowing, and understanding in medical geography. *Social Science and Medicine* 37:719–24.

———. 1998. The changing face of Cuban socialism: Tourism and planning in the post-socialist era. In CLAG *Yearbook,* ed. D. Keeling and J. Wiley. Austin: University of Texas Press, pp. 87–110.

———. 2000a. Heritage, Property Taxes, and Revitalization: Land Valuation in Historic Cartagena de Indias. Prepared for the Lincoln Institute for Land Policy, Inc., July.

———. 2000b. On the transformation of socialist cities. *Urban Geography* 21:659–69.

———. 2000c. Reshaping *Habana Vieja*: Revitalization, historic preservation, and restructuring in the socialist city. *Urban Geography* 21:724–44.

———. 2001, writer and producer. *Urban Design and Planning in Havana, Cuba: An Historical Perspective.* VHS (39 minutes). Department of Geography, College of Natural Resources, Virginia Tech.

———. 2003. Architecture, design, and planning: Recent scholarship on modernity and public spaces in Latin America. *Latin American Research Review* 38:236–50.

Scarpaci, J. L., and Frazier, L. J. 1993. State terror: Ideology, protest, and the gendering of landscapes. *Progress in Human Geography* 17:1–21.

Scarpaci, J. L., A. Gaete, and R. Infante. 1988. Planning residential segregation: The case of Chile. *Urban Geography* 9:19–36.

Scarpaci J. L., and A. Z. Hall. 1995. Cycling in Havana: "Green" transportation by policy default. *Sustainable Transport* (Institute for Transportation Policy and Sustainable Development, New York) (Summer): 4–6.

Scarpaci, J. L., R. Segre, and M. Coyula. 2002. *Havana: Two Faces of the Antillean Metropolis.* Chapel Hill: University of North Carolina Press.

Schlüter, R. G. 2000. The immigrants' heritage in South America: Food and culture as a new sustainable tourism product. *ReVista: Harvard Review of Latin America* (Winter): 46–48.

Schnore, L. F. 1965. On the spatial structure of cities in the two Americas. In *The Study of Urbanization,* ed. P. M. Hauser and L. F. Schnore. New York: Wiley, pp. 347–98.

Schumacher, E. F. 1973. *Small Is Beautiful: A Study of Economics as if People Mattered.* London: Blond and Brigg.

Schwartz, R., 1997. *Pleasure Island: Tourism and Temptation in Cuba.* Lincoln and London: University of Nebraska Press.

Scobie, J. 1974. *Buenos Aires: Plaza to Suburb, 1870–1910.* New York: Oxford University Press.

Segre, R. 1981. *Latin America in Its Architecture.* New York: Holmes and Meier.

———. 1994. Preludio a la modernidad: Convergencias y divergencias en el contexto caribeño (1900–1950). In *Arquitectura neocolonial: América Latina, Caribe, Estados Unidos, memorial,* ed. A. Amaral. San Pablo, Mexico: Fondo de Cultura Económica, pp. 95–107.

———. 1995. *La Plaza de Armas de La Habana: Sinfonía urbana inconclusa.* Havana: Editorial Arte y Literatura.

———. 1999. *América Latina fin de milenio: Raíces Y perspectivas de su arquitectura.* Havana: Editorial Arte y Literatura.

Segre, R., and S. Baroni. 1998. Cuba y La Habana: Historia, población y territorio. *Ciudad y territorio* (Buenos Aires) 30 (116): 351–79.

Serageldin, I., E. Shluger, and J. Martin-Brown. 2001. *Historic Cities and Sacred Sites.* Washington, D.C.: World Bank.

Shanks, C. 2002. Nine quandaries of tourism: Artificial authenticity and beyond. *ReVista: Harvard Review of Latin America* (Winter): 16–19.

Smith, M., and J. R. Feagin. 1987. *The Capitalist City.* Oxford and New York: Basil Blackwell.

Smith, N. 1979. Toward a theory of gentrification: A back-to-the-city movement by capital, not by people. *Journal of the American Planning Association* 45:538–48.

———. 1987. Of yuppies and housing: Gentrification, social restructuring, and the urban dream. *Environment and Planning D: Society and Space* 5:151–79.

Soubbotina, T. P. 2000. *Beyond Economic Growth: Meeting the Challenges of Global Development.* Washington, D.C.: World Bank.

Southworth, M., and E. Ben-Joseph. 1997. *Streets and the Shaping of Towns and Cities.* New York: McGraw Hill.

Stanislawski, D. 1950. The anatomy of eleven towns in Michoacán. *Latin American Studies X.* Austin: University of Texas Press, pp. 1–3, 40–48, 71–75.

———. 1956. The origin and spread of the grid-pattern town. *Geographical Review* 36:105–20.

Szlenyi, I. 1982. *Urban Inequities under State Socialism.* Oxford: Oxford University Press.

Téllez, G., and E. Moure. 1982. *Repertorio formal de arquitectura doméstica en Cartagena de Indias.* Bogotá: Corporación Nacional de Turismo.

Theobold, R. 1990. *Corruption, Development, and Underdevelopment.* Durham, N.C.: Duke University Press.

Theodorson, G. A. 1982. *Urban Patterns: Studies in Human Ecology.* University Park: Pennsylvania State University Press.

Trumball, C. 2001. Prostitution and sex tourism in Cuba. Paper presented at the Association for the Study of the Cuban Economy (ASCE), Miami, Fl., August 3.

Tung, A. 2001. *Preserving the World's Great Cities: The Destruction and Renewal of the Historic Metropolis.* New York: Clarkson Potter Publishers.

Turner, L., and J. Ash. 1975. *The Golden Hordes.* London: Constable.

UNESCO 1984. Convention Concerning the Protection of the World Cultural and Natural Heritage, World Heritage Committee, Eighth Ordinary Session, Buenos Aires,

Argentina October 29 to November 2, 1984, Report at the Rapporteur (http://www.unesco.org/whc/archive/repcom84.htm#285) (accessed December 2003).

Urry, J. 2002. *The Tourist Gaze,* 2nd ed. Thousand Oaks, Calif.: Sage Publications.

US/ICOMOS (United States/International Commission on Monuments and Sites). 2000. *Conservation and Tourism Development Plan for Cape Coast.* A design and planning workshop organized by US/ICOMOS and cosponsored by Conservation International Trust and the Ghana Heritage Conservation Trust. A project funded by the United States Agency for International Development (USAID). Washington, D.C.: US/ICOMOS.

Venegas, H. 1973. Apuntes sobre la decadencia trinitaria en el siglo XIX. *Islas* 46:214–23.

Vilagrasa J., and P. J. Larkham. 1995. Post-war redevelopment and conservation in Britain: Ideal and reality in the historic core of Worcester. *Planning Perspectives* 10:149–72.

Viñuales, G. 1990. Buenos Aires. In *Centros históricos: América Latina,* ed. G. Carboneil. Bogotá: Junta de Andalucía, Universidad de los Andes, pp. 256–71.

Violetta, B., and J. L. Scarpaci. 1999. Havana construction boom in old city. *Cuba-News,* December (Washington, D.C.): Target Research Group, p. 4.

Violich, F. 1944. *Cities of Latin America: Housing and Planning to the South.* New York: Rienhold.

Virilio, P. 1997. The overexposed city. In *Rethinking Architecture: A Reader in Cultural Theory,* ed. N. Leach. London: Routledge, pp. 289–300.

Waisman, M. 1994. Neocolonial y moderno: Falacias y realidades. In *Arquitectura neocolonial: América Latina, Caribe, Estados Unidos,* ed. A. Amaral, Mexico City: Fondo de Cultura Económica, pp. 277–86.

Ward, P. 1993. The Latin American inner city: Differences in degree or kind? *Environment and Planning A* 25:1131–60.

Waters, M. 2000. *Globalization.* London: Routledge.

Weil, C., and J. Scarpaci. 1992. *Health and Health Care in Latin America during the "Lost Decade."* Minneapolis: Prisma Institute, University of Minnesota.

Weiss, J. 1950. *Medio siglo de arquitectura cubana.* Havana: Universidad de La Habana.

———. 1978. *Technos coloniales cubanos.* Havana: Editorial Arte y Literatura.

Weymouth, L. 2000. Interview: Battling "the bad guys." *Newsweek,* February 14, p. 50.

Woolf, S., 1996. *Nationalism in Europe, 1815 to the Present: A Reader.* London: Routledge.

Yin, R. 2002. *Case Study Research: Design and Methods.* Newbury Park, Calif.: Sage.

Zanetti, O., and A. García. 1998. *Sugar and Railroads: A Cuban History, 1837–1959.* Chapel Hill: University of North Carolina Press.

Zhao H. 1995. The dual-structured land market in Shenzhen City, China. *Regional Development Studies* (Tokyo Institute of Technology) 1:17–29.

Index

accesorias, 195, *see also* tenement houses
advertising, 3; mass, 232
aesthetic, 236; visual, 102
airport, 212; of Montevideo, 115
Almendares River, 64; 78
Analco, 73, 77
Ancón Beach, 71, 208–210; Peninsula, 207, 226;
Andalusia, 17, 195
Angelópolis, 75
antiquity, 55, 56
apartment, 199–200
Appadurai, Arjun, 128
Arano, Mario, 93–94, 112
architect, 14,15, 40, 95, 145, 207, 213, 236
architecture, 8, 12, 33, 40, 123; and conquest, 39–40; blend, 212; colonial, 38, 98, 110, 114, 188; republican, 98; Spanish American, 39–40; vernacular, 21, 227; republican, 98
Argentina, 14, 86, 108, 125, 137
Art Deco, 15, 98
Art Nouveau, 35, 98
art, 8, 12, 88; African, 35
authenticity, 129, 190; defining, 96
automobile, 65, 122, 227–229
Aztecs, 41, 203
Azuay Province, 4, 5, 133, 136

Baghdad, looting of, 29
balcony, 12, 109, 103, 199

Bamiyan, Afghanistan, 29
Banco Hipotecario, 112–113
banking, 66, 132, 134, 182
barbacoas, 106
Baroque, 40, 98
Barranquilla, 78, 181
barrio, 18, 94, 99, 119, 220
Barrio Candelaria, 57–62; 229
baseball, 51, 53
Bastida, Roberto López, ch.7, n1
bay window, 171; types, ch.5, n3
Beaux Arts, 15, 91
bed-and-breakfast, 3, 117, Table 3.4; in Trinidad, 211
beef, 87, 88
belle époque, 91
Benetton, 236, Figure 6.4a
Benítez, Nancy, 208, 212, 214–215
best practices, 229–231
black marketeering, 181, 190, 190
blockade, *see also* embargo, 194
bodega, 67; *see also* mom-and-pop grocer, 100
Bogotá, 59, 123, 114, 181; name, ch.2, n3; road type, 58;
Bourbon reform, 69, 88, 95
bourgeoisie, European, 4
Brasília, 14, 16
Brazil, 14–15, 20, 125, 150; slave quarters in, 29
Bromley, Rosemary, 121
Brutalism, 15

Buenos Aires, 11, 15; Figure 2.1a; 86–88; buildings, 109–110

building, 27, 30, 41, 112, 118, 153, 209; attributes, 103; code 41; colonial, 195; good-condition, 111; government, 100–101, 113; height, 113–115, 222; historical, 80; permit, 151; residential, 27; material, 175; modern, 112, 114; office, 114

built environment, 8, 10, 22, 38, 94, 118, 190, 220, 221; alluring, 228; commodifying, 201; modern and traditional aspects of, 37; of Havana, 185

bulwark, 39, 63

Burnham, Daniel, 41

bus, 57, 164, 211–212; British, 91; electric, Figure 2.17b

cabildo, 32, 101

café, 55, 87, 100, 107

Calthorpe, Peter, 100

Calvary Square, 51, *see also* Tres Cruces

Camagüey, 71, 212, 216

Cañari, 81–82

Canary Islands, 88

Cancún, 182

candomblé, Table 8.1

capital, 23, 26, 132, 143; British, 91, 95, 220; cultural, 20, 235; international, 27; internationalization of, 186; transnational, 26; United States, 95

capitalism, 128; industrial, 3, 4, 232; global, 292; post-Fordist, 26; transition to, 16

caracoles, Table 3.4

Caribbean, 114, 185, 192; port, 148; coast 78; folklore, 203; heritage, 203; Sea, 45, 53–54, 71, 183, Figure 7.1; war-free and surf-zone, 170

Carnaval, 161

Carpentier, Alejo, 125

Carrasco, 112; 115, 222

Carta de Quito, 9, 96, 224–225

Cartagena, 11, 27, 35, 58, 63, 69, 77, 114, 116, 118, 139–140, 150, 229; and, real-estate advertisement, Figure 1.2; and money-launderers, 26; Bay, 78; brothel, 55; Chamber of Commerce, 181; defining heritage in, 181–182; Disneyfied, 183; neighborhoods, 45, 153–161; organic pattern, 45; private sector, 182; real-estate market, 151–153; traditional mom-and-pop retailing, 222

Carter, Jimmy, 50–51, 204

casa-almacén, 21, 187

casco antiguo, 117, 220; histórico, 220; ch.1, n1

Casilda (town), 70; Bay, 45

Castillo San Felipe de Barajas, 163

castle, 127, 234

cathedral, 21, 39, 89, 127, 234

Catholics, 39; burial sites for, 32

CBD (Central Business District), 12; Latin American, 182

CDR [Revolution Defense Committee], 197

ceiling, 106; high, Figure 8.1; heights, in tropics and highlands, 118

Central Business District (CBD), 12, 21, 229; *see also* CBD,

Centro Habana, 186, 222

centro histórico, 4, 8, 18, 23, 27, 41, 57, 91, 116, 117, 220; ch.1, n1; and disparity in building quality, 113; and municipal governments, 26; and nation state, 26; architectural writings, 97–98; change and population growth, 49; dignity of, 22; globalization, 26; in Quito, 109; landscape, 236; Latin American, 114; pedestrian-friendly, 100; regularities and anomalies, 115–117; residential composition, 21; sense of order, 45; urban geography, 32

Cerro, 89, Figure 2.23

Charles III (1759–1788), 69

charm, 100; Trinidad, 212

Chicago, 15, 41

church, 21, 32, 39, 40, 50, 56, 74, 100, 108, 144; steeple, 119

CIAM Congrès International d'Architecture Moderne (International Congress of Modern Architecture), 112, 119, 228–229

Cienfuegos, 70, 71

cities, Cuban, 118; layered in meaning, 35; Moorish, Figure 2.2

City Historian [Havana], 67, 139, 141, 188

City Restoration Office, 207, 212; budget, 214–215

city, edge, 84, 220; European, 27; Latin American, 81, 94, 228

cityscape, 10; beautifying, 66; look of, 118

Ciudad Amurallada, 77, 148

ciudad nueva, 89

Ciudad Vieja [Montevideo], 35, 88, 112, 113, 115; ghetto aspect, 222

ciudades universitarias, 14

civil society, 204, 236

class, 128, 184, 203; solidarity, 227

Clinton, Bill, 131

cocaine, 78, 148, 159

coding, 49, 98

collapse, of building, 188

Colombia, 125; and private historic preservation, 111; Caribbean coast of, 59; cash-strapped, 130

colonia, 75

colonnaded galleries, 10

column, 12, 103; load-bearing, 114; Figure 8.2

Committee for the Defense of the Revolution, 204

commodify, 205

community, and gentrification, 226–227; in Habana Vieja, 202; input, 227; participation, 176, 226; planned, 18; restructuring, 203; suburban, 41

condominium, 153, 200

conflict, 176, 208

Congrés International d'Architecture Moderne (CIAM), 40–43

Constitution, of Colombia in 1991, 166

content analysis, 144–145

convent, 21, 32, 101, 121

conventillos, 90, see also tenement houses

convention center, 75–76; in Puebla, 165

Coporación Barrio La Candelaria, 60–61

corruption, 66, 184

corsairs, 63, 69

Cortés, Hernán, 41, 68

Cosgrove, Denis, 17

Costanera, 115, 223

courtyard, 102, 127, 162, 196; see also patio, 196

coyote, 4, 133; defined, ch.4, n2

creolization, 124

crowding, 195, 200; see also overcrowding

cruise line, in Havana, 64

cruise ship, passengers, 192; terminal, 188; visited Cartagena, 164

cuarterías, see also tenement houses, 195

Cuba, 31, 125, 131; antiurbanism of, 184; centrally planned economy, ch.1, n2; civil society in, 204; hotel capacity in the Caribbean, 206; human rights of, 138; latecomer to conservation, 11; post-Soviet, 121; remittances from relatives, 136; Revolution, 23; socialist, 202

Cuban Americans, 205, 232

Cuenca, 4, 5, 81–85, 133, 136, 140; churches of, 85; experience with

globalization, 136; industry in, 84;
  marginalized, 83; population growth,
  82; twentieth-century, 84
cuentapropistas, 53, 194
cultural geography, 120; new, 33, 35;
cultural heritage, 14, 165, planning and
  paying for, 148–150
culture, 48–57; and class structure, 49;
  black, in Uruguay, 91–92; global consumer, 236; low, 230
Cuzco, 10, 43, 64

Dallas Morning News, ch.6, n11
dancing, 88, 107
Darwin, Charles, 86
de Velázquez, Diego, 45
debourgeoisement, 184
demolition, 112, 196, in Habana Vieja,
  Table 8.3
deregulation, 130
design, 12; Gothic, 40; issues, 169–176;
  neoclassical, 40, 89; Spanish, 72
development, 115; sustainable, 28, 216;
  uneven, 194
discotheque, 159, 236
disembedding, 127
Disney World, 18
Disneyfication, 203
displacement, 226
dollar, 190, 203; 215; 236; decriminalization, 194
dollarization of Latin America, 130–
  131; 137–138
doorway, 98, 115
Duany, Andres, 18, 100

Eastern Europe, 218, 219
Eclecticism, 15
economic development, 211, 220,
  236
ecotourism, 234
Ecuador, 78, 111, 133

El Arquitecto, 124
elderly, 50, 88
elite, 18; homes, 212; families, colonial
  Trinidad, 70; residences, 40
enforcement, land-use 9; zoning, 9
engineer, 40, 213
entertainment, as visually constructed,
  102–103
Escambray Mountains, 45, 206, 213
Europeans, 3, 146, 227
extramuros, 65

façade, 7, 56, 104, 111–113; quality of,
  102–103, 118; neocolonial, 224
FARC [Fuerzas Armadas Revolucionarias
  de Colombia], 165
field notes, 48–57
field research, 139–140
finance, 223–224
focus group, 37, 141–143, 146, 226
Ford [Company], 28; Larry, 100
foreign investment, , law, 190; sociological results of, 203
Foreign Ministry, in Cuba, ch.6, n10
foreigner, rent apartments, 200
fortress, 21, 39, 121
fountain, 10; Figure 5.6d; Italian marble
  200
Fraser, Valerie, 15;
freedom, 204–205
frigorificos, see also meatpacking houses,
  87
Ft. Lauderdale Sun-Sentinel, ch.6, n11

Gabo, 173; see also Gabiel García
  Marquez
gallery, 108, 127, 144
Gap, 236
García Márquez, Gabriel, 54, 55, 175,
  183; house, Figure 5.14a, Figure
  5.14b; lot, Figure 5.15a; *see also* Gabo
garrison, 39, 63, 88;

gentrification, 20, 96, 140, 186, 226, 227; social effect of, 178

geographers, 120; 125–126; 128, 213; test broad supposition, 232

geography, economic and social, 118; heritage, 17–27, 205

George, Henry, 162; 166

Getty, 28

ghetto, 21, 110

ghost town, 161, 169

Giedion, Sigfried, 14

glass, 14, 73

globalization, 125–130, 145, 147, 220; and globalism, 127; and globality, 127; and heritage, 25–27, 232–236; defined, 7, 26, homogenizes, 235; scales of, 227; slippery concept, 26; theorization, 233;

gold, 58, 64, 82

Golden Tulip, 51, 129, 235, 236

governance, 139

government, military, 112; municipal, 224; national mandates, 219

green site, 41, 228

Greenwich Village, Latinized, 56

grid, 32, 44, 228; colonial, 85; in Bogotá, 58, see also *cuadrícula*

grocer, mom-and-pop, 54; see also *bodega*, 67

Gropius, Walter, 41

guerilla, 130, 148, 151; righist and leftist, 78

Habaguanex, 67, 123, 139, 188, 194, 196–197, 203, 204, 205, 232; ch.6, n11; strategy, 192

Habana Vieja, 35, 49, 62–68, 98, 216, 229; and housing, 105–106; colonial life, 64; European multinationals in, 26; commodified, 203, 227; contested spaces, 210; like Beirut, 50; foreign investment, 227; new housing, 199;

residents, 205 190; United States influence, 66; walled city, 65; see also Old Havana, 24

Habermas, Jürgen, 74;

Halliburton, 132

Hardoy, Jorge Enrique, 98

Haussmann, Baron Georges-Eugène, 4, 41

Havana Bay, 63, 192

Havana, 11, 58, 71, 77, 88, 115, 212; and trade with United States, 65; as a parasite, 184; British in, 64; coast of arms, 64; modern architecture in, 123–124; more of a North American city, 196; organic pattern, 45

Hemingway, Ernest, 20, 191, 202, 232

heritage, 23, 96, 162, 188; local, 27; site, 9, 27, 121; urban, 128

heritage preservation, 182; and local planning, 224–226; steady involvement in, 222

heritage tourism, 7, 18, 20, 27–31, 96, 121, 125–130, 140, 143, 193, 202, 216, 220, 227, 236; at local offices, 218; circuit in Cuba, 106; ebb and flow of, 223; immigrant, 20; venue, 20; duality of, 20; and economic capital, 23; local resident, 29; niches, 235; policies, 27; programs, Table 8.1; Third World, 21; United Nations conference, Table 1.1

Herzog, Lawrence A., 18

highway, elevated, Figure 2.1c; interstate, 112

Hilberseimer, Ludwig, 41

hinterland, 95

hispanidad, 15

historian, 17; architectural, 9, 12, 98

historic centers, 8, 21, 30; residents of, 12

historic district, 127, 175; becomes a ghost town, 108; land use anomalies in, Table 3.4, 116

historic preservation, 8, 20, 22, 23,140,
165, 181, 182, 186, 193, 200, 203,
216; agencies, 111; conflict between
economic growth and, 77; gut-and-
preserve, Figure 2.11; paradigm, 11;
project, 18; interdisciplinary, 28
history, architectural, 38; economic,
220
Hitchcock, Henry, 15
Holy Week, 52, 53, Figure 1.5b
home, gentrified, 174; restaurant, 145;
second, 173
Homo turisticos, 127
hospital, 21, 32, 121
hotel, 76, 108; Ancón, 208–209; Las
Cuevas, 209–210; operator, 176;
housing, 15; affordable, 75, 88; in
Habana Vieja, 195; market, 150;
mass, 13; prefabricated, 209; public,
18, 194, 232; residential, 105–106
hustler, 195, 202, ch. 6, n1; *see also*
jineteros, 195
hut, 21; *see also bohío*, 65

Iberian Peninsula, 39; Moorish occupation of, 44
Ibero-American Tourism Summit, 31
ideologies, 78–79
immigrants, 90; European, 89; in
Uruguay, 91; Italian, 50–51, 91; Spanish, 91
imperialism, 39
import-substitution, 84
INAV (National Housing Institute), 184
Independence War, 59; of Cuba, 70
industry, leisure, *see also* tourism, 202
infrastructure, 114–115; aging, 148
Inter-American Development Bank, 28,
138, 150, 177
interest rate, 152–153
International Monetary Fund [IMF], 138,
181

investment, 151; private 111, productive,
121, real-estate, 110
investor, 121, 146, 150, 190, 193, 207,
214; attracting, 212–213

Jacobs, Jane, 100
Jesuits, 43–44
jet set, 143, 73
jinetera, *see also* prostitute, 50
jineteros, 128; 202
joint venture, 190, 195; Italian-Cuban,
200
Jones, Gareth, 77, 121, 150
Jorge Tadeo University, 79, 117
José Antonio Echeverría Polytechnic University, 51

Kostof, Spiro, 41
Kunstler, James Howard, 100

L'Enfant, Pierre Charles, 41
La Cabaña [Fortress], 24, 25, 63
labor, 220, 236; headquarters, 108; international division, 202–203;
land use, 57, 221–223; abandoned, 109;
abandoned, under construction, or in
demolition, 102; commercial, 101;
commercial, 108–109; defined, 97;
eminent domain, 41; in Cartagena,
161–162; institutional, 100; institutional, 108; methodology, 97–105;
park, or open space, 101; parking,
102; patterns, 105–111; rent-
generating, 167; residential, 100;
restaurant, 100
land value, on capturing, 150–151,
183
landmark, 27, 29, 221, 229; global, 35;
national, 96
landscape, 33; 35, 115, 128, 213; as text,
33; highbrow aspects of, 25; homogenous and ubiquitous, 205

Latin America, 8, 41, 49; symbolism, 40; urban spaces in, 120;
Law of the Indies, 43, 88–89
Law Process 8,000, 151, 227
Le Corbusier, 40–43, 112, 229
legislation, 20, 90
leisurescape, 234
lifestyle, 96, 121, 236
Lima, 58, 64, 88
location, relative, 212–213
Lonja de Comercio, 191–192
López, Roberto "Macholo", 215

Macondo, 183
Malecón, 188
mampostería, 65, 114, 187
mansion, 21, 65, 87
Marín, Victor, 33
market economy, 30, 202, 227
Márquez, Gabriel García, 226
master plan, 40–41; 177; 188
mayordomo, Figure 7.6
McDonald's, 56, 236
McDonaldization, ch.6, n7
menemismo, 107
Mexico, 63, 111, 125
Mexican-American War, 72–73
Mexico City, 43, 58, 73
Miami, 66, 182
Miamification, ch.6, n7
micro-brigade, 49–50
militia, 121, 130, 225
Millán, Guadalupe, 74–75
Ministry of Foreign Investments (MINVEC), 190
Modern Movement, 114, 119, 123; 228–229
modernity, 40, 77, 91,123, 220, 223, 229
modernization, 85, 220; socialist, 185; theory, 201
Mogollón, María Pía, 165
Montevideo, 112, 193; and abandoned buildings, 109–110; exudes a European atmosphere, 91; plaza unlike Buenos Aires, 89; *see also* Ciudad Vieja, 88–94
monument, 29, 30, 118, 163
Moors, 32, 39
motif, 39; buccaneer, 233
multinational firm, "logic of the market", 236
museum, 35, 101, 117, 153, 212; curator, 28; living, 203; sugar, 214
music, 56, 88; Afro-Latina, 233

National Assembly, 188–190
nation-state, 127; abilities of, 26
neighborhood, change, 141; immigrant, 111–112; of Puebla, 73
New Orleans, 66
New Urbanism, 96
New World, 39, 40
New York, 66, 83, 193
newspaper, 139, 140
NGO, (non-governmental organization), 100, 108; cultural, 161
Niemeyer, Oscar, 15
nightclub, 161, 236
nonprofit organization, 195
North American Free Trade Agreement, 18

oil, 131–132
Old Havana, spiral shape, 45; *see also Habana Vieja*, 20
Old San Juan, Puerto Rico, 205
Ordenanzas, 43; *see also* master plan *and* ordinance
ordinance, 119; noise, 161
Organization of American States, 9
orthogonality, 38, 45
overcrowding, 106, 169

painters, French and Italian, 214
paja toquillo, see also Panama hat, 83

palace, 21, 65, 79
Palermo, 115, 222
Panama, 31, 137
paradigm, 12, 122,127
Paris, 3, 83,193
park, 21, 102, 157, Figure 1.6
parking lot, 102, 115, 196
Parque Central Hotel, 51
Parque Central, 51, 129, 193, 236
Paseo del Río de San Francisco, 75, 77
paternalism, 140
patio, 91; Figure 5.6d
pedestrian, 56, 100, 196
pedestrianization, 123, 229
peso, 56; Cuban, 214
Peters, Philip, 137
pirate, 69, 232
Plan Colombia, 138
Plan Montevideo, Table 2.2
planner, 28, 81, 95, 125–126, 176,
    195, 205, 213, 225, 232; Montevideo,
    92
planning, 12, 125, 141–142, 183, 236;
    "best practices", Table 8.1; goals in
    Trinidad, 218; in Colombia, 143; law,
    176; local-level, 204; socialist, 205;
    tourism, 218; town, 15, 32; urban, 10,
    22–23, 139; urban and regional, 97,
    184
plaster, 103, 199
Plater-Zyberk, Elizabeth, 18, 100
plaza, 18, 40, 43, 48–57, 74, 94, 117,
    144, 220
Plaza, Bolívar, Figure 2.7; de Armas, 40,
    50, 64, 188, 191; de Cristo, 49–50; de
    la Catedral, 50, 64, 191; de la Con-
    stitución, 89; de las Tres Cruces, 51;
    Figure 5.1; see also Calvary Square
    and Tres Cruces; de los Sapos, 122; de
    Mayo, 55, 86, 112; San Francisco,
    188, Figure 6.4b; Dorrego, 55, 88;
    Grande, Table 3.4; Mayor, 215, Figure

7.9; Trinidad, 53; Santo Domingo,
    Figure 8.4; Vieja, 142, 188, 196–200
plazuela, 102
pleasurescape, 234–235
plusvalía, 202
police, 51, 121, 159, 182
political economy, 37, 195; new, of Cuba,
    215
pollution, air, Figure 2.17b; air and noise, 81
Portes, Alejandro, 147
postmodernism, 12
POT (Plan de Ordenamiento Territorial),
    176–177
Potosí, 79, 84, 88
poverty, in the Latin American city, 21
preservation, in Mexico and Ecuador,
    111; municipal governments, 121; see
    also historic preservation
preservationist, 29, 33
privatization, 138
promenade, 27, 77
property, owner, 181; tax, 167–168;
    unreported, 181; value 169
prostitute, 50; see also jinetera
prostitution, 184, 236, 195
public place, 39, 48–57, 223; debate over
    need to create, 202; in Habana Vieja,
    Cartagena, and Cuenca, 147; of
    Habana Vieja, 201; social con-
    struction of, 49
Puebla, 71–77, 114, 122; Figure 1.6;
    land-use changes, 74; public space, 22;
    regional planning, 75

Queens, [New York] 5, 133
quinceañeras, 166
Quito, 79–81, 83, 84, 118, 150, 193,
    229; mayor, 81; relative location, 79;
    traffic, Figure 2.17a; retailing, 222

rampart, 53–54, 153
redlining, 180

remittance, 7, 132–137, 146,190, 223
Renaissance, 44
residents, 108; illegal, 165; local, 176
restaurants, 54, 76, 100, 107–108, 158
Restoration Office, in Trinidad, 223
restoration, 164; in Habana Vieja, 195–197
restructuring, 186. 193, 205; and tourism, 202; defined, 186; geographic, 203
retailing, 101, 118, 134; mom-and-pop, 22, 109; twenty-four-seven, 221
retired, 101, 107
revitalization, 139, 140, 148, 176, 186, 196, 200, 205; cornerstones of, 231; defined, 186; in Montevideo, 93–94; Old Havana, 188; outcome, 200;
revivalism, 124–125
Revolution, 184, 185, 209; antiurban biases, 67; Cuban, 67, 200
Revolutionary Armed Forces, 225
Río de la Plata, 86, 88, 112
River Plate, 35, 38; see also Río de la Plata
Rodó, Jose Enrique, see also Ariél, 15
Rodríguez, Luis, 123
roof, 195; mansard, 92
Royal Crown, 32, 88

sampling error, 103
San Diego, 19; Park, land use conflict, 157–160; 236; Plaza, 225
San Felípe de Barajas, 78, 164
San Francisco [Puebla], 77
San Francisco de Quito, see also Quito, 79
San Francisco Square, 50–51, 64, 191, 192
San Miguel Bastion, 164
San Pedro, 79, 164
San Telmo, 20, 35, 86, 88, 111, 222

Santa Clara Convent, [in Havana], 27, 64, 155–156, 225
Santa Clara Hotel, 117, 129, 160
Santa Isabela Hotel, 50–51
Santa Teresa, Convent, 154; Hotel, 117
Santiago de Cuba, 63, 71, 216
Santo Domingo, 205; Plaza, 43, 154
scale, 35; sorting-out process, 222
school, 100, 108, 116–117
Segre, Roberto, 16
self-employed, 194, 202; see also cuentapropistas
señora de la chalupa, 225, Figure 1.6
September 11, 2001, 29, 218
Sert, José Luis, 67
settlement, 86; pre-Columbian, 43; colonial, 113
sewage, 114–115, 211
shantytown, 184; in Cartagena, 78
shopkeeper, 57; Figure 1.6
shopping, 74, 81; gallery, see also caracoles, 93
Sierra Madre Oriental, 71
skyline, 12, 114, 113, 222, 223; measurement, 103–104
slave, 77, 91
slavery, in Cuba, 70; in Havana, 37
smuggler, 78, 181
soccer, 91; see also fútbol
social justice, 185, 226
social theory, and material life, 230
socialist, 16, 96; bloc, 194; society, 209
Society for Public Improvements of Cartagena, 164 ch.5, n2; see also Sociedad de Mejoras Públicas de Cartagena
Sofitel, 27, 143, 157, 158–160; 225, 235
solares, 195; see also tenement
Southern Cone, 91, 95, 114, 222
souvenir 57; shop, 3
Soviet Union, 67, 111, 206, 209, 218, 229
space, 21; city, 86; contested, 121–123,

200; contrived cultural, 232; local, 125–130; open, 21, 101; 102; public, 13, 21; ubiquitous, 129

Spain, 10, 40; Catholic, 39

Spanish America, 39; belief system, 39–40

Spanish-American-Cuban War, 98

Special Period, 51, 194, ch.6, n9

Starbucks, 236

state, 216–217

steamship, travel to Havana, Figure, 2.10

stock market, *see also* Lonja de Comercio, 191

stone, 113–114

storefront, converted into housing, 67

street, 234; cobbled, 127, 212, 227, Figure 2.21, Figure 7.4; gated, 211,; name, 45–46; Native American, 44; vendor, 21; Figure 1.6

streetcar, 65, 81, 89, 196

subsidies, 27, 88

suburbanization, 89–90; of Havana, 65–66

suburbs, elites to, 95; in Havana, 196

sugar, 64–65,132,191, 212

sugar mill, 70; *see also ingenio*

Sugar Mill Valley, 69, 208; *see also* Valle de los Ingenios, 208

supermarket, 74, 100

Supreme Court Palace, 59

sustainability, 188; 223

symbol, 40, 203, 233

symbolism, 117, 203

synagogue, 100, 108

Taliban, 29

tango, 55, 107, 223; table 8.1

tax, 41, 214, 223–224; amnesty, 169; assessing, 162; collection, 180; ethos in Colombia of, 182; policy, 148; property, 134, 169; vendor, 21

technology, 3, 26, 234

tenement, 169; *see also cuaterías*, 145

textile, 73, 101; workshop, 79

The Cuzco Commitment, 31

Third World, 13, 236

Three Crosses Square, Figure 1.5a; *see also* Tres Cruces *and* Plaza de las Tres Cruces

Three Kings Day, 157

Tijuana, 4, 19

Tomebamba [River], 81–82;, 101

tourism, 25, 78, 84, 127, 164, 182, 185, 186, 195, 205; ebb and flow of, 217; four S's of tropical, 128; global, 205; industry, 205; international, 125, 208; Latin American, 31; pole, 207; promoting, 8; sexual, 20, 195; sun-and-surf, 218, 234

tourist, 3, 21, 55, 56, 108, 145, 146; car rentals, 196; European and Canadian, 190; gaze, 203; gastronomic, 20; heritage, 20; international, 35, 37; international, 122, 164; maintaining heritage sites, 217; neighbors and, 101; pole, 71

town square, 8, 10, 101; cultural expression, 49; unpaved, Fig. 1.5b

tradition, 220, 229; Creole, 8

traffic, 15; congestion, 95

tram, 89; *see also* steetcar *and* trolley

transparency, 132, 151; in Quito, 81

travel, agency, 145; international, 4

Tres Cruces, 219, Table 8.1, Figure 1.5b; *see also* Three Crosses *and* Plaza de las Tres Cruces, 212

Trinidad Restoration Office, 213

Trinidad, 27; 68–7, 114, 123, 229; charm, 208; isolation, 206; organic pattern of, 45; waste system, 71

trolley, 81

U.S. News and World Report, ch.6, n11

UNESCO World Heritage Site, 148, 207

UNESCO, 10, 22, 29, 67, 80, 85, 96, 160, 163, 182, 185, 190, 195, 209, 213, 218, 221, 224–225, 229; and Trinidad, 71
unit of analysis, 98, 104
United States, 203; Information Agency, 161; Interests Section, 205; migration to, 4; Treasury, 205
Universidad Benemérita Autónoma de Puebla, 73
University of Chicago, 122
university, 100, 101, 108
urban, design, 14, 31, 41, 123, 203; ecologist, 110; economics, 97; fabric, 203; geography, 97, 120; and spatial organization school, 226; morphology, 38–48, 230; primacy, 73, 90; renewal, 96
urbanization, 80, 115, 117, 223
Uruguay, 90, 92–93, 125
USSR, 186, 219

validity, defined,104; instrumental, 103, 104
Valle de los Ingenios, 71; *see also* Sugar Mill Valley
Varadero, 71, 137, 212
Varley, Ann, 121
Vedado, 115, 197, 222

vendor, 3, 22, 53, 57, 75, Table 8.1; ambulant food, 158; *ventanas de panza*, 171, 229
Veracruz, 63;, 69, 71, 75, 77, 205
villa, 45, 206
village, 113; feudal, 24; medieval, 24

Walt Disney Corporation, 18
Ward, Peter, 150
warehouse, 123, 121, 187; port, 119
waste removal, 65, 75
water, 65; main, 49; treatment, 75
waterfront, 101, 161
Weiss, Joaquín, 98
welfare state, 90, 169
Williamsburg, Virginia, 24
Worcester, 25, 193
World Bank, 26, 28, 150, 204, 218
World Heritage Sites, 10, 45, 67, 71, 85, 134, 213, 224–225, ch.5, n2

young Cuban American (YUCAS), 193, ch.6, n7
young urban professional (yuppies), 193; ch.6, n7
zócalo, 19, 40; in Puebla, 56

zoning, 80, 224; *see also* land use

About the Author

Joseph L. Scarpaci is a Professor of Geography at Virginia Tech in Blacksburg, Virginia. An internationally known expert on Cuba, he has focused on researching the social and political correlates of historic preservation there since 1990. He has also taught at the Universidad Interamericana de Puerto Rico, Rutgers University, and the University of Iowa. He received his Ph.D. from the University of Florida in 1985. He has coordinated study abroad programs in Chile and Cuba and has testified before the U.S. State Department and congressional staffers on the nature of the Cuban economy and civil society.

A Fulbright award in 1983–84 placed Scarpaci in Chile during the Pinochet era as part of a broader research project on social services privatization in the Southern Cone. Subsequent grants from the National Institutes of Health, National Science Foundation, Social Science Research Council, and the Lincoln Institute for Land Policy have helped him acquire extensive field research in Chile, Argentina, Uruguay, Brazil, Colombia, Ecuador, Mexico, and Cuba.

The most recent of his six books is *Havana: Two Faces of the Antillean Metropolis*, with Cuban architects Mario Coyula and Roberto Segre (University of North Carolina Press, 2002), which earned a Choice Outstanding Academic Book Award and was lauded as a "breakthrough urbanography" by *Lingua Franca*. In 2004, the Conference of Latin American Geographers gave Scarpaci the Carl O. Sauer award for excellence in scholarship and international research. In 2005, *Plazas and Barrios* won the Al Sturm Award given by the Phi Beta Kappa Mu Chapter for the Outstanding Faculty Publication at Virginia Tech.